Drupal 7 Development by Example

Beginner's Guide

Follow the creation of a Drupal website to learn, by example, the key concepts of Drupal 7 development and HTML 5

Kurt Madel

PUBLISHING

BIRMINGHAM - MUMBAI

Drupal 7 Development by Example
Beginner's Guide

First published: May 2012

Production Reference: 1160512

Published by Packt Publishing Ltd.
Livery Place
35 Livery Street
Birmingham B3 2PB, UK.

ISBN 978-1-84951-680-8

www.packtpub.com

Cover Image by Asher Wishkerman (wishkerman@hotmail.com)

Credits

Author

Kurt Madel

Reviewers

Nedo Laanen

Danny Pfeiffer

James Roughton

Ronald J. Simon

Reid Braswell

Acquisition Editor

Sarah Cullington

Lead Technical Editor

Joanna Finchen

Technical Editor

Lubna Shaikh

Project Coordinator

Alka Nayak

Proofreaders

Aaron Nash

Mario Cecere

Indexer

Rekha Nair

Production Coordinator

Prachali Bhiwandkar

Cover Work

Prachali Bhiwandkar

About the Author

Kurt Madel is a Senior Manager and developer for Captech Consulting in Richmond, VA. He has worked on open source CMS projects for over six years. Kurt contributes regularly to `Drupal.org`, and is the maintainer of several modules. In addition to Drupal, Kurt has been doing Java EE development since 2000, and has focused on mobile web development over the last two years. When he is not writing or programming, Kurt enjoys cycling and spending time with his wife and four boys.

About the Reviewers

Nedo Laanen graduated from college in 2003, where he studied Applied Mathematics and Computer Science. First, he worked as a Novell Engineer, and later made the switch to Linux and Open Source technology. In 2011, Nedo started his own one-man company, providing services based on Linux and Open Source technology. At the moment, he is working as a freelance Linux Engineer at Morpho in Haarlem.

Nedo was also a reviewer on the following Packt publishing books:

- *The GIMP 2.6 Cookbook*
- *Drupal 7 – Social Networking*

Danny Pfeiffer started off his career as a developer, after which he transitioned to working as a contractor doing information architecture and usability work for Fortune 500 companies across the country. This experience, while sometimes dry, underscored the importance of architecture and proper planning as part of the overall project cycle.

With over 10 years of web development experience, Danny has amassed a tremendous wealth of knowledge, dating back to the days of tables, iFrames, and server side includes. These days, he focuses primarily on building dynamic websites and applications using the latest technologies, HTML5, CSS3, AJAX, PHP, MySQL, and of course, Drupal.

In 2007, Danny had drawn enough boxes and arrows, and decided to apply that experience towards a new venture, focused exclusively on Drupal development. He and his brother, Mike, started Denver-based Rehab Creative and enjoy continually introducing new clients and staff to the exciting world of Drupal.

James Roughton, MS, CSP, CRSP-R, CHMM-R, CIT, CET, Six Sigma Black Belt, jr@gotsafety.net, received his Bachelor of Science degree in Business Administration from Christopher Newport College, and his Masters in Safety Science degree from **Indiana University of Pennsylvania (IUP)**.

James is also a published author. Two of his most notable books include, *Developing an Effective Safety Culture: A Leadership Approach* and *Job Hazard Analysis: A Guide for Voluntary Compliance and Beyond*. He is currently working on a new book *Developing an Effective Safety Culture: Implementing Safety Through Human Performance Improvement*, which is to be completed by December 31 2012.

In addition, he is looking to develop a new book on social media that will outline all of the useful productivity tools on the Internet, such as dropbox, evernote, Google alerts, Google reader, and so on, that he has found. Based on his experience and presentations, these elements are not considered as a part of social media, and therefore, are not usually on the radar as productivity tools and he wants to change this perception.

As he sees it, there is the need for a more practical, down-to-earth guidance that weaves together the numerous techniques and methods necessary for understanding the social media in a different light. His goal is to help individuals get from point A (having a strong professional expertise but limited knowledge of social networking) to point B (where they can use your new knowledge to enhance and broadcast their message to their intended audience more effectively).

This idea was formed from his personal vision and research:

To live my life with PURPOSE and the PASSION to help others succeed.

You can follow James on the following sites:

- ◆ Social Media website: http://www.jamesroughton.com/
- ◆ Safety-related website: http://www.safetycultureplus.com
- ◆ YouTube video feed!: http://www.youtube.com/user/MrJamesroughton/feed
- ◆ Facebook: http://www.facebook.com/james.roughton
- ◆ Twitter: http://twitter.com/jamesroughton
- ◆ LinkedIn: http://www.linkedin.com/in/jamesroughtoncsp

Ronald J. Simon has been working with the development of shared information and database design dating back to the days before the Internet, and has worked in many different areas of information management and writing documentation to support users.

Ron is also an Adjunct Instructor for Grand Valley State University, and has worked in the legal field in Document Management and Security. Ron has been an editor for the book *Drupal 7 Social Networking*.

Currently, Ron is evaluating a major program rollout for a large retail chain. He is also the owner of RJS Designs, which is a small business consulting company.

I would like to thank both of my parents for teaching me how to learn and have fun at the same time.

www.PacktPub.com

Support files, eBooks, discount offers and more

You might want to visit www.PacktPub.com for support files and downloads related to your book.

Did you know that Packt offers eBook versions of every book published, with PDF and ePub files available? You can upgrade to the eBook version at www.PacktPub.com and as a print book customer, you are entitled to a discount on the eBook copy. Get in touch with us at service@packtpub.com for more details.

At www.PacktPub.com, you can also read a collection of free technical articles, sign up for a range of free newsletters and receive exclusive discounts and offers on Packt books and eBooks.

http://PacktLib.PacktPub.com

Do you need instant solutions to your IT questions? PacktLib is Packt's online digital book library. Here, you can access, read and search across Packt's entire library of books.

Why Subscribe?

- Fully searchable across every book published by Packt
- Copy and paste, print and bookmark content
- On demand and accessible via web browser

Free Access for Packt account holders

If you have an account with Packt at www.PacktPub.com, you can use this to access PacktLib today and view nine entirely free books. Simply use your login credentials for immediate access.

Table of Contents

Preface

This book is a hands-on, example-driven guide to programming Drupal websites. Discover a number of new features for Drupal 7 through practical and interesting examples while building a fully functional recipe sharing website. Learn about web content management, multi-media integration, and new features for developers in Drupal 7.

With this book you will:

- Learn to build cutting edge websites with Drupal 7
- Discover important concepts for HTML5 and why it's time to start building websites with HTML5, if you haven't already
- Learn the important patterns for JavaScript and AJAX in Drupal 7
- Realize interesting ways to integrate multi-media with Drupal 7
- Find out how becoming more involved with the Drupal development community can help you build better websites
- Set up a development environment, and learn to use Git and Drush
- Uncover how much fun it can be to build websites with Drupal 7

What this book covers

Chapter 1, Getting Set up, walks through setting up a Drupal development environment before diving into Drupal development.

Chapter 2, Custom Content Types and an Introduction to Module Development, will explain how to configure Drupal content types and begin Drupal development with an introduction to creating custom Drupal modules.

Chapter 3, HTML5 Integration for Drupal 7 and More Module Development, will continue with some Drupal development examples, and show how we can integrate HTML5 with Drupal 7.

Chapter 4, Introduction to Drupal 7 Theme Development, will explain about custom theme development and Drupal 7 render arrays.

Chapter 5, Enhancing the Content Author's User Experience, will configure WYSIWYG for Drupal 7 and show how we can improve the content author user experience with some custom development examples.

Chapter 6, Adding Media to our Site, will explain how the Drupal 7 Media module makes multi-media integration for Drupal better than ever, keeping in mind that a site without any multimedia is just text.

Chapter 7, How Does it Taste – Getting Feedback, will show some ways to provide visitor site interaction in Drupal as one way to extend the amount of time a visitor spends on your site is to provide ways for them to interact with it.

Chapter 8, Recipe Lists and More with Views, will show some of the more advanced features of the Views module, and find out why Views is the most popular contrib module on drupal.org.

Chapter 9, Rotating Banners and Project Promotion, will show how to use Views to display images in a compelling way, because the Views module offers a lot more than just displaying some fields.

Chapter 10, Test Your Code with SimpleTest, will test the custom code that you have written.

Chapter 11, Introduction to the Features Module and Configuration Management, will show how the Features module can help us manage the code that you have written for the Drupal site that you created.

What you need for this book

Programs/applications:

- MAMP 2.0.5: http://www.mamp.info/downloads/releases/ MAMP_MAMP_PRO_2.0.5.zip

- XAMPP 1.7.7: http://www.apachefriends.org/download.php?xampp-win32-1.7.7-VC9.7z

- Homebrew: https://github.com/mxcl/homebrew/wiki/installation

- Git for Mac (just use Homebrew from above to install it): brew install git

- msysgit, Git for Windows: http://code.google.com/p/msysgit/downloads/ detail?name=Git-1.7.9-preview20120201.exe&can=2&q=

- Drush for Mac: brew install drush

- Drush Windows Installer (easy way to get Drush working on Windows): `http://drush.ws/sites/default/files/attachments/Drush-5.x-dev-2012-02-21-Installer-v1.0.13.msi`

- Drupal 7.12: `git clone  http://git.drupal.org/project/drupal.git d7dev`

- Aptana Studio 3 IDE: `http://www.aptana.com/products/studio3/download`

- `drupal_aptana_formatter_profile.xml` (provides Drupal code formatting for Aptana Studio): `http://drupalcode.org/sandbox/kmadel/1249414.git/blob_plain/HEAD:/drupal_aptana_formatter_profile.xml`

- Google Chrome: `https://www.google.com/chrome`

Drupal contributed modules (Drush was used to install all contributed modules):

- Chaos tool suite (ctools) 7.x-1.0-rc1
- Coder 7.x-1.0
- Colorbox 7.x-1.x-dev (2011-Oct-10)
- Devel 7.x-1.2
- Elements 7.x-1.2
- Entity API 7.x-1.0-rc1
- Features 7.x-1.0-beta6
- Field group 7.x-1.1
- File entity (fieldable files) 7.x-2.0-unstable3
- Fivestar 7.x-2.x-dev (2012-Feb-16)
- HTML5 Tools 7.x-1.1
- Libraries API 7.x-1.0
- Media 7.x-2.0-unstable3
- media_youtube 7.x-1.0-beta1
- Microdata 7.x-1.0-alpha4
- Omega Tools 7.x-3.0-rc4
- Views 7.x-3.3
- Views Field View 7.x-1.0-rc1
- Views Slideshow 7.x-3.0
- Voting API 7.x-2.6
- Webform 7.x-3.16
- Wysiwyg 7.x-2.1

Drupal Contributed theme:

- ◆ Omega: Responsive HTML5 Base Theme 7.x-3.1

JavaScript Libraries:

- ◆ `ckeditor`: http://ckeditor.com/download
- ◆ `colorbox`: http://jacklmoore.com/colorbox/colorbox.zip
- ◆ `jquery.cycle`: http://malsup.github.com/jquery.cycle.all.js

Who this book is for

This book is for people who have some experience building websites and who want to learn to do so with Drupal 7. You should have experience with HTML markup, CSS, and jQuery. Experience with previous versions of Drupal would be helpful, but is not necessary.

Conventions

In this book, you will find several headings appearing frequently.

To give clear instructions of how to complete a procedure or task, we use:

Time for action – heading

1. Action 1
2. Action 2
3. Action 3

Instructions often need some extra explanation so that they make sense, so they are followed with:

What just happened?

This heading explains the working of tasks or instructions that you have just completed.

You will also find some other learning aids in the book, including:

Pop quiz – heading

These are short multiple-choice questions intended to help you test your own understanding.

Have a go hero – heading

These practical challenges and give you ideas for experimenting with what you have learned.

You will also find a number of styles of text that distinguish between different kinds of information. Here are some examples of these styles, and an explanation of their meaning.

Code words in text are shown as follows: " You may notice that we used the Unix command `rm` to remove the `Drush` directory rather than the DOS `del` command."

A block of code is set as follows:

```
# * Fine Tuning
#
key_buffer = 16M
key_buffer_size = 32M
max_allowed_packet = 16M
thread_stack = 512K
thread_cache_size = 8
max_connections = 300
```

When we wish to draw your attention to a particular part of a code block, the relevant lines or items are set in bold:

```
# * Fine Tuning
#
key_buffer = 16M
key_buffer_size = 32M
max_allowed_packet = 16M
thread_stack = 512K
thread_cache_size = 8
max_connections = 300
```

Any command-line input or output is written as follows:

```
cd /ProgramData/Propeople
rm -r Drush
git clone --branch master http://git.drupal.org/project/drush.git
```

New terms and **important words** are shown in bold. Words that you see on the screen, in menus or dialog boxes for example, appear in the text like this: "On the **Select Destination Location** screen, click on **Next** to accept the default destination.".

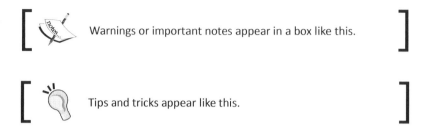

Warnings or important notes appear in a box like this.

Tips and tricks appear like this.

Reader feedback

Feedback from our readers is always welcome. Let us know what you think about this book—what you liked or may have disliked. Reader feedback is important for us to develop titles that you really get the most out of.

To send us general feedback, simply send an e-mail to `feedback@packtpub.com`, and mention the book title through the subject of your message.

If there is a topic that you have expertise in and you are interested in either writing or contributing to a book, see our author guide on `www.packtpub.com/authors`.

Customer support

Now that you are the proud owner of a Packt book, we have a number of things to help you to get the most from your purchase.

Downloading the example code

You can download the example code files for all Packt books you have purchased from your account at `http://www.packtpub.com`. If you purchased this book elsewhere, you can visit `http://www.packtpub.com/support` and register to have the files e-mailed directly to you.

Errata

Although we have taken every care to ensure the accuracy of our content, mistakes do happen. If you find a mistake in one of our books—maybe a mistake in the text or the code—we would be grateful if you would report this to us. By doing so, you can save other readers from frustration and help us improve subsequent versions of this book. If you find any errata, please report them by visiting http://www.packtpub.com/support, selecting your book, clicking on the **errata submission form** link, and entering the details of your errata. Once your errata are verified, your submission will be accepted and the errata will be uploaded to our website, or added to any list of existing errata, under the Errata section of that title.

Piracy

Piracy of copyright material on the Internet is an ongoing problem across all media. At Packt, we take the protection of our copyright and licenses very seriously. If you come across any illegal copies of our works, in any form, on the Internet, please provide us with the location address or website name immediately so that we can pursue a remedy.

Please contact us at copyright@packtpub.com with a link to the suspected pirated material.

We appreciate your help in protecting our authors, and our ability to bring you valuable content.

Questions

You can contact us at questions@packtpub.com if you are having a problem with any aspect of the book, and we will do our best to address it.

1
Getting Set up

In this chapter, we will focus on setting up a development environment, so that you can begin writing the code for a Drupal-powered website, and we will explore some other aspects of what it means to be a Drupal developer.

In this chapter, we will:

- ◆ Install and configure the settings for a web server, PHP, and the MySQL database
- ◆ Install and use Git
- ◆ Install and use Drush
- ◆ Install Drupal 7
- ◆ Install the Aptana IDE, and set up a PHP-based Drupal project
- ◆ Explore `http://drupal.org/` from a developer's perspective

So let's get started and get a Drupal development environment set up so we can move onto some cool development examples in the following chapters.

Installing an Apache, MySQL, and PHP stack

Although you can use a number of different web servers and databases, we are going to use the commonly used combination of Apache, MySQL, and PHP, often referred to as the ***AMP** stack.

Mac OS X AMP stack

For Mac OS X, we will use the MAMP package to install an AMP stack.

The instructions for setting up a development environment for Mac OS X are very similar to setting a development environment for a Linux distribution. They are both Unix-based operating systems. If you aren't already tied to a particular Linux distribution, and would like to set up a development environment in Linux, then I highly recommend the Ubuntu **distribution (distro)**. There are excellent directions on setting up a Drupal development environment, available at http://groups.drupal.org/node/6261, and if you don't already have Ubuntu installed, there is a **Quickstart** virtual machine available as part of the Drupal Quickstart project. More information can be found at http://drupal.org/project/quickstart.

Time for action – downloading the latest version of MAMP

1. First, download MAMP from http://www.mamp.info/en/downloads/index. html. Once MAMP has completed downloading, double-click on the downloaded .zip file, expand the 64bit folder, and then double-click the MAMP.pkg file. This will launch the MAMP installer as shown in the following screenshot:

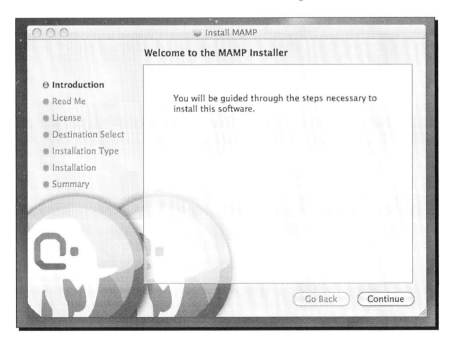

2. Next, click on **Continue** on this screen and the next screen, then click on **Continue**, and click on **Agree** to agree to the terms of the software license agreement, and then click on **Continue** once again on the next screen. It is important on the next screen to click on the **Customize** button, and on the very next screen, un-check the **MAMP Pro 2.0.1** checkbox.

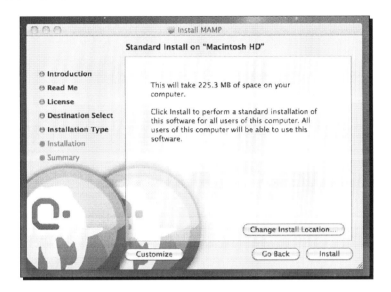

3. After that, click on **Install**. After the installation completes, click on **Close**. Go to your `Applications` folder and the **MAMP** folder, and double-click on the **MAMP** application. After the Apache and MySQL servers have started, you will see the following MAMP start screen load in your default web browser:

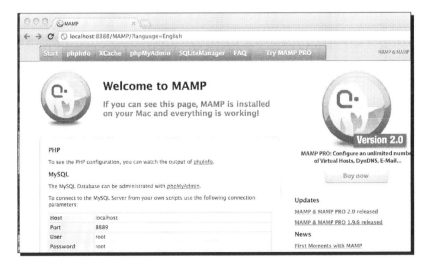

Windows AMP stack

For Windows, we will use XAMPP.

 This is a disclaimer of sorts. I do most of my Drupal development on Mac OS X. I also believe that developing on a Unix-based operating system, such as OS X, is a better fit for Drupal development, as there are many development-oriented aspects of Drupal that either depend on Unix or are Unix-centric. From `cron` to Unix-based permissions, a lot of documentation on `http://drupal.org/` will be biased towards the Unix operating systems.

Time for action – downloading the latest version of XAMPP

1. First, download XAMPP from `http://www.apachefriends.org/en/xampp-windows.html`. Scroll down the page until you get to the **XAMPP for Windows** section, and click on the **Zip** download. After the `xampp-win32-1.7.4-VC6.zip` file has completed downloading, right-click on it and select **Extract All...**, enter `C:\` as the destination, and click on **Extract**. Note that the extraction process will take a few minutes.

 WAMP (`http://www.wampserver.com/en/`) is also a good choice for setting up an AMP stack on Windows.

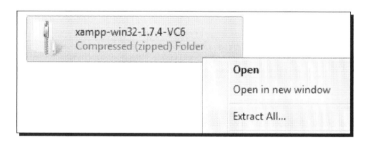

2. Now, navigate to the `C:\xampp` directory, and double-click on the `xampp-control` application to start the **XAMPP Control Panel Application**:

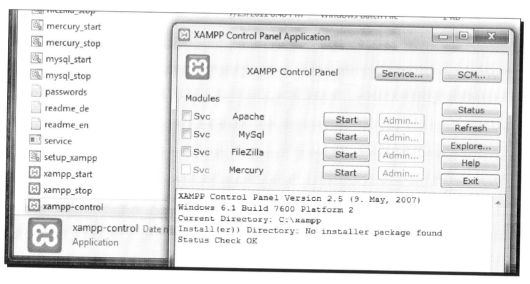

3. Inside the **XAMPP Control Panel Application**, click on the **Start** buttons next to Apache and MySQL. Now, open up your favorite web browser, navigate to `http://localhost`, and you should see something similar to the following screenshot:

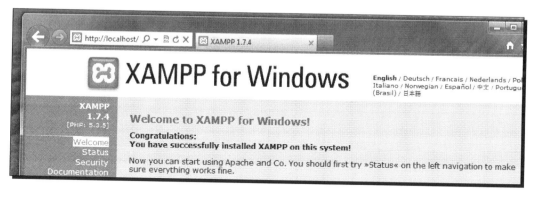

4. There is one last step with XAMPP before we move on; we need to set the `admin` password for MySQL. In your favorite web browser, open `http://localhost/security/index.php`:

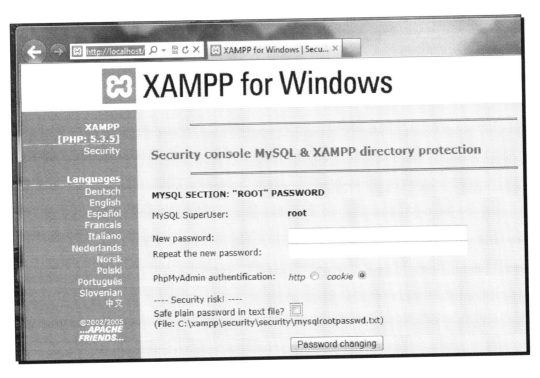

5. Enter the new password as `root,` and click on the **Password changing** button to submit the change. You should see the following message:

```
The root password was successfully changed. Please restart MYSQL
for loading these changes!
```

What just happened?

Congratulations! You now have a working AMP stack installed.

PHP configuration

Drupal 7 recommends PHP version 5.3. The latest version of MAMP includes PHP version 5.3.6 (it also includes PHP version 5.2.13, and allows you to switch between them). The latest version of XAMPP for Windows includes PHP version 5.3.5. Although this version of PHP meets the requirements of Drupal 7, there are some PHP-related settings that need to be tweaked before we install Drupal, to ensure that things will run smoothly.

Time for action – modifying php.ini settings

Mac OS X: Use your favorite text editor to open the `php.ini` file located at `/Applications/MAMP/bin/php/php5.3.6/conf`. If you are using Apple's `TextEdit` application, then I recommend that you take a look at `Smultron-http://www.peterborgapps.com/smultron/`, which is inexpensive and available in the Mac App Store. Other favorite text editors for the Mac include `TextMate-http://macromates.com/` and `Coda-http://panic.com/coda/`, among many others.

Windows: Use your favorite text editor to open the `php.ini` file located at `C:\xampp\php`. I like Sublime Text and Notepad++.

Navigate to the **Resource Limits** section, and edit the settings to match the following values:

```
max_execution_time = 60;
max_input_time = 120;
memory_limit = 128M;
error_reporting = E_ALL & ~E_NOTICE
```

Drupal 7 is a bit slower in some ways than Drupal 6. So, it is important that you make these changes to the `php.ini` file for your Drupal 7 development site to run smoothly.

MySQL configuration

Although it is possible to run Drupal 7 on several different databases, including some NoSQL databases (such as MongoDB), we will use the most commonly used database, MySQL. For Drupal 7, MySQL version 5.0.15 or higher is recommended, and both of the AMP stacks chosen for Mac OS X and Windows include MySQL versions higher than that. Now, let's tweak some MySQL configuration settings to ensure a smooth running development environment.

Time for action – modifying the MySQL my.cnf settings

Mac OS X: MAMP does not use a `my.cnf` file by default. So you must copy the file at `/Applications/MAMP/Library/support-files/my-medium.cnf` to `/Applications/MAMP/conf/my.cnf` (notice the new name of the file).

Windows: For XAMMP, open the `my.ini` file located at `C:\xampp\mysql\bin`.

 You may want to make a back-up copy of this file before you begin to edit it.

Open the `my.cnf/my.ini` file in your text editor, and find and edit the following settings to match these values:

```
# * Fine Tuning
#
key_buffer = 16M
key_buffer_size = 32M
max_allowed_packet = 16M
thread_stack = 512K
thread_cache_size = 8
max_connections = 300
```

One of the real gotchas for the Drupal MySQL configuration is the `max_allowed_packet` setting. This has always been a source of bewildering errors in the past for myself and many other Drupal developers that I know, and it is a setting that is specifically mentioned on the `http://drupal.org/requirements#database` page, under the **Database server** section.

 When you are ready to take your site live, there are some excellent performance tuning tips available on drupal.org at `http://drupal.org/node/2601`.

Time for action – creating an empty MySQL database

Before we can install Drupal, we need to create a new and empty MySQL database.

Both MAMP and XAMPP include `phpMyAdmin`—a web-based administration tool for MySQL. We will use `phpMyAdmin` to create an empty database for Drupal.

Mac OS X: With MAMP running, open your favorite web browser, and go to `http://localhost:8888/phpMyAdmin`.

Windows: With XAMPP running, open your favorite web browser, and go to `http://localhost/phpmyadmin/`.

You will see the following screen:

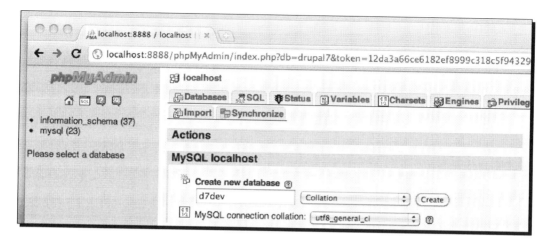

The default page of **phpMyAdmin** includes a form for creating a database as shown. Enter the name d7dev for your database, and click on **Create**. You will then see the following screen:

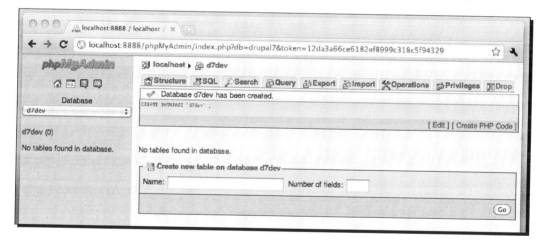

What just happened?

You have installed a fully-functional AMP stack that has been configured specifically for Drupal, and you have created an empty MySQL database as a preliminary step for installing Drupal.

Installing Git

Git is a source control and versioning software that has become very popular over the last few years. In February of 2011, `drupal.org` migrated from the outdated CVS versioning system to Git. The migration to Git has enabled a completely new way for Drupal developers to interact with `drupal.org`, and we will highlight this enhanced interaction throughout the book. However, we will also immediately start using Git to facilitate setting up a Drupal development environment. So, if you don't already have Git installed on your computer, let's get it set up.

Time for action – installing Git for Mac OS X

To install Git for the Mac, we are going to use Homebrew (an open source package manager for Mac OS X) with installation instructions available at `https://github.com/mxcl/homebrew/wiki/installation`.

1. Once you have Homebrew installed, installing Git is as easy as opening up the `Terminal` application (in `/Applications/Utilities`), and typing the following command:

    ```
    brew install Git
    ```

2. Type the following to see if it worked:

    ```
    Git version
    ```

Downloading the example code

You can download the example code files for all Packt books you have purchased from your account at `http://www.packtpub.com`. If you purchased this book elsewhere, you can visit `http://www.packtpub.com/support` and register to have the files e-mailed directly to you.

Time for action – installing Git for Windows

For Windows, we are going to use `msysgit` available at `http://code.google.com/p/msysgit/downloads/list`.

1. Download the most recent version of the full installer for the official Git, currently `Git-1.7.6-preview20110708.exe`, and then double-click on the **downloaded file** link to begin the installation process.

2. Click on **Next**, and then click **Next** again on the **GNU General Public License** screen.

3. On the **Select Destination Location** screen, click on **Next** to accept the default destination.

4. On the **Select Components** screen, accept the defaults again, and click on **Next**.

5. On the **Adjusting your PATH Environment** screen, select **Run Git and included Unix tools from the Windows Command Prompt** as this will allow Git to work with Drush, which we will cover next.

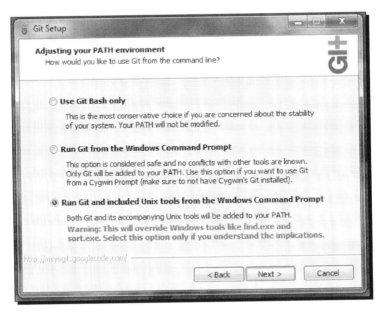

What just happened?

You have installed the Git version control system—a tool that will greatly facilitate interaction with the existing contributed code at `Drupal.org`.

Installing Drush

Drush, a portmanteau of the words Drupal and shell, is a command line utility that facilitates the management of a Drupal environment from your favorite shell (the `Terminal` application on Mac OS X and the `Command Prompt` application on Windows). For example, installing a contributed module on `drupal.org` could be as easy as running the following commands from the command line:

```
drush dl modulename
drush en -y modulename
```

Time for action – installing Drush for Mac OS X

To install Drush for Mac, we are going to use Homebrew again. With Homebrew, installing Drush is as easy as opening up the `Terminal` application (in `/Applications/Utilities`), and typing the following command:

```
brew install drush
```

Time for action – installing Drush for Windows

Installing Drush for Windows is a bit more involved than it is for Mac OS X. We will be following the directions available at `http://drush.ws/sites/default/files/attachments/Drush%20Installation%20Guide.pdf` for installing Drush on Windows.

1. Download the Drush installer from `http://drush.ws/drush_windows_installer`, and follow the instructions in the **Drush Installation Guide PDF**. On the **Custom Setup** screen, make sure that you select to install the **cwRsync Optional Components** and **Register Environment Variables**, as shown in the following screenshot:

2. After the installation has completed we are going to use Git to update Drush to a newer version because the version included with the Drush Installer has some issues (as of July 2011). Open the Command Prompt application for Windows and enter the following commands:

```
cd /ProgramData/Propeople

rm -r Drush

git clone --branch master http://git.drupal.org/project/drush.git
```

 You may notice that we used the Unix command `rm` to remove the `Drush` directory rather than the DOS `del` command. When we installed Drush with the Windows installer, we also enabled several Unix commands for Windows, including `rm`.

3. By using Git, you will now be able to easily keep your Drush installation up-to-date. To check if it is out of date, you can just run `git status`.

What just happened?

You have installed Drush - a very powerful tool that eases the management of a Drupal development environment from the command line.

Installing Drupal 7

All right, now we are getting somewhere. Now that we have created a database, installed Git, and installed Drush, we have everything in place to install Drupal 7.

Time for action – installing Drupal 7

We are going to use a combination of Drush and Git to install Drupal.

1. **Mac OS X**: Open up the **Terminal** application, and type the following command:

```
cd /Applications/MAMP/htdocs
```

Windows: Open the Drush command prompt application, and type the following command:

```
cd /xampp/htdocs
```

2. Now, we are going to use Git to locally clone the Drupal core Git repository into a new `d7dev` folder (this will take a few minutes, or so, depending on your network bandwidth):

```
$ git clone  http://git.drupal.org/project/drupal.git d7dev
Cloning into d7dev...
remote: Counting objects: 131301, done.
remote: Compressing objects: 100% (36527/36527), done.
remote: Total 131301 (delta 98528), reused 119725 (delta 88369)
Receiving objects: 100% (131301/131301), 38.73 MiB | 554 KiB/s,
done.
Resolving deltas: 100% (98528/98528), done.
$ cd d7dev
```

3. Next, we want to use Git to switch to the latest Drupal 7 release. First, we will list all of the available releases:

```
$ git tag -l 7.*
7.0
~
7.1
7.10
7.11
7.12
7.2
7.3
7.4
7.5
7.6
7.7
7.8
7.9
```

4. From this list (I removed all of the `alpha`, `rc`, and unstable releases), you will see that the latest release is `7.12`, but you should substitute whatever the latest release may be for you, and use that in the following Git command:

```
$ git checkout 7.12
Note: checking out '7.12'.


You are in 'detached HEAD' state. You can look around, make experimental

changes and commit them, and you can discard any commits you make in this

state without impacting any branches by performing another checkout.


If you want to create a new branch to retain commits you create, you may

do so (now or later) by using -b with the checkout command again. Example:

  git checkout -b new_branch_name


HEAD is now at 4d4080b... Oops. Not yet. ;) Revert "Back to 7.13-dev."
```

 By using Git, we are linking your download of Drupal to drupal.org's Git repository for your local core Drupal install. This will facilitate an easy update process for future Drupal core updates.

5. Next, we are going to go through the web-based installation process to set up Drupal.

Mac OS X: Open `http://localhost:8888/d7dev/` in your web browser.

Windows: Open `http://localhost/d7dev/` in your web browser.

You should see the following screen:

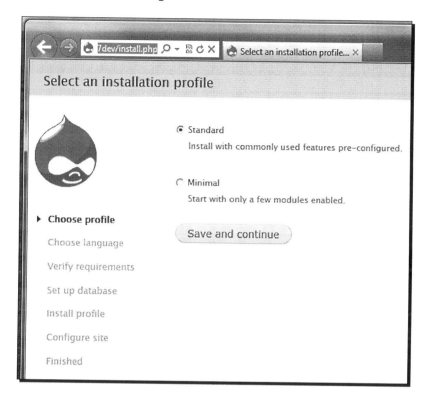

6. Select the **Standard** profile, and click on **Save and Continue**.

7. On the **Choose language** screen, select your language, and click on **Save and Continue**.

8. On the **Database configuration** screen, select **MySQL**. Enter d7dev for the database name, and root as the database username and password. Click on **Save and Continue**.

For a local development site, it is quite convenient to use the root MySQL user. However, for a live/production site, you should always create a unique MySQL user and password for your Drupal database.

9. On the **Configure site** screen, enter the following values (the e-mail address doesn't have to be real, but must appear valid):

- ❑ **Site name**: d7dev
- ❑ **Site e-mail address**: a valid email address
- ❑ **Username**: admin
- ❑ **E-mail address**: same as used for **Site e-mail**
- ❑ **Password** and **Confirm password**: admin (this is only a development environment, so keep it simple)

10. Fill out the rest of the form, and click on **Save and continue**. Your Drupal site installation is complete. So click on the **Visit your new site** link to see the site.

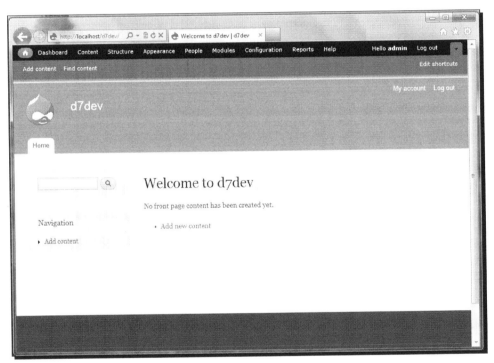

What just happened?

You used Git to get a brand new Drupal 7 site up and running. In the coming chapters, you will see how useful Git, along with Drush, can be for day-to-day Drupal development.

Installing the Aptana Studio IDE

Aptana Studio is an **Integrated Development Environment** (**IDE**) that supports PHP development. An IDE combines many useful tools for development in one application - from a syntax-aware text editor to integrated debugging, and version control.

Time for action – installing the Aptana IDE

Go to `http://www.aptana.com/products/studio3/download`, and download the correct version of the Aptana Studio IDE for your operating system. Double-click on the file once it has completed downloading, and follow the installer directions to install Aptana Studio.

> By no means should you feel like you have to use Aptana Studio. There are a number of other good IDEs out there, and you may already be using a different IDE or may just be happy using your favorite text editor. However, I will be using Aptana Studio throughout the book, so it may be easier to follow along if you are also using Aptana Studio.

Time for action – creating a new Aptana Studio PHP project

Upon opening Aptana Studio for the first time, you should see the following screen:

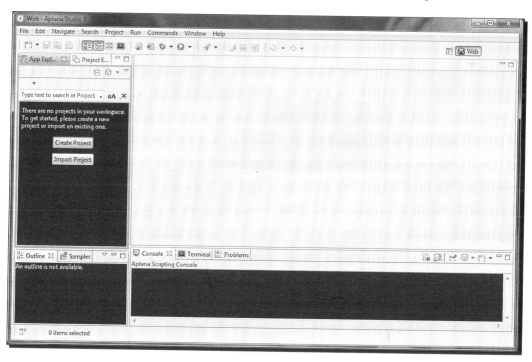

1. Click on the **Create Project** button, select **PHP Project**, and click on **Next**. At this point, you will see the **New PHP Project** window:

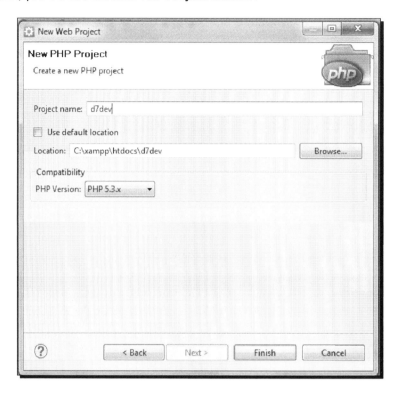

2. You must uncheck the **Use default location** checkbox, and browse to your new Drupal 7 install location. For Windows, it is `C:\xampp\htdocs\d7dev`, and for Mac OS X, it is `/Applications/MAMP/htdocs/d7dev`. After you have selected the location of your new Drupal 7 installation, click on **Finish**.

You will now have a project listing as shown in the following screenshot:

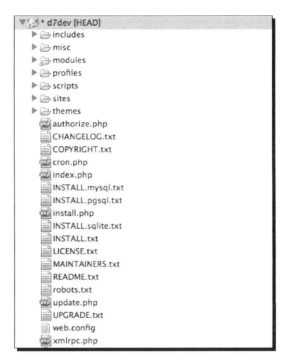

What just happened?

You have set up an IDE and have created a Drupal 7 project. Now, we are ready to start doing some Drupal development!

Drupalize Aptana Studio

Now that you have a new project pointing to your `d7dev` Drupal installation, let's take a look around. In your `project` folder, go to the `modules/aggregator` folder, and open the `aggegrator.module` and `aggegrator.pages.inc` files. You will notice that the `aggegrator.module` file does not have any syntax coloring, while the `aggegrator.pages.inc` file does. Aptana is not set up to recognize the Drupal-specific file types, such as `*.module` and `*.install`, as PHP files. Also, there are some simple formatting-related settings that don't follow the Drupal coding standards as specified at `http://drupal.org/coding-standards`.

Time for action – setting up the Drupal content type associations

Content type associations are used in Eclipse-based IDEs, so that the correct file editor is used for a specific set of file types. The PHP editor is typically only associated with the `.php` and `.inc` file suffixes, but for the Drupal development, we will also want the `.install` and `.module` suffixes associated with the PHP editor.

1. In Aptana Studio open up the **Preferences** menu; for Windows, it is under **Window | Preferences**, and for Mac OS X, it is under **Aptana Studio 3 | Preferences**. Navigate to **General | Content Types**.

2. Expand the **Text** section in the **Content types** list, scroll down to **PHP Source**, and select it.

3. Click on the **Add...** button.

4. Type `*.install` for the new **Content type** association, and click on **OK**.

5. Repeat *steps 4* and *5* by substituting *.module for the new **Content type** association.

6. Your final configuration should look similar to the following screenshot:

Time for action – installing the Drupal-specific Aptana formatter profile

The **Aptana formatter profile** will align the Aptana Studio PHP formatting with the Drupal coding standards (as outlined at http://drupal.org/coding-standards) as much as possible.

1. In your web browser, go to http://drupalcode.org/sandbox/ kmadel/1249414.git/blob/HEAD:/drupal_aptana_formatter_profile. xml, right-click on the drupal_aptana_formatter_profile.xml link, select **Save as...** or **Save link as...** (depending on your browser), and click on **Save**.

2. In Aptana Studio, open up **Preferences**, and go to **Aptana | Formatter**.

3. Click on the **Import...** button, navigate to and select the file downloaded in the first step, and click the **Open** button.

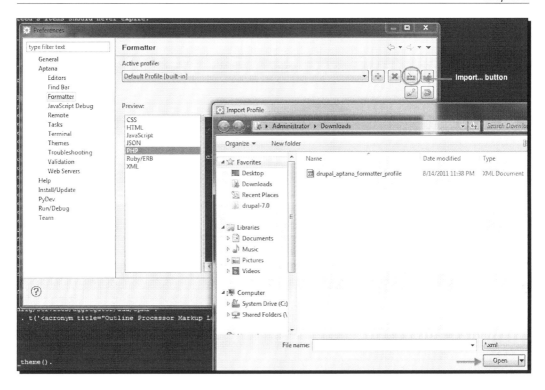

4. The **Active profile:** will now show that it is using the Drupal Profile [built-in]. Click on **OK** to save the settings.

5. For the settings to take effect, you will have to quit and then re-open Aptana Studio.

What just happened?

You have customized Aptana Studio for Drupal development, and the code we write will be following the Drupal coding standards to the degree that is possible with automatic Eclipse-based formatting.

Drupal.org from a developer's perspective

If you are new to the Drupal development, the first thing that you should understand is that being a good Drupal developer means being a part of the Drupal community. Drupal development is very much an open source process, and, as such, it is a community driven process.

`Drupal.org` has numerous resources to assist developers of all experience levels. However, before we can take advantage of all of these resources, you need to be a member of `drupal.org`. So, if you haven't already joined `drupal.org`, now is the time to do so at `http://drupal.org/user/register`. Once you are a member, and have logged in to `drupal.org`, you will see two primary tabs - **Drupal Homepage** and **Your Dashboard**:

As we move forward with the Drupal 7 development, we will return to your `drupal.org` dashboard on many occasions to keep a track of issues of the contributed modules that we are using. We will also utilize the new sandbox development feature that Drupal has added as part of the migration to Git. Before Drupal switched to Git, a lot of developers hosted their projects on GitHub as well as in the Drupal CVS-based repository. Working with CVS on day-to-day development of code became more and more tedious as compared to using new tools, such as Git. In addition to the numerous developer assets provided by drupal.org, you will find a number of Git related documentation and tools. We will find in the chapters to come how important Git is as a tool for using and contributing Drupal code. The following is a screenshot of one of my Git-enabled sandbox projects on drupal.org:

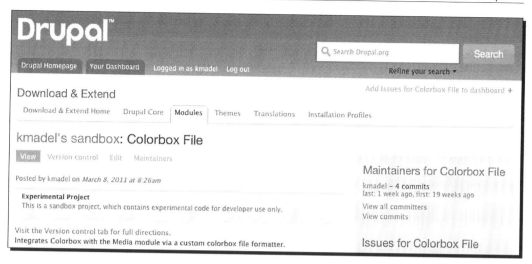

Make sure that you know the answers to the following questions before you continue.

Pop quiz – PHP and MySQL configuration for Drupal

1. What is the biggest MySQL configuration 'gotcha' in regards to Drupal?

   a. Setting `max_connections` to `300`

   b. Setting `max_allowed_packet` to `16M`

   c. Setting `innodb_buffer_pool_size` to `300M`

Summary

You have reached the end of *Chapter 1*! You should now have a working Drupal 7 website and an Aptana Studio IDE-based PHP project to begin doing custom Drupal development. I know that we haven't actually written any code yet, so I am excited to get started with some cool development examples in the next chapter. However, this chapter has given us some tools and configuration tweaks to make the development process much easier and more fun. Now, we are ready to begin developing for Drupal in earnest.

2
Custom Content Types and an Introduction to Module Development

The ability to easily define custom content types is a core feature of Drupal, and what makes Drupal a great system for managing web content. However, prior to Drupal 7, the contributed CCK module was required to create custom fields on content types. Now, field-able content types are baked right into Drupal 7core.

This chapter will walk you through the content types included with Drupal core, and the creation of a custom Recipe content type. Content type creation will include an overview of the different field types available in Drupal 7. However, the more interesting aspect of this chapter will include an initial introduction to module development. We will develop a custom module to provide a custom field formatter for a field type, provided by the Drupal core field module. If you don't already know what a field formatter is or what a field type is, don't worry about it. They will be explained when we walk through the example. Finally, we will have a brief introduction to the most popular contributed Drupal module - **Views** - and begin to explore how the **Devel** module (`http://drupal.org/project/devel`) makes Drupal development easier.

In this chapter we will:

- ◆ Define a custom content type
- ◆ Introduce module development with the creation of a custom field formatter
- ◆ Give a quick introduction to the Views module
- ◆ Use the Devel module to automatically generate content for development purposes

Creating custom Recipe content type

In this section, we are going to explore the creation of a custom recipe content type. As we make our way through each chapter, we will build a website to showcase recipes, and this Recipe content type will server as the foundation for our Drupal 7 recipe website. But before we get started, I would like to introduce you to a new administrative feature introduced with Drupal 7: the **administrative toolbar**. The administrative toolbar was born out of the d7UX project (http://www.d7ux.org/). The d7UX project for Drupal 7 focused on improving the user experience for frequent Drupal administrative tasks. Throughout this book, I will be directing you to the administrative or admin toolbar. For more in-depth documentation on the new administrative toolbar for Drupal 7, see http://drupal.org/documentation/modules/toolbar.

Time for action – creating a custom Recipe content type

The admin toolbar is pictured in the next screenshot, and we will use it to initiate the creation of a new content type.

1. Click on **Structure** in the admin toolbar, and then click on **Content types**.

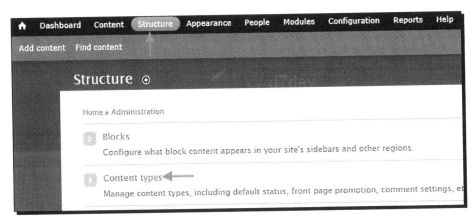

2. On the **Content types** screen, click on the **Add content type** link.

3. Enter Recipe as the **Name**.

4. Enter `A simple recipe content type based on the schema.org base HTML5 Microdata schema for Recipes at: http://schema.org/Recipe/.` for the **Description**.

5. For the **Title** field label, enter `name`.

The reason for changing the default text for the **Title** field label from `Title` to `name`, is because we are going to model our Recipe content type from the HTML5 Microdata-based spec defined at `http://schema.org/Recipe`. This will provide a semantic definition of our content for enhanced search results (Google, Yahoo, and Microsoft are some of the major backers of schema.org). If you would like to learn more about Microdata, please see the W3C spec at `http://www.w3.org/TR/html5/microdata.html`, or read the in-depth article at `http://diveintohtml5.org/extensibility.html`.

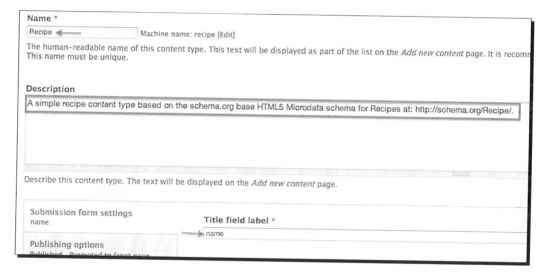

6. Click on the **Save and add fields** button (for now we will go with the default content type configuration for everything else).

7. Next, delete the **Body** field that is automatically added to our content type, by clicking on the **delete** link, and then confirming by clicking on the **Delete** button on the next screen.

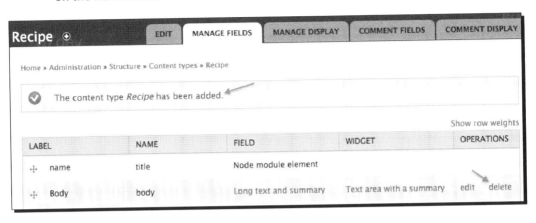

8. Now, we will add some new fields to our Recipe content type. We will use the Recipe schema property names as our field names. The first property listed in the table at `http://schema.org/Recipe/` is `description`. In the **Add new** field input, type `description`. Next to the **field_ prefix** label in the **Name** column, once again type `description`. Select **Long text** from the **Select a field type** drop-down, **Text area (multiple rows)** as the widget, and click on the **Save** button. On the next screen, click on the **Save field settings** button.

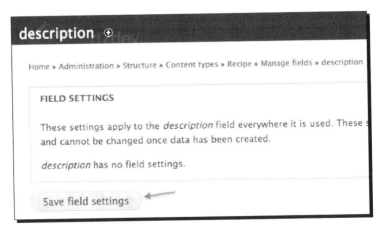

9. On the **RECIPE SETTINGS** page, enter A short description of the item. as the **Help text**. Accept the rest of the default settings, and then click on the **Save settings** button at the bottom of the page.

10. Now, we will move on to the image property. We are going to use an existing field for this property. In the **Add existing field** section, enter image for the **Label**. Select **Image: field_image (Image)** from the **Field to share** drop-down, and click on the **Save** button.

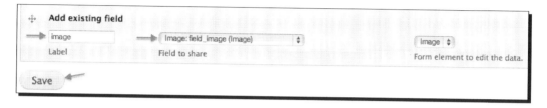

11. Click on the **Save field settings** button to accept the default settings on the **FIELD SETTINGS** page.

12. On the next page, click on the **Save settings** button to accept the default settings for **RECIPE SETTINGS** and **IMAGE FIELD SETTINGS**.

13. The **datePublished** and **author** properties will be captured by the core Drupal node properties, and we will be skipping the rest of the **Properties from CreativeWork** for now.

14. For the **cookTime** property, the settings will be—label: cookTime, name: field_cooktime, type: Integer, widget: Text field (the default).

15. Click on **Save**, and accept the default settings on the next page, by clicking on the **Save field settings** button.

16. On the next page, enter The time it takes to actually cook the dish in minutes. as the **Help text**, enter minute|minutes as the **Suffix** under **RECIPE SETTINGS**, and click on the **Save settings** button.

17. Along with cookingMethod, we will be skipping the nutrition, recipeCategory, recipeCuisine, and totalTime properties for now. We will add these properties later on in the book.

18. For the `ingredients` property, the settings will be—label: `ingredients`, name: `field_ingredients`, type: `Text`, widget: `Text field` (the default). Click on the **Save** button. On the next screen, accept the default setting of `255` for **Maximum length**, and click on the **Save field settings** button.

19. On the **RECIPE SETTINGS** page, enter `An ingredient used in the recipe.` as the **Help text**, and `Unlimited` for the **Number of values**. Accept the rest of the default settings, and click on the **Save settings** button at the bottom of the page.

20. For the `prepTime` property, the settings will be—label: `prepTime`, name: `field_preptime`, type: `Integer`, widget: `Text field` (the default). Click on **Save**, and accept the default settings on the next page by clicking on the **Save field settings** button. On the next page, enter `The length of time it takes to prepare the recipe in minutes.` as the **Help text**, and `minute|minutes` as the **Suffix** under the **RECIPE SETTINGS**. Click on the **Save settings** button.

21. For the `recipeInstructions` property, the settings will be—label: `recipeInstructions`, name: `field_recipeinstructions` (uppercase letters are not allowed for field names), type: `Long text`, widget: `Text area` (multiple rows). Click on **Save**, and accept the default settings on the next page by clicking on the **Save field settings** button. On the next page, enter `The steps to make the dish.` as the **Help text** under the **RECIPE SETTINGS** page, and click on the **Save settings** button.

22. For the `recipeYield` property, the settings will be—label: `recipeYield`, name: `field_recipeyield`, type: `Text`, widget: `Text field` (the default). Click on the **Save** button. On the next screen, accept the default setting of `255` for **Maximum length**, and click on the **Save field settings** button.

23. On the **RECIPE SETTINGS** page, enter `The quantity produced by the recipe (for example, number of people served, number of servings, and so on).` as the **Help text**. Accept the rest of the default settings, and click on the **Save settings** button at the bottom of the page.

24. You should now have a **Manage Fields** screen for our Recipe content type that looks similar to the following screenshot:

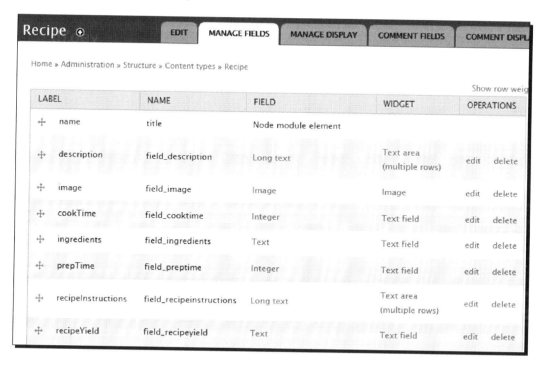

What just happened?

Now that we have created the new Recipe content type and modified its fields, let's create a new recipe by clicking on the **Add content** link in the shortcut bar, and then click on the link for Recipe. Here is my recipe for **Awesome Sauce** that you may use, but you are welcome to add any recipe you like:

- ♦ **Name**: Awesome Sauce
- ♦ **Description**: A deliciously sweet and spicy sauce that makes everything you put it on that much awesomer. A little goes a long way...

- **Ingredients**:
  - One ghost pepper (optional)
  - Two habanero peppers
  - Three Thai peppers
  - Four jalapeno peppers
  - Four garlic cloves
  - Three cups of rice vinegar
  - One tea spoon of fish sauce
  - One cup of sugar

- **recipeInstructions**:
  1. Remove the stems from the peppers.
  2. Add the peppers and garlic to a food processor, and blend until pureed.
  3. Add vinegar, sugar, fish sauce, and puree to a small saucepan, and bring to a simmer over low heat.
  4. Simmer sauce for 20 to 30 minutes, until the sugar has completely dissolved.
  5. Remove the saucepan from the burner, and let stand for 10 minutes.
  6. Your Awesome Sauce is ready to serve, or it can be refrigerated for up to three weeks.

     Thai peppers and fish sauce are typically available in most Asian markets. Ghost peppers are typically considered to be the hottest pepper in the world, and may be left out for those that have a little less tolerance for heat, or if you aren't able to find them.

- **Yield**: 12 Servings
- **prepTime**: 10 minutes
- **cookTime**: 30 minutes

When you are done, you will have a recipe page that looks similar to the following screenshot:

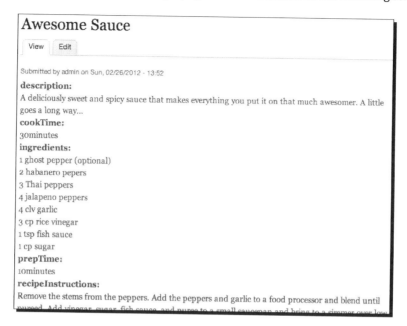

What just happened?

We created a custom Recipe content type, and added a recipe to the site.

Developing a custom module

Although the integer field type seems to be the best choice for the duration-related fields (`cookTime` and `prepTime`) in our Recipe content type, it would be nice if 60 minutes was displayed as 1 hour, and 90 minutes was displayed as 1 ½ hours. One way we can make this happen is to develop a custom module to create a custom field formatter that will display the duration related fields of `cookTime` and `prepTime` as hours, instead of minutes.

Module development is an important building block of the Drupal CMS, and it is helpful to understand that, generally speaking, there are three different types of Drupal modules:

1. A **core** module is any module that comes pre-packaged with Drupal.

2. A **contrib** or **contributed** module is any module that is available to download from `http://drupal.org/download`, and is not part of the Drupal core.

3. A **custom** module is basically any module that is not a core or contrib module, and is the type of module we will be developing in this chapter. Sometimes, a custom module will be contributed to Drupal.org, but there are many custom modules that will be so specific to your Drupal site that it does not make sense to share them as contrib modules. We will be developing a custom module to format our duration-related Recipe content type fields.

Now that we know what type of module we are developing, there are some minimum requirements for Drupal module development that we need to understand, so that our custom module is correctly recognized as a module by Drupal. A custom module requires two files in a folder of the same name, which is placed in a modules directory, located somewhere within the `sites` directory. Typically, custom and contrib modules are placed in the `sites/all/modules` directory, but they may also be placed in a `sites/{name_of_site}/modules` (a sub-site directory) directory for multi-site Drupal installations, where you would like them to only be available to those particular sites. More importantly, the two required files for a functional Drupal module are as follows:

◆ **The** `.info` **file**: This is a configuration file that allows you to specify certain defined properties—some required and some optional, which provide information for Drupal to process/handle the custom module

◆ **The** `.module` **file**: This is the file that will have all of the PHP code for our custom module

When developing the custom code that interacts with the existing Drupal core module code or contrib module code, you will typically use a Drupal programming mechanism referred to as a **hook**. A hook provides a way to inject your custom code into the processing of the existing code. A list of the core `field.module`-related hooks is available at: `http://api.drupal.org/api/drupal/modules--field--field.api.php/7`.

In the case of the custom module that we are going to develop, we will be implementing two hooks from the core `field.module`:

1. `hook_field_formatter_info`: This hook informs Drupal that our custom module has a field formatter.

2. `hook_field_formatter_view`: This hook is called by Drupal as part of the rendering process, for any field with our custom formatter applied to it.

Time for action – developing a custom module

Now we are ready to develop a custom Drupal module for our `d7dev` site!

1. Open **Aptana Studio**.

2. In the `sites/all/modules` directory, create a new folder named `custom`, and then create a new folder named `d7dev` within that folder.

3. Now, in the `d7dev` folder create two new files – `d7dev.info` and `d7dev.module`, by right-clicking on the `d7dev` folder and selecting **New file** from the contextual menu.

4. Open the `d7dev.info` file, and add the required info file properties of `name`, `description`, and `core`, and add the optional `package` property as displayed in the following code snippet:

    ```
    name = d7dev
    description = Custom module for misc custom functionality.
    core = 7.x
    package = Custom

    files[] = d7dev.module
    ```

 Although the `package` property is an optional property, adding it will make the management and organization of modules easier to maintain, as any custom module that you develop and associate to the `Custom` package will be organized as such on the Modules administrative screen.

Now, we will turn our attention to the module file. Any time that you implement a hook in your code, you just replace the prefix `hook` with the name of your module, so the two hooks that we will be implementing will become the `d7dev_field_formatter_info` and the `d7dev_field_formatter_view` functions. We can use the code from the core Drupal `number.module` (part of the field module) as a starting point for developing the code for these two hooks.

1. In **Aptana Studio**, open the `number.module` file located in the `d7dev/modules/field/modules/number` directory.

2. For our first hook, find the `number_field_formatter_info` function, copy the first 15 lines of the code, and paste them at the top of our custom `\d7dev.module` file.

3. Replace the 'number' part of the function name with `d7dev`.

4. Remove the comma on *line 16*.

   If you don't see any line numbers in your editor in **Aptana Studio**, right-click on the left margin area of the Aptana Studio PHP editor screen, and select **Show Line Numbers** in the displayed dialog-box. See the following screenshot for reference:

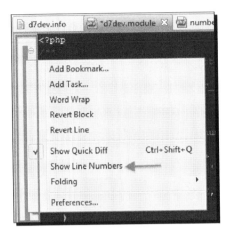

5. Close the array being returned, with a right parentheses and a semi-colon.

6. Next, close the function with a right curly bracket.

7. Then, remove the `settings` sub-array.

8. Next, rename the 'label' from `Default` to `Duration`.

9. Finally, rename the formatter from `number_integer` to `d7dev_integer_duration`.

   At this point, your code should look similar to the following:

```php
<?php
/**
 * Implements hook_field_formatter_info().
 */
function d7dev_field_formatter_info() {
  return array(
    'd7dev_integer_duration' => array(
      'label' => t('Duration'),
      'field types' => array('number_integer'),
    )
  );
}
```

Now, we will move on to the second hook that we will be implementing.

1. Copy the `number_field_formatter_view` function from the `number.module`, and paste it after our `d7dev_field_formatter_info` function.

2. Once again, rename the function to reflect our module name.

3. Next, in the `switch` statement, remove the `case` statements for `number_integer` and `number_decimal`.

4. Rename the `case` for `number_unformatted` to match the name for our custom formatter – `d7dev_integer_duration`.

5. Now, we will add some simple math to convert the integer-based field to hours and minutes, with the following code at the top of the `foreach` loop:

```
//some simple math to covert the duration minutes to hours and the
//remainder as minutes
$hours = floor($item['value']/60); //divide by minutes in 1 hour
//and get floor


$minutes = $item['value']%60;  //use the modulus to get the //
remainder of minutes
```

6. Next, we want to convert the remainder of minutes to a fraction of an hour, but we will first need to add the following helper function to get the greatest common denominator of our remainder minutes over `60`:

```
//simple helper function to get gcd of minutes
function gcd($a, $b) {
  $b = ( $a == 0 )? 0 : $b;
  return ( $a % $b )? gcd($b, abs($a - $b)) : $b;
}
```

7. Now, we can convert our remainder of minutes to a fraction of an hour with the greatest common denominator, and format the results to be returned as the markup for our custom formatter:

```
//get greatest common denominator of minutes to convert to //
fraction of hours
$minutes_gcd = gcd($minutes, 60);

//&frasl; is the html entity for the fraction separator, and we //
use the sup and sub html element to give
//the appearance of a fraction
```

```
$minutes_fraction = '<sup>' . $minutes/$minutes_gcd .
  '</sup>&frasl;<sub>' . 60/$minutes_gcd . '</sub>';

$markup = $hours > 0 ? $hours . ' and ' . $minutes_fraction . '
  hours' : $minutes_fraction . ' hours';

//finally, return our formatted value as the markup for this field
//formatter
$element[$delta] = array('#markup' => $markup);
```

8. When you are done, the `d7dev_field_formatter_view` function should look similar to the following:

```
/**
 * Implements hook_field_formatter_view().
 */
function d7dev_field_formatter_view($entity_type, $entity, $field,
  $instance, $langcode, $items, $display) {
  $element = array();
  $settings = $display['settings'];

  switch ($display['type']) {

    case 'd7dev_integer_duration':
      foreach ($items as $delta => $item) {
        //some simple math to covert the duration minutes to hours
        //and the remainder as minutes

//divide by minutes in 1 hour and get floor
        $hours = floor($item['value']/60);

//use the modulus to get the remainder of minutes
        $minutes = $item['value']%60;

//get greatest common denominator of minutes to convert to
fraction of hours
        $minutes_gcd = gcd($minutes, 60);

//&frasl; is the html entity for the fraction separator, and we //
use the sup and sub html element to give the appearance of a //
fraction
        $minutes_fraction = '<sup>' . $minutes/$minutes_gcd .
          '</sup>&frasl;<sub>' . 60/$minutes_gcd . '</sub>';
```

```
        $markup = $hours > 0 ? $hours . ' and ' . $minutes_
fraction . ' hours' : $minutes_fraction . ' hours';

//finally, return our formatted value as the markup for this field
//formatter
        $element[$delta] = array('#markup' => $markup);
      }
      break;
  }

  return $element;
}
```

We are not quite done. Now that we have created a custom formatter, we need to use it. We need to enable our new module by clicking on **Modules** in the **Admin** toolbar.

1. Now, on the **Modules** admin screen, scroll down to the **Custom** section, and check the **ENABLED** checkbox next to our d7dev module.

2. Earlier we used our new custom formatter with our Recipe content type fields. We need to click on **Configuration** in the **Admin** toolbar, click on **Performance** under the **DEVELOPMENT** section, and then click the **Clear all caches** button.

   Drupal caches the field formatters that are available for a given field type, and we must clear this cache in order for our new custom formatter to be available in the upcoming steps.

3. Now, with our new module enabled, select **Structure** in our administrative toolbar, and then select **Content Types**.

4. On the **Content types** screen, select **manage display** for our Recipe content type.

5. Now, for the two duration related fields, `cookTime` and `prepTime`, select **Duration** as the **FORMAT**, and click on the **SAVE** button.

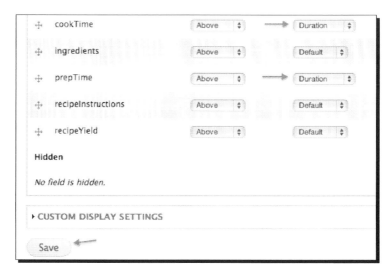

6. Now, view the Recipe content item that we created earlier, and you will see something similar to the following screenshot:

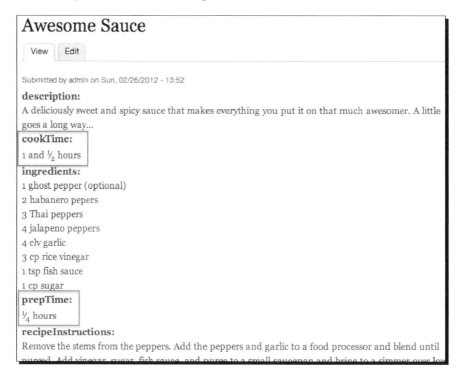

What just happened?

We have created a custom module that will allow us to format our Recipe content duration fields the way we want – integers converted to hours and fractions of hours.

Quick introduction to Views

It is with good reason that the **Views** module is the most-installed Drupal 7 contributed module. The Views module offers a very unique way to create custom 'views' of your content that is powerful, flexible, and easier than ever with the new version of Views for Drupal 7. In later chapters, we will dive deeper into custom development for Views, but for now, we will just use Views to quickly create a block, listing all of the site's Recipe content to be displayed on the front page.

> A **block** refers to one of the primary site components of a Drupal site. For the most part, any content on a Drupal page that is not part of the content item or node being displayed, is usually a block. Drupal core includes a number of system blocks, and the Views module allows you to create views as blocks. If you are not familiar with blocks, take a second to familiarize yourself with the blocks administrative page at /admin/structure/block.

Time for action – installing the Views module

We are going to use **Drush** to download and install the Views module. Start by opening a Command Prompt for Windows or Terminal for Mac. Change to your d7dev project directory, and type the following command:

```
C:\xampp\htdocs\d7dev>drush dl views

Project views (7.x-3.3) downloaded to [success]

C:/xampp/htdocs/d7dev/sites/all/modules/views.

Project views contains 2 modules: views, views_ui.
```

> It is worth mentioning that Drupal 7 added the ability to install and update modules that are hosted on Drupal.org, directly with the administrative UI. You should definitely check it out. But once you begin custom development for Drupal, and start using Drush, you will find it to be an indispensable time saver.

You will see that Views includes two modules: `views` and `views_ui`. We want both the modules, so to save typing an extra `Drush` command, we will enable the `views_ui` module, and Drush will automatically take care of enabling all module dependencies – in this case, `views` and `ctools`. When prompted to download the unmet dependencies, type `y`, and hit *Enter*.

```
C:\xampp\htdocs\d7dev>drush en views_ui

The following projects have unmet dependencies:

views_ui requires ctools

Would you like to download them? (y/n): y

Project ctools (7.x-1.0-rc1) downloaded to               [success]

C:/xampp/htdocs/d7dev/sites/all/modules/ctools.

The following extensions will be enabled: views_ui, ctools, views

Do you really want to continue? (y/n): y

ctools was enabled successfully.                    [ok]

views_ui was enabled successfully.                  [ok]

views was enabled successfully.                     [ok]
```

So now that you have the most popular Drupal module downloaded and enabled, let's create a Views block of recipes to be displayed on the front page.

Time for action – creating a recipe block listing with Views

We will see just how easy the new Views modules makes it to display a list of recipes on our d7dev site.

1. If you aren't already logged into your site, log in as `admin`, click on the **Structure** link in the **Admin** toolbar, and click on the **Views** link in the subsequently loaded **Structure** menu page.

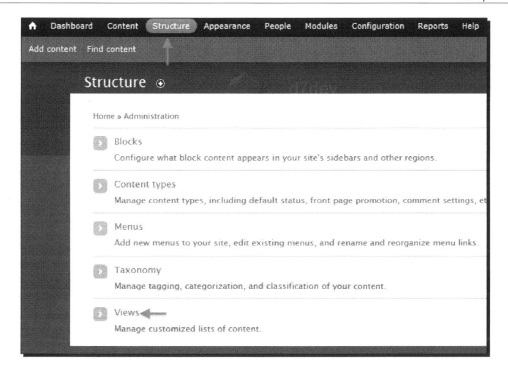

2. On the next screen, the **Views** listing pages, click on the **Add new view** link near the top of the page.

3. Next, you will see the new creation wizard page for Views 3. Enter `Recipe List` as the **View name**.

4. Select **Recipe** as the **of type** dropdown.

5. Uncheck the **Create a page** checkbox.

6. Check the **Create a block** checkbox.

7. Accepting all of the default values for creating a block, your page should look similar to the following screenshot. If everything is entered correctly, click on the **Save & exit** button.

Now, we need to configure our d7dev site, so that our Recipe List Views-based block shows up on the front page.

1. Click on the **Structure** link in the **Admin** toolbar, and select **Blocks**.

2. On the next page, scroll to the bottom of the page, and click on the configure link for the **View: Recipe List block** (the block we just created with Views).

3. Leave the **Block** title field blank because that way, the title will default to the title we added above in the Views creation wizard.

4. Under **REGION SETTINGS**, select **Sidebar second** from the **Bartik (default theme)** dropdown.

5. Under the **Visibility settings** and the **Pages** tab, select **Only the listed pages** radio button under **Show block on specific** pages, and enter `<front>` in the text area. Check that your screen should look similar to the following screenshot, and click on **Save block**.

What just happened?

You have now created a Views-based block of recipes, and configured it so that it will only be displayed on the front page. Now, when you visit the front page of our d7dev site at http://localhost/d7dev/, you will have a nice **Recipe List** block on the right side of the page.

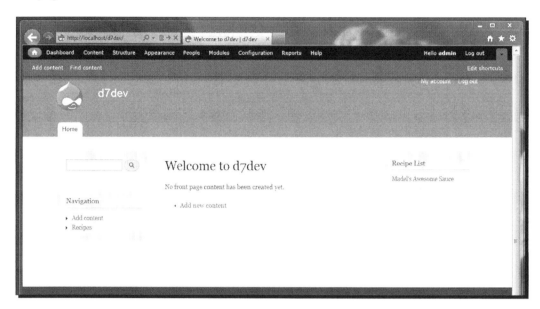

Introducing the Devel module

So, in the previous section, we saw how easy it was to create a custom Views-based block for displaying a list of the recipes on the front page. One thing that you will notice right away is that there is only one recipe showing up, because, so far, we have only created one. You may also recall that when we created the Recipe List block with Views, we left the setting for **Items per page** at the default value of 5. Now, it would be nice to be able to test that setting, without needing to manually create four more recipe items. Enter the Devel module - http://drupal.org/project/devel. The Devel module includes a number of sub-modules that makes Drupal development easier; and the one we are interested in to help us out with content creation for development purposes is the devel_generate module.

Time for action – installing the Devel Generate content module

Using Drush to install modules should start becoming somewhat routine at this point. We will use Drush to download and install the Devel module to include its devel_generate sub-module.

```
C:\xampp\htdocs\d7dev>drush dl devel

Project devel (7.x-1.2) downloaded to              [success]
C:/xampp/htdocs/d7dev/sites/all/modules/devel.

Project devel contains 3 modules: devel_generate, devel, devel_node_
access.

C:\xampp\htdocs\d7dev>drush en devel_generate

The following extensions will be enabled: devel_generate, devel

Do you really want to continue? (y/n): y

devel_generate was enabled successfully.              [ok]

devel was enabled successfully.                       [ok]
```

Now, with the `devel_generate` module enabled, we are going to generate some Recipe content, so that we can test the number of items in our Recipe List block.

Time for action – generating content with the devel_generate module

Now, with the `devel_generate` module enabled, we are going to generate some Recipe content, so that we can test the number of items in our Recipe List block view.

1. First, click on the **Configuration** link in the admin toolbar, and then click on the **Generate content** link under the **DEVELOPMENT** section.

2. On the **Generate content** page, uncheck all of the **Content types** checkboxes, except for the one for Recipe.

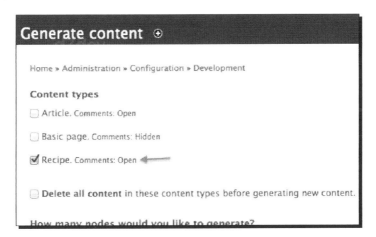

3. Stick with the default values for all of the rest of the settings, and click on the **Generate** button at the bottom of the page.

4. Now, navigate to the home page, and you will see the Recipe List block fully populated.

What just happened?

Although this is a very simple example of using the `devel_generate` module, being able to generate content can be a big time saver when testing custom code that requires multiple content items. We just used the `devel_generate` module to generate some dummy content, based on our custom Recipe content type, and now our Recipe List block on the home page should look similar to the following screenshot:

Summary

In this chapter, we have explored some fundamental Drupal concepts around content types and fields, and had a quick introduction to the Views and Devel modules. But more importantly, we have started doing Drupal development by developing a module that provides a custom field formatter for integer fields. In the chapters to come, we will continue to build on our module development skills, and eventually learn what it takes to develop a contrib module versus a custom module.

3
HTML5 Integration for Drupal 7 and More Module Development

HTML5 is not exactly new on the technology scene. If you have done any mobile web development, then you will certainly know how prevalent HTML5 is becoming. Even though there is an active initiative around HTM5 for Drupal 8 (`http://drupal.org/community-initiatives/drupal-core/html5`*), the adoption of HTML5 was not far enough along to be included as part of Drupal 7 core.*

HTML5 is one of the main ingredients of many of the upcoming development examples in this book.

In this chapter, we will explore some of the different modules and options for using HTML5 with Drupal 7, and we will enhance our custom-developed `d7dev` module to include certain HTML5 features.

Modules are a key element of what makes Drupal so attractive for both developers and non-developers. The multitude of available contributed modules makes Drupal attractive to non-developers looking for certain features, while the ease of module development and integration of such modules, with Drupal core, and other contributed modules, is what makes Drupal popular with developers.

Evidence of this popularity is displayed by the availability of almost 10,000 contributed modules on `http://drupal.org/project/modules/`. Therefore, in addition to updating our existing module with the HTML5 features, we will continue the development emphasis on module development. We are going to develop a new compound field module.

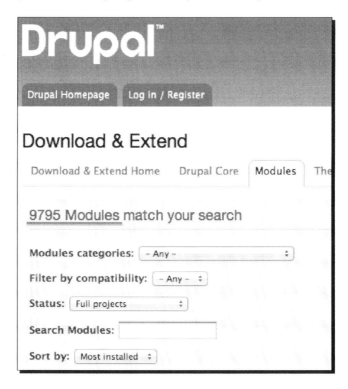

This chapter, with its HTML5-driven code examples, will serve as a foundation for many of the code examples in the following chapters.

First things first—changing our DOCTYPE

The DOCTYPE of our content may seem like an odd thing to be mentioning at this point. However, since HTML5 will be a major concept and building block for the rest of this book, it is important to get off to a good start. This all starts with the HTML5 DOCTYPE.

Drupal 7 defaults to an XHTML DOCTYPE:

```
<!DOCTYPE html PUBLIC "-//W3C//DTD
XHTML+RDFa 1.0//EN"    "http://www.w3.org/
MarkUp/DTD/xhtml-rdfa-1.dtd">
```

Whereas the HTML5 DOCTYPE is much simpler:

```
<!DOCTYPE html>
```

The HTML5 DOCTYPE is fully supported by all modern browsers, so at this point, there is not a good reason for not using it.

The DOCTYPE is hardcoded in the `html.tpl.php` file, and can be overridden in any theme, by creating your own version of that template file. However, we aren't currently using a custom theme (that's coming in the next chapter), and we don't want to modify any of the core themes (see the following information box for an explanation of why you shouldn't modify or hack core). So, there is a simple solution: the contrib HTML5 Tools module.

Do not hack core. This is a phrase that you will come across time and time again, as you do more and more custom Drupal development. The basic idea behind the phrase is that Drupal provides so many ways to modify the behavior of a Drupal site without modifying any core modules, themes or other files, that you will only cause yourself unnecessary grief in regards to upgrading core, and dealing with possible core issues if you start modifying core. An in-depth explanation of why it is a bad practice to hack core can be found at `http://drupal.org/best-practices/do-not-hack-core`.

Time for action – installing the HTML5 Tools module

The HTML5 Tools module (`http://drupal.org/projects/html5_tools`) will provide an HTML5-compliant `DOCTYPE` and will provide support for other HTML5 features.

Once again, we will use Drush to download and enable the module.

```
C:\xampp\htdocs\d7dev>drush dl html5_tools
Project html5_tools (7.x-1.1) downloaded to              [success]
C:/xampp/htdocs/d7dev/sites/all/modules/html5_tools.


C:\xampp\htdocs\d7dev>drush en html5_tools
The following projects have unmet dependencies:
html5_tools requires elements
Would you like to download them? (y/n): y
Project elements (7.x-1.2) downloaded to                [success]
C:/xampp/htdocs/d7dev/sites/all/modules/elements.
The following extensions will be enabled: html5_tools, elements
Do you really want to continue? (y/n): y
elements was enabled successfully.                       [ok]
html5_tools was enabled successfully.                    [ok]
```

In addition to providing an HTML5-compliant `DOCTYPE` (that is enabled, by default, just by enabling the module), the HTML5 Tools module, and its dependent Elements module (`http://drupal.org/projects/elements`), a number of other HTML5 features provided by the HTML5 Tools module include the following:

- Overrides Drupal core forms with HTML5 counterparts
- Simplifies the `head` markup for HTML5 specified `style`, `javascript`, and `meta` tags
- Uses the new HTML5 `time` element for content and comments publication dates

For a more comprehensive listing and explanation of what the HTML5 Tools modules does, take a look at the administrative configuration page for **HTML5 Tools** by selecting **Configuration** from the **Admin** toolbar, and selecting the **HTML5 Tools** link from the **Markup** section.

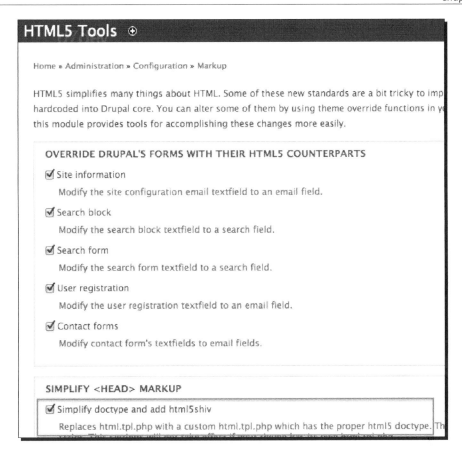

HTML5, RDFa, and Microdata

As we discussed in the previous chapter, one aspect of HTML5 is semantic markup, or the ability to describe your content in a meaningful way with a vocabulary, and apply the vocabulary to the markup of your content. Drupal 7 has such a semantic capability baked right into core, and it is called **RDFa**. However, the way that RDFa is integrated with Drupal 7 is not HTML5-compliant. Furthermore, although RDFa will be supported by HTML5, the HTML5 Microdata specification (http://dev.w3.org/html5/md/) was specifically designed with HTML5 in mind, and there is a Microdata module for Drupal 7 (http://drupal.org/project/microdata).

So, let us enhance our `d7dev` Recipe content type with some HTML5 Microdata that will make it semantically identified as an `http://schema.org/Recipe` item.

This section is not intended to start a flame war, and is not trying to make the point that Microdata is better than RDFa. Or, that Drupal 7 made a big mistake by including the XHTML flavor of RDFa instead of HTML5 RDFa or Microdata. The HTML5 version of RDFa, and for that matter Microdata, didn't even exist when the new feature set for Drupal 7 was frozen. The point of this section is that things change in the web world between major Drupal releases, and sometimes those changes need to be addressed sooner rather than later. This is the real point of this section: *showing how easy it is to adapt Drupal to the latest and greatest new web standards*. The Microdata schema that we are going to associate with our Recipe content type is part of the schema.org project that is backed by Google, Yahoo, and Microsoft. If you would like to learn more about Microdata, you can find an excellent introduction to understanding and using Microdata at: `http://diveintohtml5.org/extensibility.html`.

Time for action – installing the Microdata module

Once again, we are going to use Drush to download and install the Microdata module. Start by opening a Command Prompt for Windows or Terminal for Mac, change to your `d7dev` working folder, type the following commands, and you should see the following responses:

```
C:\xampp\htdocs\d7dev>drush dl microdata

There is no recommended release for project microdata.

Choose one of the available releases:
 [0]  :  Cancel
 [1]  :  7.x-1.x-dev     -  2012-Feb-24  -  Development
 [2]  :  7.x-1.0-alpha4  -  2012-Feb-22  -  Supported
```

2

```
Project microdata (7.x-1.0-alpha4) downloaded to          [success]
C:/xampp/htdocs/d7dev/sites/all/modules/microdata.


C:\xampp\htdocs\d7dev>drush en microdata
The following projects have unmet dependencies:
microdata requires entity
Would you like to download them? (y/n): y
Project entity (7.x-1.0-rc1) downloaded to          [success]
C:/xampp/htdocs/d7dev/sites/all/modules/entity.
The following extensions will be enabled: microdata, entity
Do you really want to continue? (y/n): y
entity was enabled successfully.                    [ok]
microdata was enabled successfully.                 [ok]
```

> Drush will actually modify the database of your Drupal installation when running certain commands, such as drush en. In order for Drush to modify the correct database, you must run the Drush command within the root Drupal install folder of your Drupal site. Otherwise, you would have to include which specific Drupal instance you would like Drush to modify with the -r argument: drush -r /Applications/MAMP/htdocs/d7dev

What just happened?

We have now installed the Microdata module and the Entity module as its dependency. Now that we have installed the Microdata module, let us put it to use, before we move on to some more development examples. We will configure our Recipe content type and its fields to utilize the functionality of the Microdata module.

Time for action – configuring Microdata for our Recipe content type

1. Navigate to the **Structure | Content Types** page, and select the **edit** link for our Recipe content type.

2. On the **Recipe content type edit** page, select the **Microdata settings** tab, and you will see a screen similar to the following, only without values in the **Field property(s)** input:

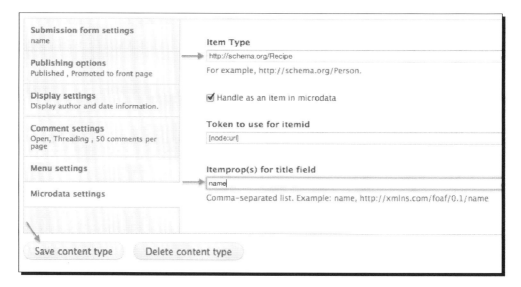

3. Type `http://schema.org/Recipe` as the value for the **Item Type** field, and `name` as the value for the **Itemprop(s) for title field** field. Click on the **Save content type** button.

4. Now, click on the **Home** button at the far left of the **Admin** toolbar, and select any of the Recipe content items from our Recipe List block on the right side of the page.

5. Next, right-click anywhere on the recipe item page, and select **View source (IE)** or **View Page Source** from your browser's menu.

6. In the source view of our page, scroll down to approximately *line 182*, and look for the following markup. You will see that the Microdata `itemscope` and `itemtype` attributes have been set on the enclosing `DIV` of our recipe content node:

```
<div id="node-51" class="node node-recipe node-promoted node-full
  clearfix" itemid="/d7dev/node/51" itemscope=""
  itemtype="http://schema.org/Recipe">.
```

7. However, if you inspect the HTML source any further, you will notice that none of the fields of our Recipe content node have any Microdata attributes applied to them. For example, the `DIV` wrapper for our `description` field will look as follows:

```
<div class="field field-name-field-description field-type-text-
long field-label-above">
```

8. As previously mentioned in this chapter, the Microdata module supports the ability to specify the `itemProp` values for any text field type. So, from the **Admin** toolbar, select **Structure | Content types**, and select the **manage fields** link for our Recipe content type.

9. Click on the **edit** link for the **description** field, and scroll down to the **Description Microdata Mapping** section on the **description field edit** page. Referring to the `http://schema.org/Recipe` definition, we will set the **Field property(s)** input to **description**, as shown in the following screenshot:

 The `node id` will most likely not be exactly the same in your environment, so look for a `DIV` element with the class as specified previously.

10. Click on the **Save settings** button to save the updated configuration for the **description** field.

11. Now, we will repeat the same steps for the rest of the text fields for our Recipe content type, setting **Field property of each** under the **Description Microdata Mapping** section accordingly:

ingredients	ingredients
recipeInstructions	recipeInstructions
recipeYield	recipeYield

12. Now, to test the output of the Microdata module, we will once again click on the **Home** button at the far left of the **Admin** toolbar, and select any of the recipe content items from our Recipe List block on the right side of the page.

13. Next, right-click anywhere on the **recipe item** page, and select **View source (IE)** or **View Page Source** from your browser's menu.

14. In the source view of our page, scroll down to approximately *line 191*, and look for the following markup:

```
<div class="field field-name-field-description
  field-type-text-long field-label-above">
  <div class="field-label">
description: 
</div>
<div class="field-items">
  <div class="field-item even" itemprop="description">
```

What just happened?

We enhanced our Recipe content type with Microdata metadata.

Earlier in its development, the Microdata module did not support the Drupal core number_integer field type, the field type that we used for the prepTime and cookTime fields of our Recipe content type. In order to provide the ability to enable the Microdata field properties for the cookTime and prepTime integer fields on our Recipe content type, we just need to implement the hook_field_info_alter hook, just as the Microdata module did for image and text fields.

The latest release of the Microdata module at the time of the publishing of this book, `7.x-1.0-alpha4`, actually included support for integer fields. Therefore, you will not need to add the following code to your custom `d7dev` module; rather, this code example illustrates the power of the Drupal community at work, by showing how local changes can eventually make their way back into core and the contributed module code.

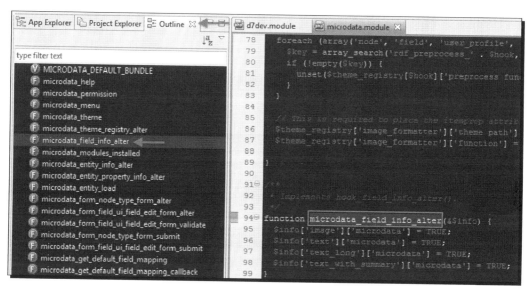

Take a close look at this screenshot, and you will see that at one point, the Microdata module only supports field mappings for the image field and text fields. So, in order to add support for the `number_integer` field, all we would have to do is implement the `hook_field_info_alter` hook just as the Microdata module. But for the `number_integer` field, the code would look something as follows:

```
/**
 * Implements hook_field_info_alter().
 */
function d7dev_field_info_alter(&$info) {
  $info['number_integer']['microdata'] = TRUE;
}
```

That is all it would take to add the Microdata support for core integer fields.

Drupal Shortcut Bar

There are many Drupal core hooks that require you to clear the Drupal cache in order for them to take effect. The `hook_field_info_alter` hook is such a hook, and it can get somewhat tiresome navigating to the **Performance administrative** page over and over again, when testing some new code. Luckily, Drupal 7 added the administrative UX component called the **shortcut bar**. The shortcut bar allows you to create a shortcut link to any administrative page. So, we can use this functionality to add the **Performance settings** page to our shortcut bar. Click on the plus icon next to the **Performance** heading, and it will show up as a link in your shortcut bar.

And notice after you add it, there is a minus icon next to the Performance heading. Therefore, you can easily remove the shortcut if you decide you don't use it much anymore, or your shortcut bar is getting crowded.

Anytime that you find yourself going to a certain administrative configuration page over and over, you should add it to your shortcut bar.

Drupal development and the Drupal community

As discussed in *Chapter 1*, *Getting Set up*, being a good Drupal developer means being aware of and active in the Drupal community. We have an opportunity to share this small bit of code we wrote with the Drupal community by adding an issue to the Microdata project issue queue (`http://drupal.org/project/issues/microdata`), suggesting that the Microdata module should add support for the core number field. This will not only help other Drupal users who would like this capability, it will also be custom code that we will no longer have to support by ourselves if it gets added to the Microdata module.

Time for action – creating issues in Contrib modules' issue queues

I am going to follow my own advice, and walk you through the process of adding an issue to a Drupal module's issue queue.

1. Open a browser, log into `http://drupal.org`, and navigate to `http://drupal.org/project/issues/microdata`.

2. Click on the **Create new issue** link under the **Issues for Microdata** heading.

3. Next, fill out all of the fields for **Create Issue form**. Here is a screenshot of the issue that I submitted for adding support for number field types:

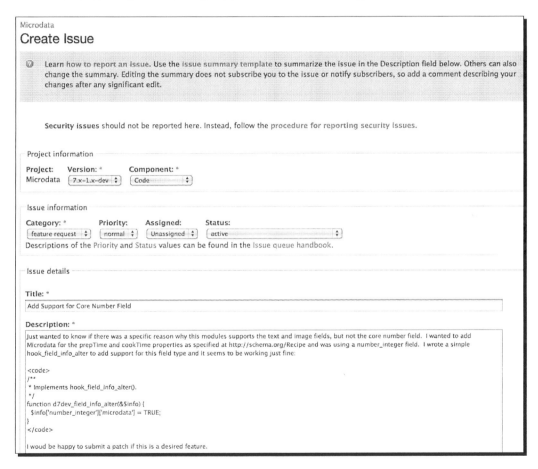

4. After you are done filling out the form, click on the **Save** button at the bottom of the page.

What just happened?

We created an issue in the Microdata module issue queue, and if we follow up with the issue at `http://drupal.org/node/1291634`, we will see that the module maintainer has actually implemented our feature request issue.

Issue Summary

Just wanted to know if there was a specific reason why this modules supports the text and image
add Microdata for the prepTime and cookTime properties as specified at http://schema.org/Recip
simple hook_field_info_alter to add support for this field type and it seems to be working just fine

```
/**
 * Implements hook_field_info_alter().
 */
function d7dev_field_info_alter(&$info) {
  $info['number_integer']['microdata'] = TRUE;
}
```

I woud be happy to submit a patch if this is a desired feature.

Login or register to post comments

Comments

#1   Posted by linclark on *September 26, 2011 at 11:20pm*

That would be great. IIRC, the only reason I hadn't added it yet is because I haven't written t
number fields to the SimpleTest for core fields, then this would be ready to go. I'm not sure
need it.

#2   Posted by linclark on *December 21, 2011 at 3:02pm*

Status: active   » fixed

This is fixed with commit http://drupalcode.org/project/microdata.git/commit/414cdea.

Time for action – adding Microdata mappings for Recipe number_integer fields

Now that the Microdata supports the `number_integer` fields, we will update all of our Recipe content type `number_integer` fields with a Microdata mapping.

1. Now, go back to the **field settings** page for the `cookTime` field, and you will see that we now have the **Field property(s)** input. So, go ahead and enter `cookTime` in that field.

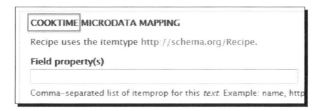

2. Now, once again we will navigate to a Recipe content item page, and view the HTML source. The `cookTime` field will look as follows:

```
<div class="field field-name-field-cooktime field-type-number-
   integer field-label-above">
   <div class="field-label">cookTime: </div>
   <div class="field-items">
     <div class="field-item even" itemprop="cookTime">
       84 and
       <sup>14</sup>&frasl;
       <sub>15</sub> hours
     </div>
   </div>
</div>
```

3. Finally, go back to the Recipe content type manage fields screen, and repeat the previous steps for the `prepTime` field.

What just happened?

We enabled the Microdata support for the `number_integer` fields of our Recipe content type.

Now, all of the fields of our current Recipe content type fields are associated with Microdata properties. With the help of the contributed Microdata module, adding Microdata support for our `cookTime` and `prepTime` Recipe fields was a straightforward task.

NutritionInformation module

One of the `http://schema.org/Recipe` properties that we did not include with our Drupal Recipe content type is the `NutritionInformation` property. The reason for that is because the `NutritionInformation` property is itself an `itemType` from `http://schema.org`, and as such is made up of a number of its own individual properties. In order to add `NutritionInformation` to our custom Recipe content type, we are going to need to create a custom Drupal compound field module that is based on the specification at `http://schema.org/NutritionInformation`.

Time for action – developing a custom module for a compound NutritionInformation field

Rather than adding the code to create this compound field to our existing module, we are going to create a new module, as it is possible that it is something that could be useful to the Drupal community as a whole, and we may want to eventually contribute it to drupal.org.

1. In **Aptana Studio**, create a new folder named `nutritioninfo` in the `/sites/all/modules/custom` directory.

2. Create the `.module`, `.info`, and `.install` files with the same name as the folder - `nutritioninfo`, and you should have a folder that looks similar to the following screenshot:

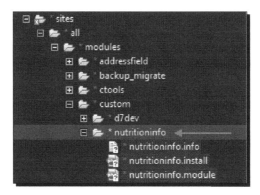

3. Now, open the `nutrtioninfo.info` file and add the following configuration:

```
name = Nutrition Information Field
description = Defines a nutrition information field type based on
the Microdata spec at http://schema.org/NutritionInformation
core = 7.x
package = Fields
```

4. I always find that development is easier when you are able to look at an example. So, we are going to use Drush to download the contributed **Address Field module** (`http://drupal.org/project/addressfield`) to use as an example for our own compound field module:

> The Address Field module is a good example of a compound field module. So, the code from that module will provide some good examples for implementing our own compound field module.

```
C:\xampp\htdocs\d7dev>drush dl addressfield-7.x-1.0-beta2

Project addressfield (7.x-1.0-beta2) downloaded to [success]

C:/xampp/htdocs/d7dev/sites/all/modules/addressfield.

Project addressfield contains 2 modules: addressfield_example,
addressfield.
```

5. So, now that we have downloaded the Address Field module, let's take a look at its code. In **Aptana Studio**, open the `addressfield.module`, and `addressfield.install` files located at `/sites/all/modules/addressfield`.

6. Next, we are going to use the following code from the `addressfield.install` file as a starting point for our `nutritioninfo.install` file.

```php
<?php

/**
 * Implements hook_field_schema()
 */
function addressfield_field_schema() {
  $columns = array(
    'country' => array(
      'description' => 'Two letter ISO country code of this
address.',
      'type' => 'varchar',
      'length' => 2,
      'not null' => FALSE,
      'default' => '',
    ),
```

7. Now, we will rename the function to `nutritioninfo_field_schema`, so that our `hook_field_schema` code looks as follows:

```php
<?php

/**
 * Implements hook_field_schema()
 */
function nutritioninfo_field_schema() {
  $columns = array(
    'country' => array(
      'description' => 'Two letter ISO country code of this
address.',
      'type' => 'varchar',
      'length' => 2,
```

```
      'not null' => FALSE,
      'default' => '',
    ),
  );

  return array(
    'columns' => $columns,
  );
}
```

8. The `hook_field_schema` hook (`http://api.drupal.org/api/drupal/modules--field--field.api.php/function/hook_field_schema/7`) allows us to define a database schema for storing our custom field information, and is automatically detected by Drupal, as long as it is in the `.install` file of our module. Now, we need to replace the `country` column as specified by the code we copied from the `addressfield_field_schema` function and add columns for the rest of the properties defined at `http://schema.org/NutritionInformation`.

9. After adding the column specifications for all of the `NutritionInformation` properties, our `nutritioninfo_field_schema` function will look as follows:

```
/**
 * Implements hook_field_schema()
 */
function nutritioninfo_field_schema() {
  $columns = array(
    'calories' => array(
      'description' => 'The number of calories.',
      'type' => 'varchar',
      'length' => 255,
      'not null' => FALSE,
      'default' => '',
    ),
    'carbohydrate_content' => array(
      'description' => 'The number of grams of carbohydrates.',
      'type' => 'varchar',
      'length' => 255,
      'not null' => FALSE,
      'default' => '',
    ),
    'cholesterol_content' => array(
      'description' => 'The number of milligrams of cholesterol.',
      'type' => 'varchar',
```

```
      'length' => 255,
      'not null' => FALSE,
      'default' => '',
    ),
    'fat_content' => array(
      'description' => 'The number of grams of fat.',
      'type' => 'varchar',
      'length' => 255,
      'not null' => FALSE,
      'default' => '',
    ),
    'fiber_content' => array(
      'description' => 'The number of grams of fiber.',
      'type' => 'varchar',
      'length' => 255,
      'not null' => FALSE,
      'default' => '',
    ),
    'protein_content' => array(
      'description' => 'The number of grams of protein.',
      'type' => 'varchar',
      'length' => 255,
      'not null' => FALSE,
      'default' => '',
    ),
    'saturated_fat_content' => array(
      'description' => 'The number of grams of saturated fat.',
      'type' => 'varchar',
      'length' => 255,
      'not null' => FALSE,
      'default' => '',
    ),
    'serving_size' => array(
      'description' => 'The serving size, in terms of the number
of volume or mass.',
      'type' => 'varchar',
      'length' => 255,
      'not null' => FALSE,
      'default' => '',
    ),
    'sodium_content' => array(
      'description' => 'The number of milligrams of sodium.',
```

```
        'type' => 'varchar',
        'length' => 255,
        'not null' => FALSE,
        'default' => '',
      ),
      'sugar_content' => array(
        'description' => 'The number of grams of sugar.',
        'type' => 'varchar',
        'length' => 255,
        'not null' => FALSE,
        'default' => '',
      ),
      'trans_fat_content' => array(
        'description' => 'The number of grams of trans fat.',
        'type' => 'varchar',
        'length' => 255,
        'not null' => FALSE,
        'default' => '',
      ),
      'unsaturated_fat_content' => array(
        'description' => 'The number of grams of unsaturated fat.',
        'type' => 'varchar',
        'length' => 255,
        'not null' => FALSE,
        'default' => '',
      ),
    );

  return array(
    'columns' => $columns,
  );
}
```

 We reformatted the NutritionInformation schema property names to be all lower case instead of camel case, as lowercase with underscores is in line with Drupal coding standards. An overview of Drupal coding standards is available at http://drupal.org/ coding-standards, and we will take a more in-depth look at Drupal coding standards in *Chapter 8, Recipe Lists and More with Views*.

10. Now we are going to move onto the nutritioninfo.module file and will open the addressfield.module to look at it implementation of hook_field_info. And once again, we will copy the contents of the addressfield function and paste it into our nutritioninfo.module file and modify it so that it looks like the following:

```
/**
 * Implements hook_field_info()
 */
function nutritioninfo_field_info() {
  $fields = array();

  $fields['nutritioninfo'] = array(
    'label' => t('Nutrition Information'),
    'description' => t('A field type used for storing nutrition
information as defined by the Microdata spec at http://schema.org/
NutritionInformation.'),
    'settings' => array(),
    'instance_settings' => array(),
    'default_widget' => 'nutritioninfo_standard',
    'default_formatter' => 'nutritioninfo_default',  );

  return $fields;
}
```

11. Now, we are going to implement two more hooks that are required by Drupal 7, when defining a custom field – hook_field_validate and hook_field_is_empty:

```
/**
 * Implements hook_field_validate().
 */
function nutritioninfo_field_validate($entity_type, $entity,
$field, $instance, $langcode, $items, &$errors) {
  //at this point we will not validate anything, but will revisit
}


/**
 * Implements hook_field_is_empty().
 */
function nutritioninfo_field_is_empty($item, $field) {
  //the nutrition field is empty if all of its properties are
empty
  return empty($item['calories'])
    && empty($item['carbohydrate_content'])
```

```
        && empty($item['cholesterol_content'])
        && empty($item['fat_content'])
        && empty($item['fiber_content'])
        && empty($item['protein_content'])
        && empty($item['saturated_fat_content'])
        && empty($item['serving_size'])
        && empty($item['sodium_content'])
        && empty($item['sugar_content'])
        && empty($item['trans_fat_content'])
        && empty($item['unsaturated_fat_content']);
}
```

12. Next, we need to tell Drupal how to handle our compound field on the node edit form. We will add hook_field_widget_info to make Drupal aware of our custom widget, and then hook_field_widget_form to actually add the form components to the node form:

```
/**
 * Implements hook_field_widget_info()
 */
function nutritioninfo_field_widget_info() {
  $widgets = array();

  $widgets['nutritioninfo_standard'] = array(
    'label' => t('Nutrition Information form'),
    'field types' => array('nutritioninfo'),     ),
  );

  return $widgets;
}


/**
 * Implements hook_field_widget_form()
 */
function nutritioninfo_field_widget_form(&$form, &$form_state,
$field, $instance, $langcode, $items, $delta, $element) {
  $settings = $form_state['field'][$instance['field_name']]
[$langcode]['field']['settings'];

  $fields = array(
    'calories' => t('Calories'),
    'carbohydrate_content' => t('Carbohydrate Content'),
    'cholesterol_content' => t('Cholesterol Content'),
```

```
    'fat_content' => t('Fat Content'),
    'fiber_content' => t('Fiber Content'),
    'protein_content' => t('Protein Content'),
    'saturated_fat_content' => t('Saturated Fat Content'),
    'serving_size' => t('Serving Size'),
    'sodium_content' => t('Sodium Content'),
    'sugar_content' => t('Sugar Content'),
    'trans_fat_content' => t('Trans Fat Content'),
    'unsaturated_fat_content' => t('Unsaturated Fat Content'),
  );

  foreach ($fields as $key => $label) {
    $value = isset($items[$delta][$key]) ? $items[$delta][$key] :
'';
    $element[$key] = array(
      '#attributes' => array('class' => array('edit-nutrition-
field'), 'title' => t('')),
      '#type' => 'textfield',
      '#size' => 3,
      '#maxlength' => 3,
      '#title' => $label,
      '#default_value' => $value,
      '#prefix' => '&lt;div class="nutrition-field nutrition-' .
$key . '-field">',
      '#suffix' => '&lt;/div>',
    );
  }
  return $element;
}
```

13. Now, we need to add some hooks for formatting our compound field, when displaying a content item. We will need to add two more hooks for that: hook_field_formatter_info **and** hook_field_formatter_view:

```
/**
 * Implements hook_field_formatter_info()
 */
function nutritioninfo_field_formatter_info() {
  return array(
    'nutritioninfo_default' => array(
      'label' => t('Default'),
      'field types' => array('nutritioninfo'),
    ),
```

```
    );
  }

  /**
   * Implements hook_field_formatter_view().
   */
  function nutritioninfo_field_formatter_view($entity_type, $entity,
  $field, $instance, $langcode, $items, $display) {
    $element = array();

    switch ($display['type']) {
      case 'nutritioninfo_default':
        $headers = array(
          t('Calories'),
          t('Carbohydrate Content'),
          t('Cholesterol Content'),
          t('Fat Content'),
          t('Fiber Content'),
          t('Protein Content'),
          t('Saturated Fat Content'),
          t('Serving Size'),
          t('Sodium Content'),
          t('Sugar Content'),
          t('Trans Fat Content'),
          t('Unsaturated Fat Content'),
        );

    $element[0]['#markup'] = theme('table', array('header' =>
  $headers, 'rows' => $items));
    break;
    }
    return $element;
  }
```

14. All right, now it is time to enable our new module. Open up our d7dev Drupal site in your favorite browser, and click on the **Modules** link in the **Admin** toolbar. Scroll down to the **Fields** section, and check the checkbox next to our new **Nutrition Info Field** module.

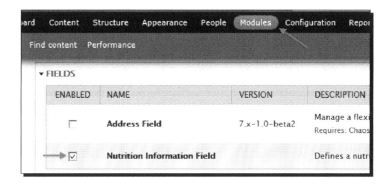

15. Finally, scroll to the bottom of the page, and click on the **Save configuration** button.

What just happened?

That was some serious development. We created a fairly complex custom module, and now have a field that offers a more complete Recipe content type.

Time for action – updating the Recipe content type to use the NutritionInformation field

Now, let's put our new module to use and add our new compound field to our Recipe content type, using our new custom `nutritioninfo` field for the `NutrionInformation` property of the `http://schema.org/Recipe` definition.

1. Go to the **Manage Fields** configuration page for the Recipe content type: `http://localhost/d7dev/#overlay=admin/structure/types/manage/recipe/fields`.

2. Now, add a new field with the following settings—label: `nutrition`, name: `field_nutrition_information`, type: `Nutrition Information`, widget: `Nutrition Information form` (the default), and click on the **Save** button.

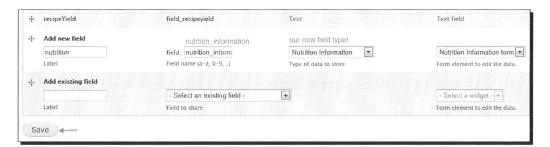

3. There is nothing to set for **Field Settings**, so just click on the **Save field settings** button. On the **Recipe Settings** screen, enter `Nutrition information about the recipe` for the **Help text**, and then click on the **Save** button at the bottom of the screen.

4. Next, click on the **Find content** link in the **Shortcuts** toolbar, and click on the **Edit** link for the first Recipe content item in the list.

5. Towards the bottom of the node edit form, you will see inputs for our new compound field.

Summary

In this chapter, we began looking at ways to support HTML5 in Drupal 7, and integrated it with our `d7dev` site in a few different ways – with existing contributed modules and with code that we wrote ourselves. We learned about some of the differences between Microdata and RDFa, and did some extensive module development. We developed a custom compound field module, based on the Microdata specification at `http://schema.org/NutritionInformation`, allowing us to enhance our Recipe content type. However, at this point, our Nutrition Information Field module is still a bit rough around the edges. In the next chapter, we will introduce some more code examples, and clean up some of those rough edges.

4

Introduction to Drupal 7 Theme Development

With regards to a recipe for food, good presentation provides a very important foundation for good taste. It is no different with a website; visitors are not going to want to explore more if they are put off by the initial presentation of the site.

Making a Drupal-based website look good starts with the theme you use. But, there is no need to build a theme completely from scratch. There are over 280 themes for Drupal 7 available on `http://drupal.org/project/themes`. *You could very well just download a theme that you thought looked nice, tweak it here and there, and be done with it. However, there are a number of themes that offer features beyond the immediate look and feel, and are intended to be sub-themed. These types of themes are referred to as* **base themes**.

You can get a quick start with your own custom theme development by using a base theme. This chapter will show you how to quickly and easily create a custom theme by utilizing Drupal's base theme capabilities, and we will explore some simple code examples for theme customization. Finally, the chapter will walk you through the new theme-related concept for Drupal 7 of 'Render Arrays', with code examples to introduce the use of the Drupal 7 `hook_preprocess_node` in our new custom theme.

Finally, we will see how the contrib Field group module can replace the need for some custom code.

Creating a sub-theme

Drupal has an extendible theming capability that allows you to sub-theme an existing theme. The sub-theme will inherit the resources (`JavaScript`, `CSS`, and `template.php` functions) of its parent theme. So, rather than downloading a contrib theme from `http://drupal.org/project/themes`, and hacking away at it, you can approach the custom theme development in the same way you approach custom module development – don't hack core or contrib modules. In other words, don't hack contrib themes! There are a number of contrib themes that are self-described base themes. A base theme is a theme that is meant to be extended and customized. The **AdaptiveTheme** (`http://drupal.org/project/adaptivetheme`) and **Omega** (`http://drupal.org/project/omega`) themes appear to be excellent choices for an HTML5-capable base theme for Drupal 7. They are also both excellent examples of a responsive theme.

If you have never heard the term responsive design or responsive grid, then you may be asking what does it mean to be a responsive theme? Responsive web design has been an emerging concept in web design for the last few years. With the steadily-increasing amount of mobile browsing, how your website is presented on mobile devices cannot be ignored. Many will go as far to say that when designing a website, you should design it for mobile first. Responsive web design builds on that, and on the idea that a website should adapt as much as possible to the device on which it is being viewed.

We will go with the Omega theme as our base theme, as it has some features that we will explore later in this chapter. So, now let's install the Omega theme, and then create a sub-theme based on Omega.

Omega is one of two recommended themes on the HTML5 Tools module page (`http://drupal.org/project/html5_tools`), and thus a good sign that it is a solid choice for an HTML5 base theme. If you recall, we installed the HTML5 Tools module in the previous chapter.

Time for action – installing a base theme

Just as you can use Drush to download and enable a contrib module, you can also use Drush to download and install a contrib theme.

1. Now, using Drush we will download and enable the Omega theme:

```
C:\xampp\htdocs\d7dev>drush dl omega

Project omega (7.x-3.0) downloaded to              [success]
```

```
C:/xampp/htdocs/d7dev/sites/all/themes/omega.

Project omega contains 5 themes: starterkit_omega_xhtml,
starterkit_omega_html5,

  starterkit_alpha_xhtml, omega, alpha.


C:\xampp\htdocs\d7dev>drush en omega

The following extensions will be enabled: omega

Do you really want to continue? (y/n): y

omega was enabled successfully.                      [ok]


C:\xampp\htdocs\d7dev>
```

2. Next, open up our d7dev site in your favorite browser, and click on the **Appearance** link in the **Admin** toolbar. Open the **Appearance administrative** page, and you will see that the newly downloaded Omega theme is available and enabled:

Now that was easy, and it is time to create our own sub-theme based on the Omega base theme.

Time for action – creating a sub-theme and setting it as our default theme

The typical way of creating a sub-theme is a completely manual process of copying and renaming certain files and directories. There are instructions in the Omega theme project for creating a sub-theme.

1. First, from within **Aptana Studio**, navigate to the `starterkits` directory of the newly installed Omega theme located at `/sites/all/themes/omega/`.

2. We are going to create a sub-theme based on the `omega-html5` starter theme. So, right-click on the `omega-html5` directory, and click on **Copy** from the menu.

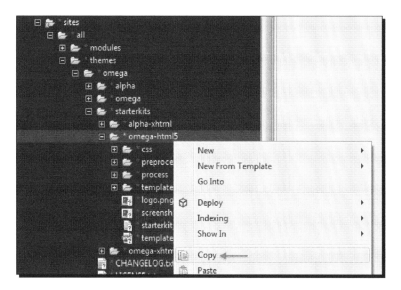

3. Next, right-click on the `/sites/all/themes` directory, and click on **Paste**.

4. Now, you will need to rename the directory to the name of our new custom sub-theme. So, right-click on the `/sites/all/themes/omega-html5` directory, click on **Rename**, and type `d7dev_theme` in the input.

5. Next, you will have to rename some files and update some settings. We will start by renaming the `starterkit_omega_html5.info` file to `d7dev_theme.info`.

6. Next, we will rename all of the CSS files that start with the text YOURTHEMENAME in the /sites/all/themes/d7dev_theme/css directory, by replacing YOURTHEMENAME with d7dev_theme. Our new d7dev_theme directory should look similar to the following screenshot:

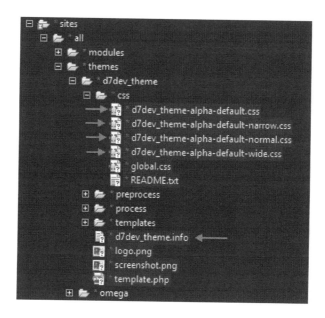

7. Now, we will need to edit the newly renamed d7dev_theme.info file, so that the first six lines look as follows:

```
name = D7Dev Theme
description = A sub-theme based on the Omega base theme to use as
theme-related development examples.
core = 7.x
engine = phptemplate
screenshot = screenshot.png
base theme = omega
```

8. Next, delete the following lines from the d7dev_theme.info file as instructed by the Omega comments:

```
; IMPORTANT: DELETE THESE TWO LINES IN YOUR SUBTHEME

hidden = TRUE
starterkit = TRUE
```

9. Finally, at the very bottom of the `d7dev_theme.info` file, delete the following configuration as it does not pertain to our custom module:

```
; Information added by drupal.org packaging script on 2011-08-23
version = "7.x-3.0"
core = "7.x"
project = "omega"
datestamp = "1314088930"
```

10. Now, open our `d7dev` site in your favorite browser, and click on the **Appearance** link in the **Admin** toolbar, then scroll down to the **DISABLE THEMES** section, and click on the **Enable and set default** link under our new **D7Dev Theme**:

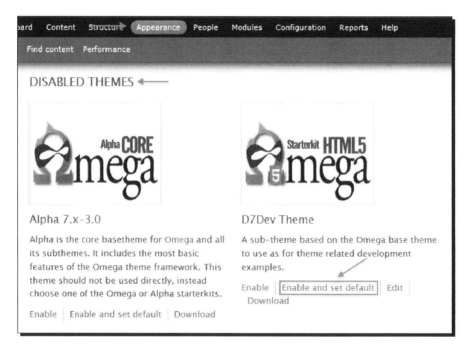

What just happened?

In this section, we created a new sub-theme and set it as the default theme for our `d7dev` site. To reinforce what a timesaving development tool Drush can be, we will use Drush to duplicate our effort of creating a sub-theme from the Omega base theme. Typically, you would have to follow the manual process we walked through previously.

However, the Omega developer(s) have created a Drupal module that adds Drush integration for sub-theme generation. Now, you may be asking yourself—*Why did we walk through the manual process of creating a sub-theme?* The answer to that question is simple—most modules are not integrated with Drush, so you should know how to do it manually. But, the Omega module is integrated with Drush, so we are going to take advantage of Omega's Drush integration.

> Before version 3 of Drush, Drush had a set of Drupal theme-specific commands. Those commands have been removed, but commands exist with the same basic functionality. Here are the mappings of the old commands to the current Drush 4.x that allow you to accomplish the same thing:

Drush 3	Drush 4
theme-enable	pm-enable
theme-disable	pm-disable
theme-info	pm-info
theme-list	pm-list –type=theme
theme-list-enabled	pm-list –tupe=theme –status=enabled
theme-set-default	vset theme_default
theme-set-admin	vset admin_theme
theme-status	status theme

Time for action – creating a sub-theme and setting as default theme with Drush

1. Before we can use Drush to generate the Omega-based sub-theme, we will need to disable the previously created d7dev_theme theme, and then delete the /sites/all/themes/d7dev_theme directory.

2. Once again, in our d7dev site, click on the **Appearance** link on the **Admin** toolbar, and click on the **Set default link for the Bartik** theme. We must set a new default theme before we can disable our **D7Dev** theme.

3. Now, with the **D7Dev** theme no longer the default theme, you will be able to disable it by clicking on the **Disable** link.

4. In **Aptana Studio**, expand the `/sites/all/themes` folder, right-click on the `d7dev_theme` folder, and select **Delete**.

5. Next, we will download and enable the Omega Tools module (http://drupal.org/ project/omega_tools) that adds Drush integration for the Omega base theme:

```
C:\xampp\htdocs\d7dev>drush dl omega_tools

Project omega_tools (7.x-3.0-rc3) downloaded to
[success]


C:/xampp/htdocs/d7dev/sites/all/modules/omega_tools.


C:\xampp\htdocs\d7dev>drush en omega_tools


The following extensions will be enabled: omega_tools
Do you really want to continue? (y/n): y
omega_tools was enabled successfully.                    [ok]
```

6. We will now use Drush to generate a new sub-theme based on the Omega theme.

```
C:\xampp\htdocs\d7dev>drush omega-subtheme "D7Dev Theme"
--starterkit=starterkit_omega_html5
You have successfully created the theme D7Dev Theme.   [status]
```

7. Next, use Drush to enable our new sub-theme:

```
C:\xampp\htdocs\d7dev>drush en d7dev_theme
The following extensions will be enabled: d7dev_theme
Do you really want to continue? (y/n): y
d7dev_theme was enabled successfully.    [ok]
```

8. Finally, we will use Drush to set our new sub-theme module as our **D7Dev** default theme.

```
C:\xampp\htdocs\d7dev>drush vset theme_default d7dev_theme
theme_default was set to d7dev_theme.            [success]
```

9. If you revisit the **Appearance** configuration page, you will now see that our new **D7Dev Theme** is set as the default theme for our site:

What just happened?

We used Drush with the help of the Omega Tools module to create an Omega sub-theme, and to set it as our `d7dev` default theme.

Time for action – configuring our Omega-based sub-theme

After you close the **Appearance** administrative screen, you will notice a few features of the Omega base theme that are useful for debugging theme development. First, the Omega theme is a grid-based theme (if you don't know what a grid-based theme is, then take a look at `http://960.gs/`), and includes the ability to highlight the columns and gutters of the grid being used. Secondly, it includes outlines of blocks representing the position of all the regions for our theme. Finally, there is a **RESIZE ME** widget at the bottom-right corner of the page that serves to highlight the Omega theme's responsiveness to different screen sizes.

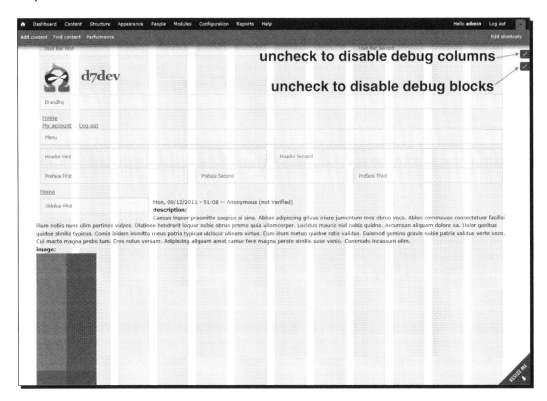

These debugging features may become useful at some point with some custom theme development, but, for now, we just want to disable these debugging features.

1. Once again, click on the **Appearance** link in the **Admin** toolbar.

2. Once the **Appearance** admin page has loaded, click on the **Settings** link for our **D7Dev** theme.

3. Next, click on the **Debugging** tab, and uncheck the checkboxes for **Enable the debugging (placeholder) block for the selected roles.** and **Enable the grid overlay for the selected roles.**.

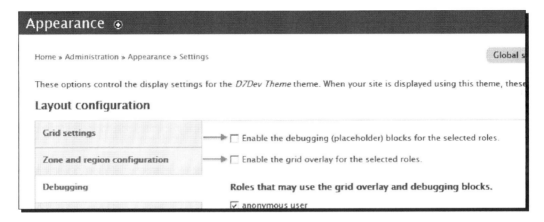

4. Finally, scroll to the bottom of the page, and click on the **Save configuration** button.

What just happened?

We disabled the Omega theme's debugging features. Now when you visit a non-admin page of our `d7dev` site, you will see that the Omega theme debugging features are gone.

Manage the display for a content type

Drupal provides an easy way to manage how the fields for a content type are displayed. The **Manage Display** administrative page allows you to drag-and-drop fields to reorder them, select how and if labels are displayed, and provides extended format settings for specific field formatters (such as providing the ability to select an image style for the image formatter).

Time for action – using the Manage Display page to update the display of our custom Recipe content type

If you go to a page of one of the Recipes that was generated by the Devel module, then you will see that every field has a label, the image is a bit larger than you might like, and the fields just aren't organized in a way that we like. To clean up the way our Recipe pages look, we are going to revisit the manage display page for our Recipe content type.

1. Click on the **Structure** link in the **Admin** toolbar, and click on the **Content types** link.

2. Next, click on the **manage display** link for our Recipe content type.

3. Click on the **Label** drop-down for the image field, and select `<Hidden>`.

4. Next, we are going to apply a different image style setting to our image field, by clicking on the **format settings** button. On **format settings**, click on the **Image style** drop down, select `medium`, and click on the **Update** button.

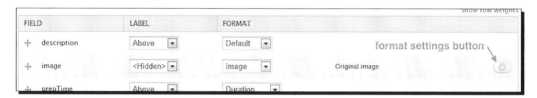

The following screenshot shows the extended format settings available for the core image formatter:

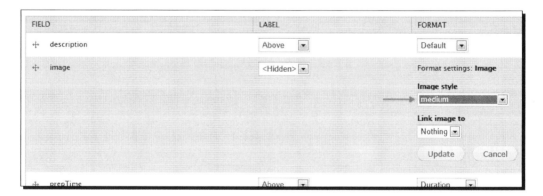

1. Now, drag the **prepTime** field above the **cookTime** field, and **recipeYield** under **cookTime**.

2. Next, select **Inline** from the **Label** drop-down for the **prepTime**, the **cookTime**, and the **recipeYield** fields.

3. The **Manage Display** screen for our Recipe content type should now look similar to the following screenshot:

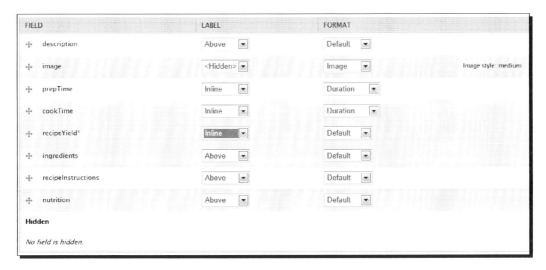

4. Now, click on the **Save** button, and close the **Manage Display** screen. You will see our new layout for our Recipe content type.

What just happened?

We used the **Content types manage display** screen for our Recipe content type to customize how the fields are displayed.

Drupal 7 Render Arrays

In the case of our Recipe content type, it would be nice to wrap the **prepTime**, **cookTime**, and **recipeYield** fields with a border, and display that box inline with the **image** field. The **manage display** settings are not going to help us accomplish this, so it is time for some more custom development, and an introduction to Render Arrays. **Render Arrays** are a new page-building data structure introduced in Drupal 7 to make it easier for developers to manipulate the content of a Drupal page as late as possible in the rendering process. Render Arrays will allow us to manipulate the output of the core modules without hacking html fragments or writing complicated CSS. In this case, we will modify the Render Array of our Recipe nodes.

Time for action – implementing hook_preprocess_node

We are going to implement the `hook_preprocess_node` hook. However, rather than adding it to a module, we are going to add it to our custom `d7dev_theme`.

 The `template.php` file is the place where you would typically add custom code to override theme-able output to include implementations of preprocess nodes. The `hook_preprocess_node` hook provides a way to manipulate the Render Array of a node before it is themed as HTML.

1. In **Aptana Studio**, open the `template.php` file in the `/sites/all/themes/d7dev_theme` directory.

2. Read the contents of the `template.php` file, and you will learn that the Omega base theme provides a custom way of handling certain aspects of adding custom functionality to your Omega based sub-theme. Specifically, it allows us to have more organization for any preprocess or process related functions that we develop.

3. Now, right-click on the `/sites/all/themes/d7dev_theme/preprocess` directory, select **New**, and click on **File**.

4. Enter `preprocess-node.inc` for the file name.

5. With the `preprocess-node.inc` file opened, type in the following code:

```php
<?php

/**
 * Implements hook_preprocess_node().
 */
function d7dev_theme_alpha_preprocess_node(&$vars) {
  // custom functionality here
}
```

6. Although we know we want to manipulate a Render Array, we are not exactly sure what the structure of that Render Array looks like. Once again, we will get a little help from the `devel` module by using the `dpm()` function to print out the `$var` variable in a collapsible display. This will allow us to explore the make up of the Render Array for our Recipe nodes. Add the following line of code to our `d7dev_theme_alpha_preprocess_node` function:

```php
dpm($vars['content']);
```

In order for the output of the dpm() function to be displayed, we must empty the Drupal cache. We will use the shortcut to the **Performance administrative** page that we created in the previous chapter to quickly navigate to the administrative page for clearing the Drupal cache.

1. Load our **d7dev** site, and click on the **Performance** link that we added to the **Shortcut** bar, then click on the **Clear all caches** button.

2. Then, load a Recipe page in your favorite browser, and reload the page once more, and you will see the output of the dpm() function:

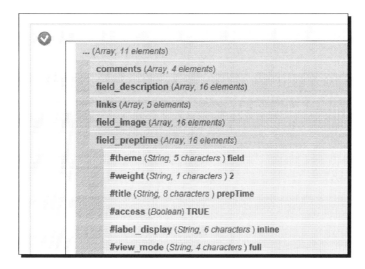

3. Okay, so now we have an idea of what we are working with. You can expand and explore all of the Render Array values for our Recipe node.

4. Now we are going to add a #prefix for field_preptime and a #suffix to the field_recipeyield. So, our complete implementation of hook_preprocess_node will look as follows:

```php
<?php

/**
 * Implements hook_preprocess_node().
 */
function d7dev_theme_alpha_preprocess_node(&$vars) {
  //add a prefix to first field to be part of the box
  $vars['content']['field_preptime']['#prefix'] =
    '<div class="time-yield-wrapper">';
```

```
//close the box by adding a suffix to the last field to be part
  //of the box
$vars['content']['field_recipeyield']['#suffix'] = '</div>';
}
```

5. Go back to our Recipe node page, and reload it twice. You will notice that nothing seems to have changed. However, if you view the source of the page, you will see the `div` based wrapper that we added:

```
<div class="time-yield-wrapper">

<div class="field field-name-field-preptime field-type-number-
  integer field-label-inline clearfix">
  <div class="field-label">prepTime: </div>
  <div class="field-items">
    <div class="field-item even">
      111 and <sup>7</sup>&frasl;<sub>12</sub> hours
    </div>
  </div>
</div>

<div class="field field-name-field-cooktime field-type-number-
  integer field-label-inline clearfix">
  <div class="field-label">cookTime: </div>
  <div class="field-items">
    <div class="field-item even" itemprop="cookTime">
      84 and <sup>14</sup>&frasl;<sub>15</sub> hours
    </div>
  </div>
</div>

<div class="field field-name-field-recipeyield field-type-text
  field-label-inline clearfix">
  <div class="field-label">recipeYield: </div>
    <div class="field-items">
      <div class="field-item even" itemprop="recipeYield">
        wU2t7ZsYijSHvCToof6Qd...
      </div>
    </div>
  </div>
</div>
```

6. Now, we need to add some CSS to our custom theme to make the new markup look the way we want. So, in **Aptana Studio**, open the `global.css` file located in the `/sites/all/themes/d7dev_theme/css` folder.

7. Enter the following CSS rules:

```
/* styles for Recipe content type */
body.node-type-recipe div.field-name-field-image{
  float:left;
}

body.node-type-recipe div.time-yield-wrapper{
  float:left;
  margin-left: 20px;
  border: 1px solid #777;
  padding: 10px;
}

body.node-type-recipe div.field-name-field-ingredients{
  clear:left;
}
```

8. Now, go back and reload the Recipe node, and it should looking something similar to the following screenshot:

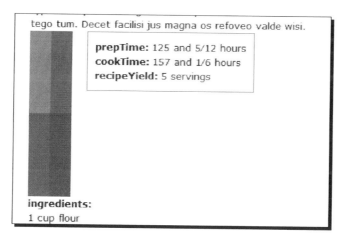

What just happened?

We used the `hook_preprocess_node` core hook to modify the Render Array of our recipe node content, and were able to wrap a number of fields to display them in a cohesive manner.

An introduction to the Drupal 7 field group module

The **field group module** (`http://drupal.org/project/field_group`) was introduced with Drupal 7 to replace similar functionality that was part of the **Content Construction Kit** (**CCK**) module for Drupal 6. For Drupal 7, much of the CCK module was added to core as the `field` and `field_ui` core modules. However, there were two major areas of functionality offered by the CCK module that were not migrated to Drupal 7 core, and those were `user/node` reference fields and field groups. The field group module enables you to add groups to wrap fields for the node edit form, and through the manage display admin screen of a given content type.

In this section, we are going to once again undo something that we have already done, and redo it another way. In order to illustrate that writing the custom code is not always the best route to take to achieve certain functionality for our site, we are going to replace our custom implementation of `hook_preprocess_node` with the built-in capabilities of the field group module.

Time for action – creating the wrapper with display suite

We are going to once again undo something that we have already done, and redo it another way. In order to illustrate that writing the custom code is not always the best route to take to achieve certain functionality for our site, we are going to replace our custom implementation of `hook_preprocess_node` with the built-in capabilities of the field group module.

1. Once again, we must start by undoing what we have already done. So, in **Aptana Studio**, open the `preprocess-node.inc` file in our `/sites/all/themes/d7dev_theme/preprocess` directory.

2. Put a `/*` before our `d7dev_theme_alpha_preprocess_node` function and a `*/` after it. This is referred to as "commenting out the code", so this function will not execute.

3. Next, we will use Drush to download and enable the field group module.

```
C:\xampp\htdocs\d7dev>drush dl field_group
Project field_group (7.x-1.1) downloaded to  [success]


C:/xampp/htdocs/d7dev/sites/all/modules/field_group.


C:\xampp\htdocs\d7dev>drush en field_group
The following extensions will be enabled: field_group
Do you really want to continue? (y/n): y
field_group was enabled successfully.          [ok]
```

4. Now, click on the **Structure** link in the **Admin** toolbar, click on the **Content types** link, and then on the **Content types admin** page, click on the **manage display** link for our Recipe content type.

5. Next, we are going to create a field group to replace the `time_yield` wrapper from our `d7dev_theme_preprocess_node` function. In the **Add new group** row, fill out the fields to match the following screenshot, and click on the **Save** button:

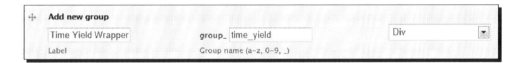

6. Now, drag our new **Time Yield Wrapper** custom field group above the **prepTime** field. Finally, drag the **prepTime**, **cookTime**, and **recipeYield** fields, so that they are indented under our **Time Yield Wrapper** field group, as shown in the following screenshot, and click on the **Save** button.

7. Now, click on the **format settings** button (the button with the cog icon under the **FORMAT** column, as pointed out in the previous screenshot) for our newly-added **Time Yield Wrapper** field group, and set it up to match the following screenshot (with the key fields highlighted), and click on the **Update** button:

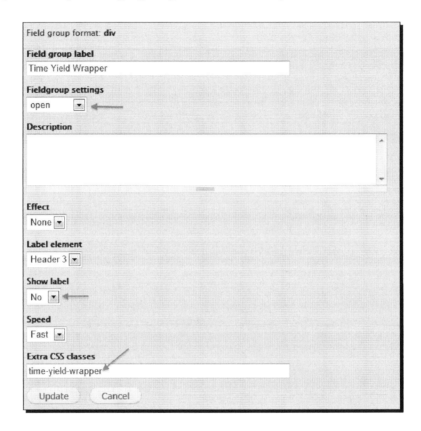

8. We will add the same CSS class that we used in our custom `d7dev_theme_preprocess_node` function – `time-yield-wrapper` – and we will now see how the HTML output for our recipe page is very similar to what was produced with our custom code:

```
<div class="field-group-format group_time_yield field-group-div
  group-time-yield time-yield-wrapper speed-fast effect-none">
  <div class="field field-name-field-preptime field-type-number-
    integer field-label-inline clearfix">
    <div class="field-label">prepTime: </div>
    <div class="field-items">
      <div class="field-item even">
```

```
      125 and <sup>5</sup>/<sub>12</sub> hours
    </div>
  </div>
</div>

<div class="field field-name-field-cooktime field-type-number-
  integer field-label-inline clearfix">
  <div class="field-label">cookTime: </div>
  <div class="field-items">
    <div class="field-item even" itemprop="cookTime">
      157 and <sup>1</sup>/<sub>6</sub> hours
    </div>
  </div>
</div>

<div class="field field-name-field-recipeyield field-type-text
  field-label-inline clearfix">
  <div class="field-label">recipeYield: </div>
  <div class="field-items">
    <div class="field-item even" itemprop="recipeYield">
      5 servings
    </div>
  </div>
</div>
</div>
```

What just happened?

We replaced the functionality of some custom code that we wrote with the existing functionality of a contrib module.

Summary

In this chapter, we have made a few steps towards enhancing the appearance of our d7dev site, and introduced you to some Drupal development concepts around theming. With the addition of an Omega-based sub-theme, our site has the ability to be responsive to the myriad mobile devices that are an ever growing percent of traffic for websites.

We have also introduced the field group module, a contrib module that actually reduces the need to develop custom code for some simple layout needs. But, more importantly, we have seen how there is always more than one way to accomplish something within Drupal. This highlights a very important aspect of writing code: the only bug-free code is code that is never written in the first place. Nevertheless, there are still plenty of interesting code examples to come in the remaining chapters.

5

Enhancing the Content Author's User Experience

*The core admin and authoring UI in Drupal 7 is greatly improved from Drupal 6, but there are still a number of enhancements that could really improve the **user experience (UX)** for content authors. This chapter will walk you through easy ways to enhance the content authoring UX to include an introduction to the fundamental Drupal construct known as **blocks**. Finally, the chapter will walk through the code for integrating a truly inline What You See Is What You Get or WYSIWYG editor through the HTML5 **contenteditable** attribute (*`http://dev.w3.org/html5/spec/Overview.html#editing-0`*), and explore some of the new JavaScript and AJAX paradigms for Drupal 7.*

Developing a custom block for adding content

Please excuse the pun, but the Drupal **blocks** component has always been a key building block of Drupal web sites. The Drupal 6 `hook_block()` - `http://api.drupal.org/api/drupal/developer--hooks--core.php/function/hook_block/6`, has been replaced with several new Drupal 7 **blocks** hooks. The details of these changes are documented at `http://api.drupal.org/api/drupal/modules--block--block.api.php/7`. However, the primary changes were the addition of `hook_block_info()` and `hook_block_view()`. In the rest of this section, we are going to learn about custom block development for Drupal 7, and see how it can help us enhance the content author UX for our d7dev site.

Sometimes, it is nice to have a streamlined process for creating and editing content. This is especially true when you have a site that has quite a few content types, but only a subset of those are used by most of your site's content authors. In the case of our d7dev site, we may want to open up the ability to add recipes to the site for any authenticated user, but don't want to overwhelm them with the default **Add content** page.

We would like to streamline the process for adding the recipe content by creating a custom block with an **Add recipe** link that replicates the **Recipe link** on the **Add content** page. We will be able to place this block on every page, so that creating a new recipe will always just be one click away. To accomplish this, we are going to create a new administratively focused `d7dev_admin` module that implements the Drupal 7 hooks: `hook_block_info()` and `hook_block_view()`.

Time for action – developing a custom block for adding recipes

Now we will use the new Drupal 7 block hooks to add a custom block with a link to create new recipe content.

1. First, open Aptana Studio, and navigate to the `/sites/all/modules/custom` folder in the **Project Explorer** tab of the Web perspective. Right-click on the `custom` folder, select **New** and then **Folder** as shown in the following screenshot. Then, enter `d7dev_admin` as the name of the folder, and click on the **Finish** button.

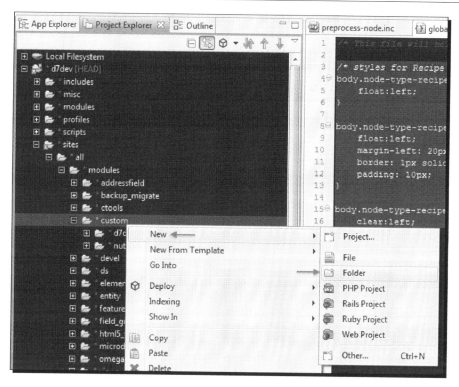

2. Next, we are going to create the necessary files for creating a Drupal module in our new `d7dev_admin` folder, by right-clicking on the folder, selecting **New | File**, entering the specified file name for each, a `d7dev_admin.info` file and a `d7dev_admin.module` file, and clicking on the **Finish** button. When you have finished, your `d7dev_admin` directory should look similar to the following screenshot:

3. Now, open the `d7dev_admin.info` file in the Aptana editor, and enter the following configuration:

   - **name**: d7dev Admin
   - **description**: Custom module for enhancing the content author UX
   - **core**: 7.x
   - **package**: Administration

4. Now, it is time to move on to the `d7dev_admin.module` file. To start, we must provide some standard Drupal module code, as follows:

```php
<?php

/**
 * @file
 * d7dev Admin module.
 *
 */
```

5. Now, we are ready to add our implementation of `hook_block_info()`. An associative array must be defined for each block defined by a custom module. For each block, an associative array-based description that contains the info key-value pair is required. In addition to the required info key-value, we will also be specifying the optional cache key-value. The other available optional key-value pairs for block descriptions are available here: `http://api.drupal.org/api/drupal/modules--block--block.api.php/function/hook_block_info/7`.

```php
/**
 * Implements hook_block_info().
 *
 * Define all blocks provided by the module.
 */
function d7dev_admin_block_info() {
  //Define an associative array for each block, in this case just
  ..//one:
  $blocks['add_recipe_content'] = array(

    // info: (requried) The name of the block.
    'info' => t('Add Recipe Content'),
```

```
    // cache: (optional) Same for every user on every page where
....//it is visible.
    'cache' => DRUPAL_CACHE_GLOBAL,

  );

  return $blocks;
}
```

6. Next, we will add the implementation of `hook_block_view()`:

```
/**
 * Implements hook_block_view().
 *
 * Return a rendered or renderable view of a block.
 */
function d7dev_admin_block_view($delta = '') {
  //$delta: what block to render as defined in hook_block_info.
  switch ($delta) {
    case 'add_recipe_content':
      // The default localized title of the block, in this case
      //NULL
      $block['subject'] = NULL;

      // The content of the block's body.
      $block['content'] = d7dev_admin_contents($delta);
    break;
  }
  return $block;
}
```

7. In the `d7dev_admin_contents` function, we will define a simple render array that builds a link to the **Create Recipe** page for the `add_recipe_content` block delta.

```
/**
 * Function that generates the content for d7dev_admin blocks.
 */
function d7dev_admin_contents($delta = '') {
  //additional blocks may be added, so base this on the block
$delta
  switch ($delta) {
    case 'add_recipe_content':
      //just a simple reander array with a link
      $add_recipe_link = array(
```

```
        '#theme' => 'link',
        '#text' => t('Add Recipe'),
        '#path' => 'node/add/recipe',
        '#options' => array(
          'attributes' => array(),
          //REQUIRED:
          'html' => FALSE,
        ),
      );
      return $add_recipe_link;
   }
}
```

8. Now that we have defined the necessary hooks for implementing a custom block, we will use Drush to enable our new d7dev_admin module.

   ```
   C:\xampp\htdocs\d7dev>drush en d7dev_admin

   The following extensions will be enabled: d7dev_admin

   Do you really want to continue? (y/n): y

   d7dev_admin was enabled successfully.              [ok]
   ```

9. Next, we need to configure our new **Add Recipe** block for our d7dev site. Open our d7dev site in your favorite browser, click on the **Structure** link in the **Admin** toolbar, and select the **Blocks** link.

10. Scroll to the bottom of the **Blocks administrative** screen, and click on the **configure** link for our custom **Add Recipe Content block**.

11. On the **Add Recipe Content block** settings page, select **Sidebar Second** for the **D7Dev Theme (default theme)** drop-down in the **REGION SETTINGS** section. Then, click on the **Roles** vertical tab, select **authenticated user** under **Show block for specific roles**, and click on the **Save block** button.

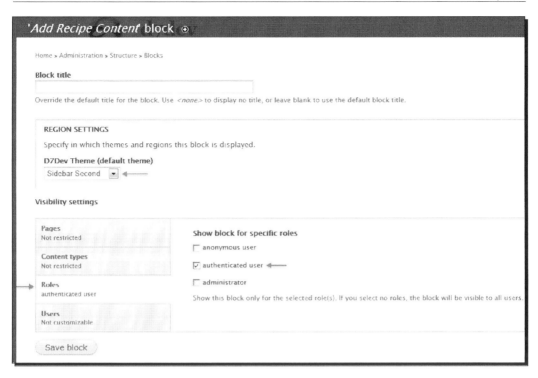

12. Now, go to `http://localhost/d7dev/`, and you will notice a new **Add Recipe** link at the top-right of the page.

What just happened?

We have explored the block-related hooks for Drupal 7, and created a custom block that displays a link for adding the recipe content.

 It is worth mentioning that the Drupal core block module provides the capability to create blocks through the **Add block** link on the **Blocks administrative screen** (admin/structure/block). Once you click on the **Add block** link, you will be presented with a page to add a new custom block, and the form will include a **Block body** field where you can enter any arbitrary HTML or even include a link to add a new recipe content item.

Introduction to the WYSIWYG module

Now that authenticated users can easily add the recipe content to our d7dev site, we will turn our attention to the **Create Recipe** form itself. What if a content author wants to add some basic formatting, such as bold or italics? A typical content author may not be expected to write the actual HTML markup for their content.

A common component of most-managed web content solutions, such as Drupal, is a WYSIWYG type interface for text area input fields. Drupal does not provide such a capability as part of core, but the excellent contrib Wysiwyg module (http://drupal.org/project/wysiwyg) fills this need quite nicely.

The Wysiwyg module is actually a WYSIWYG framework that allows you to easily plug in any of the numerous WYSIWYG plugins that it supports.

Time for action – installing and configuring the Wysiwyg module

We will now enhance the content author UX by enabling WYSIWYG for the content edit form.

1. Once again, we will use Drush to install the module.

```
C:\xampp\htdocs\d7dev>drush dl wysiwyg

Project wysiwyg (7.x-2.1) downloaded to          [success]

C:/xampp/htdocs/d7dev/sites/all/modules/wysiwyg.

C:\xampp\htdocs\d7dev>drush en wysiwyg

The following extensions will be enabled: wysiwyg

Do you really want to continue? (y/n): y

wysiwyg was enabled successfully.                [ok]
```

2. Next, click on the **Configuration** in the **Admin** toolbar, and then click on the **Wysiwyg profiles** link in the **CONTENT AUTHORING** section.

3. On the **Wysiwyg profiles** settings page you will notice that the **INSTALLATION INSTRUCTIONS** section is expanded by default. This is because no editor library has been installed—on subsequent visits to this page, you will notice that it is collapsed by default. For this example, we are going to install the CKEditor editor library. So, right-click on the **Download** link for **CKEditor**, and select **Open in a new tab**.

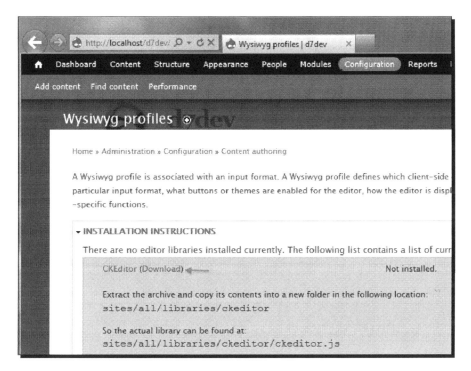

4. On the **CKEditor Download** page, click on the **Download zip** link, and close the tab.

5. Now, as per the Wysiwyg module editor library installation instructions, in Aptana Studio, right-click on the /sites/all/ folder and select **New | Folder**, enter libraries for the **name**, and click on the **Finish** button.

6. Next, extract the downloaded `ckeditor` zip file to our newly created libraries folder at `C:\xampp\htdocs\d7dev\sites\all\libraries\`. It should look similar to the following screenshot.

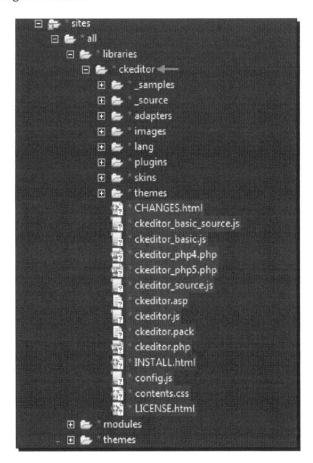

7. Now, refresh the **Wysiwyg profiles** settings page in your browser, select **CKEditor 3.x.x...** from the **EDITOR** drop-down for the **Full HTML** text format in **INPUT FORMAT**, and click on the **Save** button.

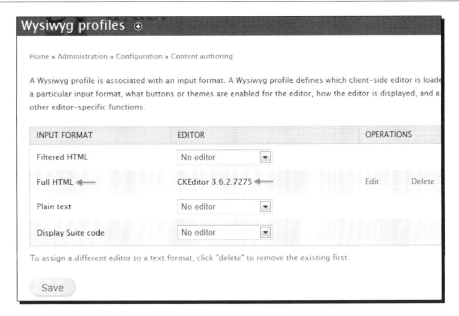

8.   You will now notice that there are **Edit** and **Delete** links for the **Full HTML** text format in **INPUT FORMAT**. Click on the **Edit** link and on the **CKEditor profile for Full HTML** settings page, expand the **BUTTONS AND PLUGINS** section, check the checkboxes as shown in the following screenshot, and click on the **Save** button.

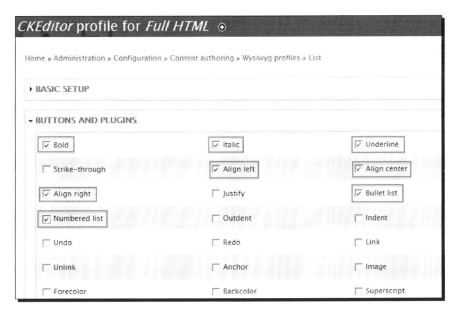

9. Now, go back to the **Configuration** page, and the click on the **Text formats** link, right above the **Wysiwyg profiles** link.

10. On the **Text formats** settings page, drag the **Full HTML** text format to the very top, above the **Filtered HTML** format, and click on the **Save changes** button. This will make the **Full HTML** text format, the default format wherever we have configured text areas fields to use filtered text.

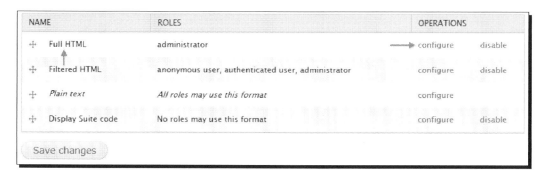

NAME	ROLES	OPERATIONS	
⊹ Full HTML	administrator	──▶ configure	disable
⊹ Filtered HTML	anonymous user, authenticated user, administrator	configure	disable
⊹ *Plain text*	*All roles may use this format*	configure	
⊹ Display Suite code	No roles may use this format	configure	disable

Save changes

11. Next, click on the **configure** link for the **Full HTML** text format, check the authenticated user checkbox under **Roles**, and scroll down and click on the **Save configuration** button. We want both administrators and authenticated users to be able to use the **Full HTML** text format.

12. Now, we are ready to configure our Recipe content type to use the WYSIWYG-enabled text format. Click on **Structure** in the **Admin** toolbar, then click the **Content types** link, and then click on the **manage fields** link for our Recipe content type.

13. Click on the **edit** link in the **OPERATIONS** column for the **description** field. Then, on the **description field** settings page, scroll down to the **Text processing** section, select the radio labeled **Filtered text (user selects text format)**, scroll to the bottom of the form, and click on the **Save settings** button. Repeat for the **recipeInstructions** field.

14. Now, we are ready to test out our new WYSIWYG-enabled text format. Click on the **Find content** link in the **Shortcuts** bar, and select the **edit** link for the first recipe listed.

15. Now, scroll down the **description** field, and you will see a WYSIWYG-enabled text area:

What just happened?

We installed the Wysiwyg module, and enabled WYSIWYG for the text area fields of our Recipe content type.

Pasting text into a WYSIWYG text area

Pasting text from applications, such as Microsoft Word, can wreak havoc on the markup that is saved in a WYSIWYG text area. For example, if you were to paste the first sentence of this tip with the title into our CKEditor WYSIWYG-enabled text area, then the HTML source markup would look similar to the following code:

```
<p></p>
<dir></dir>
<br>
<p dir="LTR" align="LEFT">
  <b>
    <font size="2" face="Calibri">
      <font size="2" face="Calibri">
        <span lang="EN" xml:lang="EN">
          Pasting Text into a WYSIWYG Text Area
        </span>
      </font>
    </font>
  </b>
</p>
```

```
<p>
  <font size="2" face="Calibri">
    <font size="2" face="Calibri">
      Pasting text from applications like
Microsoft Word can wreak
        havoc on the markup that is saved in a
WYSIWYG text area.
      </font>
    </font>
</p>
```

Wow, not pretty! But don't worry, there is a simple fix that forces all the text to be copied into any of our sites CKEditor WYSIWYG-enabled text format to only copy external text as plain text, even when you paste from Microsoft Word. Copy the following function into our `d7dev_admin.module`:

```
/**
 * Implementation of hook_wysiwyg_editor_
settings_alter().
 */
function d7dev_admin_wysiwyg_editor_settings_
alter(&$settings, &$context) {
  if($context['profile']->editor ==
'ckeditor') {
    $settings['forcePasteAsPlainText'] = TRUE;
  }
}
```

Now, clear the cache, go back, edit that same recipe, delete everything in the description field, and re-paste the first sentence and header for this tip. The HTML source markup should now look similar to the following code:

```
<p>Pasting Text into a WYSIWYG Text Area<br />
Pasting text from applications like Microsoft
Word can wreak havoc on the markup that is
saved in a WYSIWYG text area.</p>
```

A new recipe

At this point, our site is starting to take shape, as we continue to do more development related to the look and feel of our site. Now, it becomes important to have real content, so that we can get a better idea of what will look good and what will not look good. From now on, in this chapter, we will be adding one of my own personal recipes, so that we have some real content. Before we add this recipe, we are going to remove all of the recipe content that we generated with the devel module.

Time for action – deleting all Devel-generated recipe content

Before we add real recipe content we are going to remove all of the devel generated content.

1. Open our d7dev site, and click on the **Content** link in the **Admin** toolbar.

2. Next, scroll down to the **SHOW ONLY ITEMS WHERE** section, select **Recipe** from the type drop-down in the, and click on the **Filter** button.

3. After the content list is filtered for Recipe content, check the checkbox next to the **TITLE** column, select **Delete selected content** from the **UPDATE OPTIONS** drop-down, and click on the **Update** button.

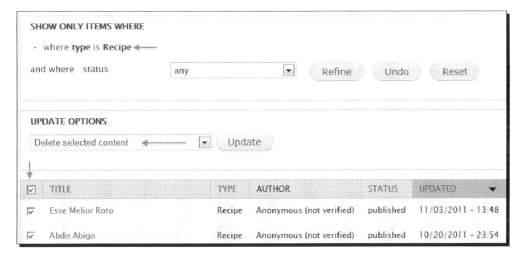

4. Scroll to the bottom of the **Are you sure you want to delete these items** page, and click on the **Delete** button.

5. The only recipe that should be left is the recipe for **Awesome Sauce**. If that is not the case, then delete any remaining devel-generated Recipe content items.

Time for action – adding my Cannellini Cumin Chicken Chili recipe

1. Open up our d7dev site.

2. Click on our **Add Recipe** link, and enter the following recipe:

    - name: Cannellini Cumin Chicken Chili

    - description: This spicy, creamy white chili is just the ticket on those first cool days for Fall

    - recipeYield: Six to Eight servings

    - prepTime: 20 minutes

    - cookTime: 150 minutes

    - ingredients:

      Two pounds of boneless chicken breasts

      One large sweet onion, diced

      Four cloves of garlic

      One yellow bell pepper

      Three large jalapeno peppers

      Half cup of fire roasted diced green chiles

      One table spoon of chopped cilantro

      Three table spoons of olive oil

Three 15.5 oz cans of cannellini (alubias) beans

Two table spoons of cumin powder

One table spoons of chili powder

One table spoons of oregano

One table spoons of crushed read pepper

Two whole bay leaves

salt

pepper

Four cups of chicken broth

Three-fourth cup half & half

One table spoons of sugar

One cup of shredded Colby cheese

One cup of sour cream

❑   instructions:

1.   Preheat oven to 350 degrees.

2.   Heat olive oil in a large Dutch oven over medium heat for two minutes.

3.   Season chicken breasts with a pinch of salt and pepper.

4.   Place chicken breasts in the Dutch oven, turn heat up slightly, and cook each side for five to seven minutes, until lightly browned.

5.   Place chicken in a baking dish, cover with aluminum foil, and bake at 350 degrees for 30 minutes, or until the internal temperature of the largest chicken breast reaches 180 degrees.

6.   Add diced onion to the Dutch oven and sauté for five minutes, stirring frequently.

7.   Add diced jalapeno and diced yellow pepper. Then, add garlic pressed through garlic press, and add ½ jalapeno by pressing through garlic press. Sauté for two minutes, stirring frequently.

8.   Add green chilies and cannellini beans. Then, add chicken broth, stir until combined, and reduce heat to low.

9.   Add the cumin, bay leaves, oregano, chili powder, crushed red pepper, and sugar.

10. Add salt and pepper to taste.

11. Add half and half, stir until combined, and continue to simmer over low heat.

12. Remove the chicken from the oven, and set aside to cool for 10 minutes.

13. Pull the chicken apart into bite size pieces, and add it to the Dutch oven.

14. Simmer over low heat for two hours, stirring regularly.

15. To serve, fill bowl, sprinkle liberally with shredded cheese, and top with a dollop of sour cream.

3. Click on the **Save** button, and enjoy some Cannellini Cumin Chicken Chili.

Developing a custom contenteditable module

In this section, we are going to develop a module that provides a field formatter for text fields that allows in-place editing of text fields through the HTML5 **contenteditable** attribute.

See `http://blog.whatwg.org/the-road-to-html-5-contenteditable` for a good summary of the contenteditable attribute.

The contenteditable attribute value of true indicates that the HTML element it is applied to is editable. However, to make this truly useful, we will need to explore a way of saving the edited content asynchronously. In doing so, we will explore some new JavaScript and AJAX development concepts in Drupal 7.

Time for action – developing an HTML5 contenteditable module

1. Open Aptana Studio, and navigate to the `/sites/all/modules/custom` folder in the **Project Explorer** tab of the **Web perspective**. Right-click on the `custom` folder, select **New**, and select **Folder**. Enter `html5_contenteditable` as the name of the folder, and click on the **Finish** button.

2. Now, we need to create the necessary files for our contenteditable module: `contenteditable.info` and `contenteditable.module`.

3. Next, add some of the basic configuration information to the `contenteditable.info` file:

   ❑ `name`: HTML5 contentEditable

   ❑ `description`: "Uses a custom formatter to allow you to make some fields editable from the display through the HTML5 contentEditable attribute."

   ❑ `package`: Fields

   ❑ `version`: "7.x-1.x-dev"

- ❏ dependencies[]: entity
- ❏ core: 7.x

4. Now, we will turn our attention to the `contenteditable.module` file, and start by adding the code for the first hook that we will implement: `hook_field_formatter_info`:

```
/**
 * Implementation of hook_field_formatter_info().
 */
function contenteditable_field_formatter_info() {
  return array(
    'contenteditable' => array(
      'label' => t('contentEditable'),
      'field types' =>
        array('text','text_long','text_with_summary','list_text'),
      'settings' => array(
        'fallback_format' => NULL,
      ),
    ),
  );
}
```

5. Basically, we are creating a new contenteditable field formatter for all the text field types. Now, we will add some settings for our new formatter with `hook_field_formatter_settings_form`:

```
/**
 * Implements hook_field_formatter_settings_form().
 */
function contenteditable_field_formatter_settings_form($field,
  $instance, $view_mode, $form, &$form_state) {
  //This gets the view_mode where our settings are stored
  $display = $instance['display'][$view_mode];
  //This gets the actual settings
  $settings = $display['settings'];
  $element = array();

  //had an issue when using this formatter in a View, results in a
  //Fatal error: undefined function field_ui_formatter_options()
  if (!function_exists(field_ui_formatter_options)) {
    module_load_include('inc', 'field_ui', 'field_ui.admin');
  }

  //fallback formatter
```

```
    // Get the list of formatters for this field type, and remove
    //our own.
    $formatters = field_ui_formatter_options($field['type']);
    unset($formatters['contenteditable']);
    $element['fallback_format'] = array(
      '#type' => 'select',
      '#title' => t('Fallback formatter'),
      '#options' => $formatters,
      '#description' => t('Select formatter to be used for users
    that don\'t have permission to edit the field.'),  //helper text
      '#default_value' => $settings['fallback_format'],
    );

    return $element;
}
```

The `field_formatter_settings_form` hook, introduced with the new Field API for Drupal 7, allows you to add any number of form-driven settings to a field formatter. In this case, we are adding a setting that will allow the site administrators to select what formatter should be used for the field when a user does not have permission to edit the field. The `field_ui_formatter_options` function allows us to retrieve all of the available formatters for the current field, and then use those as the options to select from for the value of this setting after removing our own contenteditable formatter.

> The Drupal 7 core image field uses `hook_field_formatter_settings_form` to select the image style settings to be used for displaying the image field, and whether to wrap the image with a link to the content (the parent content item of the image) or to the image file (the original non-resized image). With Drupal 6, the CCK `ImageField` (`http://drupal.org/project/imagefield`) module provided several formatters to achieve the same functionality, and each formatter had to be listed for every possible image cache setting (replaced by image style for Drupal 7). The end result was that Drupal 6, with `ImageField` and `ImageCache` (`http://drupal.org/project/imagecache`) modules, had 12 formatters to accomplish what Drupal 7 does with one.

6. Now, we need to do some Drupal field house keeping. The custom settings for our field formatter will not be accessible unless we implement `hook_field_formatter_settings_summary`.

```
/**
 * Implements hook_field_formatter_settings_summary().
 */
```

```
function contenteditable_field_formatter_settings_summary($field,
  $instance, $view_mode) {
  $display = $instance['display'][$view_mode];
  $settings = $display['settings'];
  $formatter_type =
    field_info_formatter_types($settings['fallback_format']);
//get label of fallback formater for summary info
  $summary = t('Fallback format: @fallback_format format (Select
    format to be used when not in edit mode.)', array(
    '@fallback_format' => $formatter_type['label'],
  ));
// we use t() for translation and placeholders to guard against
  //attacks
  return $summary;
}
```

Our `contenteditable_field_formatter_settings_summary` function will display the currently selected fallback formatter, and it will trigger Drupal to expose the link to the formatter settings form.

7. Ok, now it is time to get to our formatter's output with the implementation of `hook_field_formatter_view`:

```
/**
 * Implements hook_field_formatter_view().
 */
function contenteditable_field_formatter_view($entity_type,
$entity, $field, $instance, $langcode, $items, $display) {
  // See if access to edit this field is restricted,
  //if so, use the default formatter.
  if (!entity_access('update', $entity_type, $entity) ||
    !field_access('edit', $field, $entity_type, $entity)) {
    // Can't edit.
    return contenteditable_fallback_formatter($entity_type,
      $entity, $field, $instance, $langcode, $items, $display);
  }
  $element = array();
  foreach ($items as $delta => $item) {
    $element[$delta] = array('#markup' => '<div
      contentEditable="true" data-tooltip="click to edit"
      data-nid="' . $entity->nid . '" data-fieldname="' .
      $field['field_name']. '">'
      . $item['value'] . '</div>');
  }

  return $element;
}
```

8. Basically, we are just wrapping the field with a div element that has the `contentEditable` attribute set to `true`. We are also adding some custom data attributes that we will utilize later in the JavaScript for this module. You may also notice the call to the `contenteditable_fallback_formatter` function when access to edit the field is restricted. That function doesn't exist yet, so we need to write it:

```
/**
 * Format a field using the fallback formatter of the
contenteditable field.
 */
function contenteditable_fallback_formatter($entity_type, $entity,
$field, $instance, $langcode, $items, $display) {
  // Set the fallback formatter.
  $display['type'] = $display['settings']['fallback_format'];
  $formatter_type = field_info_formatter_types($display['type']);
  $display['module'] = $formatter_type['module'];

  // Clone the entity to avoid messing with it.
  $cloned_entity = clone $entity;

  return field_view_field($entity_type, $cloned_entity,
$field['field_name'], $display, $langcode);
}
```

Our `contenteditable_fallback_formatter` function sets the type and module for the display of the element based on our custom `fallback_format` setting, and uses the core `field_view_field` function to generate the correct output.

9. Now, we are at a point where we can test what we have done so far. Open up our d7dev site, and click on the **Modules** link in the **Admin** toolbar. We will use Drush to enable our custom contenteditable module:

```
C:\xampp\htdocs\d7dev>drush en contenteditable

The following extensions will be enabled: contenteditable

Do you really want to continue? (y/n): y

wysiwyg was enabled successfully.                [ok]
```

10. We can now configure the **description** field on our Recipe content type to use our HTML5 contentEditable formatter. In the **Admin** toolbar, click on the **Structure** link, then the **Content types** link, and then the **manage display** link for our Recipe content type.

11. On the **manage display configuration** page for our Recipe content type, click on the **FORMAT** drop-down, select `contentEditable`, and click on the **settings** button to see the output of our `contenteditable_field_formatter_settings_form` function:

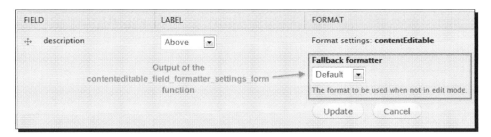

12. For now, just leave the **Fallback formatter** set to `Default`. Click on the **Cancel** button, and click on the **Save** button at the bottom of the page.

13. So, let's see what this formatter looks like. Click on the **Content** link in the **Admin** toolbar, and click on the link for the Cannellini Cumin Chicken Chili recipe that we added earlier in this chapter.

14. You will notice that the description for the recipe reads: **This spicy**, **creamy white chili is just the ticket on those first cool days for Fall**. Double-click on the word **for** and **type** of to replace it inline. Notice the changed text, and the active text cursor in the following screenshot:

15. Now, refresh the page in your browser, and you will notice that the text reverts back to the word `for`.

16. Browsers that support the `contentEditable` property, don't do anything to automatically save the edited value. As you can see in the informative screenshot from caniuse.com, there is excellent browser support for the `contentEditable` attribute—there is even support for it with iOS 5:

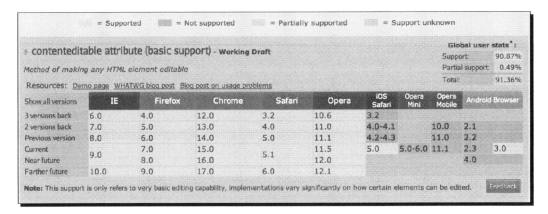

However, to save the edited value of our `contentEditable` enabled elements and for other usability enhancements, we will need to enhance our HTML5 `contentEditable` module with some Drupal 7 JavaScript and AJAX functionality.

17. In Aptana Studio, right click on the `/sites/all/modules/custom/contenteditable` folder, and add the new `contenteditable.js` file.

18. Now, we are ready to begin writing the necessary JavaScript for our module. But, first, you should understand that jQuery has been namespaced for Drupal 7, so the `$` global variable no longer refers to the jQuery object. The following code will associate the `$` variable with the jQuery object within our local function:

```
(function ($) {

})(jQuery);
```

 Namespacing jQuery for Drupal7 allows for better compatibility with other JavaScript libraries. For more information about this change for Drupal 7, see `http://drupal.org/update/modules/6/7#javascript_compatibility`.

Typically, with jQuery you would use `$(document.ready(function(){});` to ensure that the DOM is fully loaded before your JavaScript attempts to manipulate elements or bind behaviors. However, Drupal provides a wrapper for this functionality, and adds some additional features with the `Drupal.Behaviors` object.

19. So, we will now extend the `Drupal.Behaviors` object for our contenteditable module:

```
var self = Drupal.behaviors.contenteditable = {


};
```

20. For Drupal 7, the `Drupal.Behaviors` object has two handlers or methods: `attach` and `detach`. The `attach` handler is required, so we will add that now.

```
attach: function (context) {
  // Make sure it was initialized.
  if (!self.initialized) {
    self.init();
  }
  // Bind handlers and prevent elements from being processed
  //again.
  $('div[contenteditable]', context)
  .once('contenteditable')
  .bind('focusin', self.focusin)
  .bind('focusout', self.focusout);
}
```

Note the use of the `once` method. The jQuery **once** plug-in (`http://plugins.jquery.com/project/once`) has been integrated with Drupal 7, and makes it much simpler for the JavaScript developers to ensure that behaviors are only applied to an element once. Prior to using the jQuery once plugin, our code may have looked something similar to the following:

```
attach: function (context) {
  // Make sure it was initialized.
  if (!self.initialized) {
    self.init();
  }
  // Bind handlers and prevent elements from being processed
  //again.
  $('div[contenteditable]', context)
  .not('.contenteditable-processed')
  .addClass('contenteditable-processed')
  .bind('focusin', self.focusin)
  .bind('focusout', self.focusout);
}
```

The code uses jQuery to add and remove a certain class, and tests for the presence of that class with a selector to accomplish the same thing as the once plugin.

21. You may also notice that we made a call to the three methods that haven't been defined yet: `self.init`, `self.focusin`, and `self.focusout`. We will now add the code for those three methods after our `attach` method:

```
,
init: function() {
  // Create controls, store reference and bind handlers.
  var $controls = self.constructControls().add('<button>', { 'id':
    'contenteditableCancel', 'text': Drupal.t('Cancel'), click:
    self.hideControls, 'data-tooltip': 'cancel edit'})

    .add('<button>', { 'id': 'contenteditableSave', 'text':
      Drupal.t('Save'), click: self.submitHandler, 'data-tooltip':
      'save changes'});

  self.controls = $('<div id="contenteditableButtons"
    class="contenteditable_buttons"></div>').append($controls)
    .appendTo('body');

  self.initialized = true;
  self.currentField = null;
  },
focusin: function(e) {
  // Move the controls to right before the element we're editing,
  //but only when focusing in on a new field, otherwise do
  //nothing.
  if(self.currentField != $(this).data('fieldname')){
    self.active = $(this);
    $(this).addClass('contenteditableActive');
    self.currentField = self.active.data('fieldname');
    var $clone = self.controls.clone(true);
    self.controls.remove();
    self.controls = $clone;
    self.controls.hide().insertBefore(self.active).fadeIn('slow');
  }
},
focusout: function(e) {
  // TODO: handle removing the controls
}
```

The `init` method sets up the controls that will be defined in our `contenteditable.module`. These will include some basic WYSIWYG controls, such as the ability to style the text of the contenteditable element as bold, italic, and/or underline.

The focusin method actually takes care of showing the controls for the currently focused contenteditable element. The focusout method is just a placeholder for some possible future enhancements; it serves as a visual reminder that there may be room for improvement.

22. Now, we will add the code for two other methods called in the init method: self. constructControls and self.submitHandler.

```
,
constructControls: function() {
  if (!Drupal.settings || !Drupal.settings.contenteditableButtons)
  {
    throw new Error('Control settings not found.');
  }

  // Go over the settings object, construct the controls and
  //return them as 1 jQuery collection.
  var $buttons = $();
  $.each(Drupal.settings.contenteditableButtons, function(i, el) {
    var $el = $(el.wrapper, el.attributes).bind(el.event,
    el.handler ? eval('(' + el.handler + ')') :
    self.commandHandler);

  $buttons = $buttons.add($el);
  });
  return $buttons;
},
submitHandler: function(e) {
  // If they manage to press the button before an element was set
  //as active,
  // or there are no controls, throw an exception, otherwise, post
  //the data.
  if (!self.active) {
    throw new Error('Active element not found.');
  }
  if (!self.controls) {
    throw new Error('Failed to hide controls: reference not
      found.');
  }

  // Display a saving message indicator.
  $('<div id="contenteditableSaving"
    class="messages"></div>').insertBefore(self.active);
```

```
var $title;
var text = Drupal.t('Saving');
var dots = '';
$title = $('#contenteditableSaving').text(text);
var id = setInterval(function () {
  dots = (dots.length > 10) ? '' : dots + '.';
  $title.text(text + dots);
}, 500);


//disable contenteditable on active element until the ajax call
//is complete
self.active.attr('contenteditable', 'false');
// Hide the controls and trigger the hide helper
self.controls.slideUp('slow', self.hideControls);
var ajax_data = {
  'field_value': self.active.html(),
  'nid': self.active.data('nid'),
  'fieldname': self.active.data('fieldname')
}
$.ajax({
  type: 'POST',
  url: Drupal.settings.basePath + 'contenteditable/ajax',
  dataType: 'json',
  data: ajax_data,
  success: self.successHandler
});
}
```

The `constructControls` code binds either the yet to be defined `commandHandler` or a handler specified by the controls configuration in our module, to an event specified by our modules controls configuration. The `submitHandler` hides the attached controls for the associated `contenteditable` element, and then uses jQuery `ajax` to POST the updated element value and additional data to the `contenteditable/ajax` path as JSON.

If you are not familiar with the term **Asynchronous JavaScript And XML (AJAX)** and/or with jQuery, then I recommend that you read through the jQuery documentation for the `ajax()` function at `http://api.jquery.com/jQuery.ajax/`.

23. Now, switch back to `contenteditable.module`, and we will add the code that will define the controls to be set up by the `constructControls` code:

```
/**
* Hook and helper function to add the controls to Drupal.settings
*
*/
function _contenteditable_add_controls() {
  $buttons = array(
      'bold' => array(
        'wrapper' => '<button>',
        'event' => 'click',
        'attributes' => array(
          'html' => '<strong>B</strong>',
          'data-command' => 'bold',
          'alt' => 'bold',
          'data-tooltip' => t('bold'),
        ),
      ),
      'italic' => array(
        'wrapper' => '<button>',
        'event' => 'click',
        'attributes' => array(
          'html' => '<i>i</i>',
          'data-command' => 'italic',
          'alt' => 'italic',
          'data-tooltip' => t('italic'),
        ),
      ),
      'underline' => array(
        'wrapper' => '<button>',
        'event' => 'click',
        'attributes' => array(
          'html' => '<u>u</u>',
          'data-command' => 'underline',
          'alt' => 'underline',
          'data-tooltip' => t('underline selected text'),
        ),
      ),
  );
  //hook to add controls
  $additional_controls =
    module_invoke_all('contenteditable_add_controls');
  if (is_array($additional_controls)) {
    $buttons = array_merge($buttons, $additional_controls);
  }
  return $buttons;
}
```

In addition to the `$buttons` array that contains the necessary information for the `constructControls` function, we have also added our very own hook that will allow other modules to add their own controls. The `module_invoke_all` function will execute all implementations of our `hook_contenteditable_add_controls`. You may notice that we haven't actually written any code yet that calls this `_contenteditable_add_controls` function. We will do that when we integrate `contenteditable.js` with our module.

24. Next, we will add the following implementation of `hook_menu`, so that our module will respond to requests to the `contenteditable/ajax` path, as used in our `submitHandler` previously:

```
/**
 * Implementation of hook_menu().
 */
function contenteditable_menu() {

  $items['contenteditable/ajax'] = array(
    'title' => t('contenteditable AJAX'),
    'type' => MENU_CALLBACK,
    'page callback' => 'contenteditable_ajax',
    'access arguments' => array('access content'),
  );

  return $items;
}
```

25. Drupal's `hook_menu` allows you to register paths, and specify a page callback to tell Drupal how to handle the response for those paths. In this case, we are registering the path from our `submitHandler` in `contenteditable.js` with a page callback of `contenteditable_ajax`. So now we will define that function:

```
/**
 * Callback for the contenteditable_menu hook
 */
function contenteditable_ajax () {
  // Retrieve the slider value
  $field_value = $_POST['field_value'];
  $nid = (int)$_POST['nid'];
  $field_name = $_POST['fieldname'];
  $node = node_load($nid);
  $node->{$field_name} =
    array('und'=>array(array('value'=>$field_value)));
  node_save($node);
  // Return json
```

```
$json_output = array();
$json_output['nid'] = $nid;
$json_output['fieldname'] = $field_name;
$json_output['msg'] = t('The field value has been updated.');
drupal_json_output($json_output);
}
```

The `contenteditable_ajax` function gets the values from the `POST` data set by specifying `POST` for the `type` option of the `$.ajax` call in our `submitHandler`. This data is used to load the parent node of the `contenteditable` field, update the value of the field, and then save the node with the updated field value. We then create an `array()` of data to send back to the client as JSON, by passing the array to the `drupal_json_output` function.

26. Now, add the code for the call to `self.commandHandler` in `constructControls`:

```
'
  commandHandler: function(e) {
    // Executes commands attached to the controls.
    var $this = $(this),
        cmd = $this.data('command')
        cmdValue = $this.attr('cmdValue') || null,
        returnValue = document.execCommand(cmd, false, cmdValue);
    if (returnValue) {
      return returnValue;
    }
  }
}
```

The `commandHandler` code takes care of executing the actual commands that are activated by the user through the `document.execCommand` method, which is a part of the HTML Editing APIs specification (see `http://dev.w3.org/html5/spec/Overview.html#editing-apis`).

27. Next, we need to add the code for the call to `self.successHandler` and `self.hideContros` in the `submitHandler`:

```
'
successHandler: function(data, status, xhr) {
//remove saving indicator
$('#contenteditableSaving').remove();
// Highlight the edited element and show a status message.
var $el = $('div[data-nid="' + data['nid'] + '"][data-
  fieldname="' + data['fieldname'] + '"]'),
  $success = $('<div id="contenteditableSuccess" class="messages
  status">' + data['msg'] + '</div>').insertBefore($el);
```

```
$el.effect('highlight', {}, 3000);
$success.delay(2000).slideUp('slow', function() {
  $(this).remove(); });


//re-enable contenteditable on active element so it may be re-
//edited
self.active.attr('contenteditable', 'true');
},
hideControls: function() {
  // Move the controls back to the end of the body element.
  if (!self.controls) {
    throw new Error('Failed to hide controls: reference not
      found.');
  }
  self.active.removeClass('contenteditableActive');
  var $clone = self.controls
    .removeAttr('style').clone(true).appendTo('body');

  self.controls.remove();
  self.controls = $clone;
  //unset self.currentField so that the same field may be re
  //-edited
  self.currentField = null;
}
```

The `successHandler` is called by the jQuery `$.ajax` function, if it succeeds in asynchronously updating the field ,and inserts a dynamic success message before the contenteditable element being updated. The `hideControls` code hides the controls associated with the contenteditable element.

28. Now, we will update our module code to include the `contenteditable.js` when the `contenteditable_field_formatter_view` function is called. Switch back to the `contenteditable.module` file in Aptana Studio, and add the following code above the return statement `return $element` in the `contenteditable_field_formatter_view` function:

```
//use the #attached property to add the JavaScript and CSS
$path = drupal_get_path('module', 'contenteditable');
$element['#attached'] = array(
    'js' => array(
        $path . '/contenteditable.js' => array(),
        // JavaScript settings may use the 'data' key.
        array(
            'type' => 'setting',
```

```
        'data' => array('contenteditableButtons' =>
          _contenteditable_add_controls()),
      ),
    ),
    'css' => array(
      $path . '/contenteditable.css' => array(),
    ),
    //add system library, used by the successHandler method of
    //our JavaScript
    'library' => array(
      array('system', 'effects.highlight'),
    ),
  );
```

Here, we are revisiting the use of render arrays that we introduced in the previous chapter. We are using the #attached property to add our JavaScript file, custom JavaScript settings, CSS, and a system library. In order to add the contenteditable. js and contenteditable.css files, we get the path to our module with the drupal_get_path function, and append it to the names for those files. The settings are added by calling our module's private _contenteditable_add_controls function. I am not going to go over the CSS in detail, but here are the contents for the contenteditable.css file:

```
[contenteditable]:hover {
  outline: 1px dotted #CCC;
}

div.contenteditable-processed.contenteditableActive{
      box-shadow: 0 0 5px rgba(81, 203, 238, 1);
}

/*buttons css*/
div.contenteditable_buttons{
  display: none;
  -webkit-appearance: none;
  -moz-border-radius: 11px;
  -webkit-border-radius: 11px;
  -moz-background-clip: padding;
  -webkit-background-clip: padding;
  border-radius: 11px;
  background: #DDD url(images/button.png) repeat-x;
  background: -webkit-gradient(linear, left top, left bottom,
    color-stop(0, white), color-stop(1, #DDD));
```

```css
  background: -moz-linear-gradient(top center, white 0%, #DDD
    100%);
  border: 1px solid;
  cursor: pointer;
  color: #333;
  font: bold 12px/1.2 Arial, sans-serif;
  outline: 0;
  overflow: visible;
  padding: 3px 10px 4px;
  text-shadow: white 0 1px 1px;
  width: auto;
  border-color: #DDD #BBB #999;
  width:240px;
}

/*buttons for format plugin*/
#contenteditableSave,
#contenteditableCancel{
  float: right;
}

#contenteditableButtons button{
      margin: 0 2px;
}

/*override line height*/
#contenteditableButtons a:link, a:visited{
  line-height:0;
}

#contenteditableButtons button:hover:after{
  content: attr(data-tooltip);
  position: absolute;
  white-space: nowrap;
  background: -webkit-gradient(linear, left top, left bottom,
    color-stop(0, #FFFFCC), color-stop(0.9, #FFFFCC));
  background: -moz-linear-gradient(top center, #FFFFCC 0%, #FFFFCC
    90%);
  padding: 3px 7px;
  color: #777;
  border-radius: 3px; -moz-border-radius: 3px; -webkit-border-
    radius: 3px;
```

```
    margin-left: -30px;
    margin-top: -30px;
  }

  [contenteditable="true"]:not(.contenteditableActive):hover:after{
    content: attr(data-tooltip);
    position: relative;
    right:-100%;
    background: -webkit-gradient(linear, left top, left bottom,
      color-stop(0, #FFFFCC), color-stop(0.9, #FFFFCC));
    background: -moz-linear-gradient(top center, #FFFFCC 0%, #FFFFCC
      90%);
    padding: 3px 7px;
    color: #777;
  }

  #contenteditableSaving{
    background-color: #FFFCE5;
    color: #840;
    font-weight: bold;
    font-size: 16px;
    border-color: #ED5;
  }
```

29. Now, we are ready to test what we have done. Load the d7dev site in your browser, click on the **Content** link in the **Admin** toolbar, and click on the link for the Cannellini Cumin Chicken Chili recipe that we added earlier in this chapter.

30. Once again, click on the word **for** in the description. You will right away notice a few differences.

31. Now, delete the word **for** and **type** in **of**, and click on the **Save** button. Once you see the message that the field was successfully updated, refresh the page, and you will see that the value sticks.

What just happened?

Wow, that was some pretty serious module development. We created a fairly complex module that allows us to make text fields editable inline using the HTML5 `contentEditable` attribute, and we were introduced to some key Drupal 7 development concepts around JavaScript, AJAX, and a number of new **hooks**.

Summary

In this chapter, we have seen how easy it can be to enhance the UX for content authors. In some cases, it was as easy as adding and configuring additional contrib modules. We also learned some fairly advanced development that allowed us to offer a unique authoring experience for Drupal 7, and we learned a lot about how to integrate custom JavaScript with Drupal 7, as well as a bit about AJAX for Drupal 7.

In the next chapter, we are going look at some ways to enhance our d7dev site with images, by introducing the **Media** module, and developing another custom module to display the Media module-managed images in a **lightbox**.

6
Adding Media to our Site

*A **text-only** site is not going hold the interest of visitors; a site needs some pizzazz and some spice. One way to add some pizzazz to your site is to add some multi-media content, such as images, video, audio, and so on. But, we don't just want to add a few images here and there; in fact, we want an immersive and compelling multi-media experience that is easy to manage, configure, and extend. The new **Media** (*`http://drupal.org/projects/`*
`media`) *module for Drupal 7 will enable us to easily add the multi-media content to our d7dev site. The Media module is quickly becoming the de facto contributed module for managing multi-media content in Drupal 7, and it offers a solid foundation for the future of multi-media in Drupal. In this chapter, we will discover how to integrate the Media module to add images to our d7dev site, and will explore compelling ways to present images to the users. This will include taking a look at the integration of a **lightbox** type UI element for displaying the Media module-managed images, and learning how we can leverage the Drupal development community to make improvements to the existing code.*

The following topics will be covered in this chapter:

◆ Configuring the Media module

◆ Adding Media fields to your content types

◆ Code Example: Image styles for Drupal 7

◆ Displaying Media in a lightbox through a custom field formatter

◆ Using Drupal Sandbox projects, and applying patches

Introduction to the Media module

Prior to Drupal 7, integrating multi-media content with your Drupal site has been a mishmash concoction of contrib modules and configuration. Many solutions for integrating images into content only offered part of a total solution, requiring you to piece together a number of modules to get exactly what you wanted. Before Drupal 7, you couldn't even include an image with your content without adding a contrib module. The **Image** module for Drupal 6 (`http://drupal.org/pojrect/image`) filled the gap nicely, and several modules were introduced that allowed you to "insert" the Image module images in a WYSIWYG text area. Eventually, a CCK-based **ImageField** module (`http://drupal.org/project/imagefield`) was introduced, and you were able to have field-based images. In addition to the Image and ImageField modules, some other image-related modules for Drupal 6 included the **ImageCache** module (`http://drupal.org/project/imagecache`) to dynamically generate resized versions of the images, and the **Insert** module (`http://drupal.org/project/insert`) that enabled the inline insertion of ImageField images within a WYSIWYG-enabled text area.

Features provided by the Drupal 6 ImageCache and Insert modules are duplicated quite nicely by Drupal 7 core and the Drupal 7 Media module. Drupal 7 includes the addition of the new core image module, so that an image field is available with a core install. In addition to field-based images, the Drupal 7 core image module includes much of the functionality that was included with the Drupal 6 Image, ImageAPI, and ImageCache modules. Even though this was a great improvement, the core image module does not include the ability to insert images inline in the WYSIWYG text area. The Media module for Drupal 7 does provide the capability to insert images inline within a WYSIWYG text area, and it offers many other features that would have required a number of different modules for Drupal 6.

Working with dev versions of modules

There are times when you come across a module that introduces some major new features and is fairly stable, but not quite ready for use on a live/production website, and is therefore only available as a dev version. This is a perfect opportunity to provide a valuable contribution to the Drupal community. Just by installing and using a dev version of a module (in your local development environment of course), you are providing valuable testing for the module maintainers. Of course, you should enter an issue in the project's issue queue if you discover any bugs, or would like to request any additional features. Also, using a dev version of a module presents you with the opportunity to take on some custom Drupal development. However, it is important that you remember that a module is released as a dev version for a reason, and is most likely not stable enough to be deployed to a public facing site.

Our use of the Media module in this chapter is an excellent example of living on the edge with dev. The Media module has two major releases for Drupal 7, and the second release includes some massive refactoring of the code, and those large code changes are only available as a dev release. One of the major changes between the 1.x and 2.x versions of the Media module is the removal of the file entity code that has been moved into its own module, and requires the installation of the **File Entity** module (http://drupal.org/project/file_entity) in order to enable the Media module.

One thing to note in regards to Drush is that, by default, Drush will only download official module releases, so we need to get the exact version of the module we would like to download with Drush. Then, we will be able to download the dev release, and enable it with Drush, as we have already done with other contrib modules.

Time for action – using Drush to install a dev version of the Media module

We are going to use Drush to download the dev release of the Media module, so that we can add some multi-media content to our d7dev site.

1. Open the Terminal (Mac OS X) or Command Prompt (Windows) application, and go to the root directory of our d7dev site.

2. The second version of the Media module is dependent on the File Entity module. So, we will use Drush to download and enable that module.

```
$ drush dl file_entity-7.x-2.x-dev
Project file_entity (7.x-2.x-dev) downloaded to /Users/kurt/
htdocs/d7dev/sites/all/modules/file_entity.    [success]
$ drush en file_entity
The following extensions will be enabled: file_entity
Do you really want to continue? (y/n): y
file_entity was enabled successfully.               [ok]
```

3. Next, we will use Drush to get the release information for the Media module.

```
$ drush rl media
------- RELEASES FOR 'MEDIA' PROJECT -------
 Release        Date         Status
 7.x-2.x-dev    2011-Nov-23  Development
 7.x-2.0-unstab 2011-Oct-12  Supported
 le2
 7.x-1.x-dev    2011-Nov-21  Development
 7.x-1.0-rc2    2011-Oct-12  Supported, Security, Recommended
```

4. Now, with the release information, we will see the exact version of the Media module that we are interested in: `7.x-2.x-dev`. So, download and enable the 2.x dev version of the Media module with Drush.

```
$ drush dl media-7.x-2.x-dev

Project media (7.x-2.x-dev) downloaded to /Users/kurt/htdocs/
d7dev/sites/all/modules/media.            [success]

Project media contains 3 modules: mediafield, media_internet,
media.

$ drush en media

The following extensions will be enabled: media

Do you really want to continue? (y/n): y

media was enabled successfully.        [ok]
```

5. The Media module is now enabled for our d7dev site.

What just happened?

We enabled the Media module, and learned how to install a dev release with Drush. We have also learned that it is can be useful to us, and the greater Drupal community, to explore a dev release of a module.

Enhancing the Recipe content type with a Media field

Now that we have enabled the Media module for our d7dev site, let's enhance our Recipe content type with a Media field.

Time for action – adding a Media field to our Recipe content type

We will use the **manage fields** administrative page to add a Media field to our d7dev Recipe content type.

1. Open up our d7dev site in your favorite browser, click on the **Structure** link in the **Admin** toolbar, and then click on the **Content types** link.

2. Next, on the **Content types** administrative page, click on the **manage fields** link for our Recipe content type.

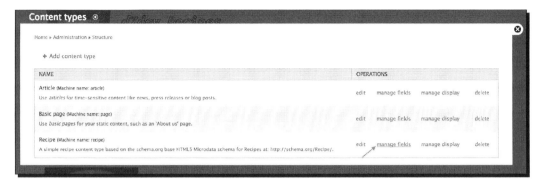

3. Now, enter `Media` as the label for the **Add new field** input type. Next to the **field_** prefix label in the **Name** column, type `media`, and select **File** from the **Select a field type** dropdown and **Media file selector** as the widget, and click the **Save** button. On the next screen, click on the **Save field settings** button.

4. On the **RECIPE SETTINGS** page, enter `Associate multimedia files with the recipe.` as the **Help text**, and then check the **Upload**, **Library**, and **View Library** checkboxes under the **Enabled browser plugins** section.

5. Next, enter `jpg` and `png` as the **Allowed file extensions for uploaded files**, and enter `recipe/media` as the **File directory**. Then, accept the rest of the default settings, and click on the **Save settings** button at the bottom of the page.

Although the Media module supports other media types besides images, such as video and audio, we are only going to work with images for now. The **File directory** setting will allow us to maintain some order for our d7dev public files director: `/sites/default/files.`.

6. So, let's add some media to a recipe. Click on the **Find content** link in the **Shortcuts** bar, and click on the **edit** link for the Cannellini Cumin Chicken Chili recipe.

7. Now, scroll down to the new Media field that we have added, click on the **Select media** button, and you will see a Media browser dialog pop up:

8. Feel free to explore the **Library** and **View Library** tabs of the media browser. However, for now, we are just going to focus on the **Upload** tab. Click on the **Choose File** button, and select a recipe photo to upload.

9. Next, click on the **Add another item** button below the **Media** field, and add another image. Repeat until all nine chili images have been uploaded, scroll to the bottom of the screen, and click on the **Save** button.

10. Now, if you scroll to the bottom of the page for the Cannellini Cumin Chicken Chili recipe, you will see that by default the media field is formatted as a generic file—that is, as a file icon with a link.

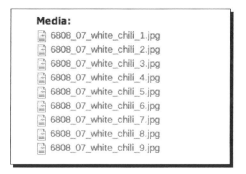

11. Let's change the formatter, and layout to something more visually appealing. Click on the **Structure** link in the **Admin** toolbar, then click on the **Content types** link and the **manage display** link for our Recipe content type.

12. Drag the **Media** field above the **image** field, and move the **image** field to the **Hidden** section.

13. Next, select **<Hidden>** for the **LABEL** and **Rendered file** for the **FORMAT** for the **Media** field. Once you select **Rendered file** for the **FORMAT**, you will notice that a **FORMAT** setting button appears. We will click on the **FORMAT settings** button to change the **View mode** from **Default** to **Preview**, and click on the **Update** button for the **Format settings**. Finally, click on the **Save** button at the bottom of the screen.

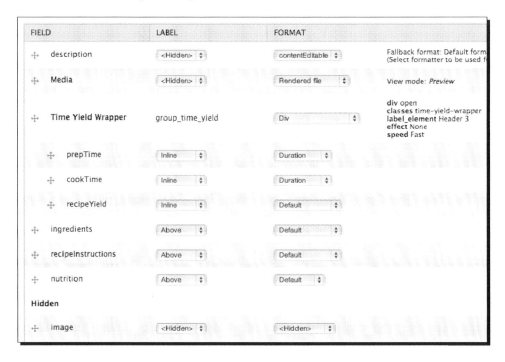

14. Reload our Cannellini Cumin Chicken Chili recipe page, and you will see a small version of the media images we uploaded, but they are all stacked on top of each other. So, we will add the following CSS just under the style for `article.node-recipe div.field-name-field-image` in the `/sites/all/themes/d7dev/css/global.css` file, to lay out the media field images in more of a grid:

```
article.node-recipe div.field-name-field-media div.file{
  float:left;
  margin: 0 5px 5px 0;
  box-shadow: 0 5px 5px -3px black;
}
```

15. Once again, reload our Cannellini Cumin Chicken Chili recipe page, and you should see something similar to the following:

What just happened?

We added and configured a Media-based field for our Recipe content type.

A new Recipe for our site

As promised in the previous chapter, here is a new recipe for this chapter: **Thai Basil Chicken**. Add it to your d7dev site, if you would like to have more real content to use as an example, and feel free to try the recipe out!

- name: Thai Basil Chicken

- description: A spicy, flavorful version of one of my favorite Thai dish.

- recipeYield: Four servings

- prepTime: 25 minutes

- cookTime: 20 minutes

- ingredients:

    - One pound boneless chicken breasts

    - Two tablespoons of olive oil

    - Tthree tablespoons of soy sauce

    - Two tablespoons of fish sauce

    - Two large sweet onions, sliced

    - Five cloves of garlic

- ❏ One yellow bell pepper
- ❏ One green bell pepper
- ❏ Four to eight Thai peppers (depending on the level of hotness you want)
- ❏ One-third cup of dark brown sugar dissolved in one cup of hot water
- ❏ One cup of fresh basil leaves
- ❏ Two cups Jasmin rice

◆ instructions:

1. Prepare the Jasmine rice according to the directions.
2. Heat the olive oil in a large frying pan over medium heat for two minutes.
3. Add the chicken to the pan and then pour on soy sauce.
4. Cook the chicken until there is no visible pinkness; approximately eight to ten minutes.
5. Reduce heat to medium low.
6. Add the garlic and fish sauce, and simmer for three minutes.
7. Next, add the Thai chilies, onion, and bell pepper, and stir to combine. Simmer for two minutes.
8. Add the brown sugar and water mixture. Stir to mix, and then cover. Simmer for five minutes.
9. Uncover, add the basil, and stir to combine.
10. Serve over rice.

Custom image styles and inline Media for WYSIWYG

As mentioned previously, the Media module offers a number of compelling features out of the box. This enables you to do more with less, and it does a lot more by itself than many of the image integration solutions for Drupal 6, and even the core image module with Drupal 7. One of those features is to allow the insertion of images into a WYSIWYG-enabled text area.

Creating a custom image style

Before we configure inline Media for the WYSIWYG module, we are going to create a custom image style to use when we add an inline image to a WYSIWYG text area. Image styles for Drupal 7, part of the core Image module, is a replacement for the Drupal 6 contrib Image Cache, Image Field, and Image modules. In my opinion, **Image Styles** is a much better name than **Image Cache**. Regardless of the name, we are now going to configure a custom image style for our d7dev site. The core image module provides four default image styles: **thumbnail**, **medium**, **large**, and **square thumbnail**, as seen in following the **Image style** configuration page:

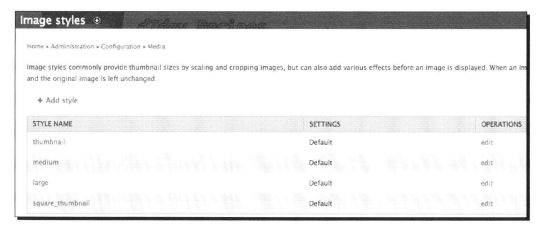

We are going to add a fifth custom image style, an image style that will resize our images somewhere between the `100x75` thumbnail style and the `220x165` medium style. We will walk through the process of creating an image style through the Image style administrative page, and walk through the process of programmatically creating an image style.

Time for action – adding a custom image style through the image styles administrative page

First, we will use the **Images styles** administrative page to create a custom image style.

1. Open our d7dev site in your favorite browser, click on the Configuration link in the **Admin** toolbar, and click on the **Image** styles link under the **Media** section.

2. Once the **Image styles** administrative page has loaded, click on the **Add style** link.

3. Next, enter `small` for the **Style name** of our custom image style, and click on the **Create new style** button.

4. Now, we will add the one and only **EFFECT** for our custom image style by selecting **Scale from EFFECT** options, and then clicking on the **Add** button.

5. On the **Add Scale effect** page, enter `160` for the width, `120` for the height, leave the **Allow Upscaling** checkbox unchecked, and click on **Add effect** button.

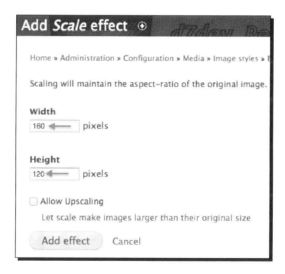

6. Finally, just click on the **Update style** button on the **Edit small style** administrative page, and we are done. We now have a new custom small image style that we will be able to use to resize images for our site.

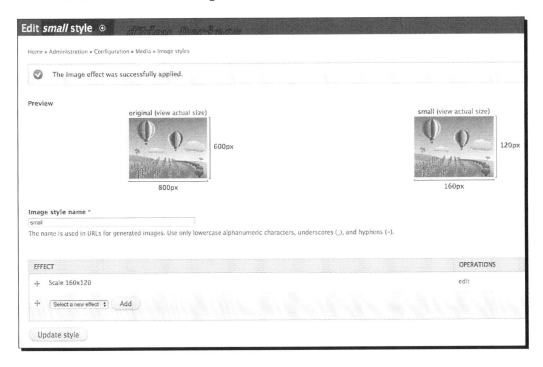

What just happened?

Ok, so we saw how easy it is to add a custom image style with the administrative UI. Now, we are going to see how to add a custom image style by writing some code. The advantage of having code-based custom image styles is that it will allow us to utilize a source code repository, such as Git, to manage and deploy our custom image styles between different environments. For example, it would allow us to use Git to promote image styles from our development environment to a live production website. Otherwise, the manual configuration that we just did would have to be repeated for every environment.

Time for action – creating a programmatic custom image style

Now, we will see how you add a custom image style with code.

1.   The first thing we need to do is delete the small image style that we just created. So, open our d7dev site in your favorite browser, click on the **Configuration** link in the **Admin** toolbar, and then click on the **Image styles** link under the **Media** section.

2.   Once the **Image styles** administrative page has loaded, click on the **delete** link for the small image style that we just added.

3.   Next, on the **Optionally select a style before deleting small** page, leave the default value for the **Replacement style** select list to **No replacement, just delete**, and click on the **Delete** button.

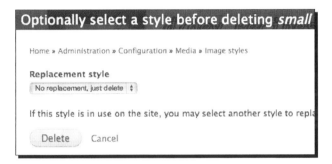

4.   Now that we have cleared the way to replace our custom image styles programmatically, open the d7dev.module file located at /sites/all/modules/ d7dev in Aptana Studio.

5.   The Drupal 7 core Image API includes a hook for programmatically creating custom image styles: hook_image_default_styles. We are going to implement the image_default_styles hook in our d7dev.module by adding the following code after our d7dev_field_formatter_view function.

```
/**
 * Implements hook_image_default_styles().
 */
function d7dev_image_default_styles() {

}
```

6. Now, the next part is pretty easy. We are going to take a look at the Drupal 7 API documentation for `hook_image_default_styles` at `http://api.drupal.org/api/drupal/modules--image--image.api.php/function/hook_image_default_styles/7`. Scroll down to the **Code** section of the page, and copy all of the code between the function curly brackets.

```
Code
modules/image/image.api.php, line 176

<?php
function hook_image_default_styles() {
  $styles = array();

  $styles['mymodule_preview'] = array(
    'effects' => array(
      array(
        'name' => 'image_scale',
        'data' => array(
          'width' => 400,
          'height' => 400,
          'upscale' => 1,
        ),
        'weight' => 0,
      ),
      array(
        'name' => 'image_desaturate',
        'data' => array(),
        'weight' => 1,
      ),
    ),
  );

  return $styles;
}
?>
```

7. Next, paste the code into our new `d7dev_image_default_styles` function, changing the name of the style from `mymodule_preview` to `small`, the width to `160`, the height to `120`, set upscale to `0`, and delete the `image_desaturate` array. The `final` function should look similar to the following code:

```
/**
 * Implements hook_image_default_styles().
 */
function d7dev_image_default_styles() {
  $styles = array();

  $styles['small'] = array(
```

```
    'effects' => array(
      array(
        'name' => 'image_scale',
        'data' => array(
          'width' => 160,
          'height' => 120,
          'upscale' => 0,
        ),
        'weight' => 0,
      ),
    ),
  );


  return $styles;
}
```

The name of our custom style, small, is provided as the key of the `$styles` array. Then, for each effect that we want to add to our image style, we pass in an effect configuration array, specifying the effect we want to use as the name key, and then passing in a data array as the settings for the effect. In the case of the `image_scale` effect that we are using here, we pass in the width, height, and upscale settings. Finally, the value for the weight key allows us to specify the order that the effects should be processed in, and although it is not very useful when there is only one effect, it becomes important when there are multiple effects.

8. Now, we will need to clear the cache for our d7dev site by going to **Configuration**, clicking the **Performance** link, and then clicking on the **Clear all caches** button. Then, go back to the **Image styles** administrative page, and you will see our programmatically created small image style.

> You could also use Drush to clear the Drupal cache. The Drush `cc` command will accomplish the same thing as clicking on the **Clear all** cache button on the **Performance** administrative page.

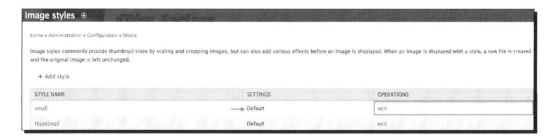

When we created our custom image style through the administrative UI, **Custom** was listed as the value for the **SETTINGS** column, and there was a link to delete the image style in the **OPERATIONS** column. Now, with our programmatic image, **Default** is listed in the **SETTINGS** column, and there is no delete link in the **OPERATIONS** column. In order to remove an image style provided by a module, you would need to disable the module. Therefore, if you are coding custom image styles, you may want to place them in their own module, so that you can disable them without disabling other features of the module. You won't be able to modify the effects without being forced to override the default; or in the case with our small custom image style, modifying the code of our `d7dev_image_default_styles`.

The programmatic approach for creating custom image styles is straightforward, and I feel that it is almost as easy as doing it through the administrative UI. However, for more complex custom image styles, the biggest issue may be figuring out the correct names to use for all of the available effects. We already saw two effect names in the code that we copied from the API documentation for `hook_image_default_styles`: `image_scale` and `image_desaturate`. The best, and only place that I am aware of to find all of the available image style effects available in the core image module is in the actual code. Open `/modules/image/image.effects.inc` in Aptana Studio, and you will see all of the available core image style effects listed in the `image_image_effect_info`. To see what data settings are available for a given effect, you must find the function that is specified as the effect callback for each `$effects` array. Here is a list of effects, and the available data settings available for those effects based on the code in the `image.effects.inc` file:

Effect name	Effect data settings
`image_resize`	`width`: An integer representing the desired width in pixels.
	`height`: An integer representing the desired height in pixels.
`image_scale`	`width`: An integer representing the desired width in pixels.
	`height`: An integer representing the desired height in pixels.
	`upscale`: A Boolean specified as `0` or `1`, indicating that the image should be upscaled, if the dimensions are larger than the original image.

Effect name	Effect data settings
image_scale_and_crop	width: An integer representing the desired width in pixels.
	height: An integer representing the desired height in pixels.
image_crop	width: An integer representing the desired width in pixels.
	height: An integer representing the desired height in pixels.
	anchor: A string describing where the crop should originate in the form of XOFFSET-YOFFSET. XOFFSET is either a number of pixels or left, center, right", and YOFFSET is either a number of pixels or top, center, bottom.
image_desaturate	No data settings.
image_rotate	degrees: The number of (clockwise) degrees to rotate the image.
	random: A Boolean, captured as 0 or 1, indicating that a random rotation angle should be used for this image. The angle specified in degrees is used as a positive and negative maximum.
	bgcolor: The background color to use for exposed areas of the image. Use web-style hex colors (#FFFFFF for white, #000000 for black). Leave blank for transparency on image types that support it.

Time for action – configuring Media-based images to use our custom small image style for our Recipe content type

Now that we have a custom image style, let's put it to use.

1. Open up our d7dev site in your favorite browser, click on the **Configuration** link in the **Admin** toolbar, and click on the **File types** link under the **Media** section.

2. Now, on the **File types** administrative page, click on the **manage file display** link for the **Image file type**.

3. On the **Manage File Display** page, click on the button for the **Small** display.

4. Next, select our custom **small** image style for the **Image style** select list for the **Image Display** settings, and click on the **Save configuration** button.

5. Now, load the Cannellini Cumin Chicken Chili recipe to see our custom image style in action.

What just happened?

We created a custom image style with some custom code. We then configured our Recipe content type to use our custom image style for images added to the **Recipe Media** field.

Inline Media with WYSIWYG

Now, we are ready to look at how easy it is to enable inline images in a WYSIWYG text area with the Media module.

Time for action – configuring WYSIWYG inline Media for the basic page content type

We are going to take advantage of the Media module's WYSIWYG integration.

1. Open up our d7dev site in your favorite browser, click on the `Configuration` link in the **Admin** toolbar, and then click on the **Wysiwyg profiles** link under **Content authoring**.

2. On the **Wysiwyg profiles** administrative page, click on the **Edit** link for the **Full HTML INPUT FORMAT**.

3. Expand the **BUTTONS AND PLUGINS** section, check the Media browser checkbox, and click on the **Save** button at the bottom of the form.

4. Next, we will create a **Basic page content item**, and add some inline media through the WYSIWYG editor. Click on the **Add content** link in the **Shortcuts** bar, and select the link for adding a Basic page.

5. Now we will create a page that will tell the visitors what our d7dev site is about. We will enter About d7dev as the **Title**, and then add the following text for the **Body**:

The d7dev site is the companion website for the Drupal 7
Development by Example for Beginners book. The website will
showcase recipes for Drupal development and recipes for your
belly. And all of this is done within the context of creating an
HTML5 Drupal 7 site.

6. Next, click on the **Add media** icon in the WYSIWYG toolbar, and the **Media** browser will appear.

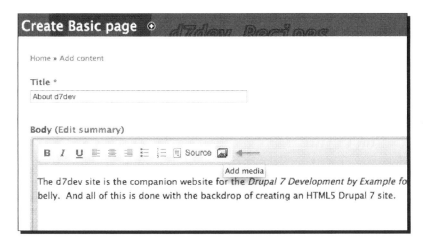

7. Click on the **Library** tab of the **Media** browser, select one of the photos we have already uploaded, and click on the **Submit** button.

8. Next, on the **Embedding** screen, select **small** as the **Current format**, and click on the **Submit** button.

9. Finally, click on the **Save** button at the bottom of the **Create Basic page** form.

What just happened?

We enabled the ability to add the Media module-based fields to content through the WYSIWYG editor.

Integrating the Colorbox and Media modules

So, the Media module has given us a nice interface for adding, browsing, and displaying media files. However, the images are taking up quite a bit of room. Let's create a pop-up gallery or lightbox, and show only one image. When someone clicks on an image, a lightbox will pop up, and will allow the user to cycle through larger versions of all of the associated images.

Drupal has a few different modules that offer an integrated lightbox solution for formatting sets of images. The following page, although somewhat outdated, offers a good overview of the different lightbox modules available for Drupal. Out of the whole bunch, I prefer the **Colorbox module**.

Time for action – installing the Colorbox module

Before we can display Media-based images in a Colorbox, we need to install and enable the module.

1. Open the Mac OS X Terminal or Windows Command Prompt, and change to our `d7dev` **directory:** `Mac: /Applications/MAMP/` or `Windows: C:\XAMPP\ htdocs\d7dev`.

2. Next, use Drush to download and enable the current dev release of the Colorbox module (`http://drupal.org/project/colorbox`).

```
$ drush dl colorbox-7.x-1.x-dev

Project colorbox (7.x-1.x-dev) downloaded to        [success]

/Users/kurt/htdocs/d7dev/sites/all/modules/colorbox.

$ drush en colorbox

The following extensions will be enabled: colorbox

Do you really want to continue? (y/n): y

colorbox was enabled successfully.   [ok]
```

3. The Colorbox module depends on the Colorbox jQuery plugin available from `http://jacklmoore.com/colorbox/`. The Colorbox module includes a Drush task that will download the required jQuery plugin to the `/sites/all/libraries` directory.

```
$ drush colorbox-plugin

Colorbox plugin has been downloaded to sites/all/libraries
[success]
```

4. Now, we will take a look at the Colorbox formatter. Click on the **Structure** link in the **Admin** toolbar, click on the **Content** types link, and click on the **manage display** link for our Recipe content type.

5. Next, click on the **FORMAT** select list for the image field, and you will see an option for **Colorbox**. Next, click on the **FORMAT** select list for the **Media** field, and you will see that there is not an option for **Colorbox**.

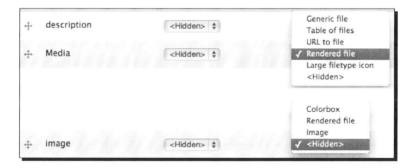

As you can see, the Colorbox module does not work with the Media module out of the box.

What just happened?

We installed the Colorbox module, and discovered that it only supports Image fields. In the next section, we will explore how we might make the Colorbox module work with the Media-based fields.

Introduction to the Colorbox File module and Drupal sandboxing

The Colorbox module for Drupal 7 only has a formatter for the core image field, so it will not work with the Media-based fields. The content of a Media module-based field may be an image, but it is still wrapped as a file type entity, as it needs to be able to support a number of different file types.

Shortly after the initial release of the Media module, I downloaded it and gave it a test drive. I wanted to compare its capabilities to some multimedia features that I was adding to a Drupal 6 site I was working on at the time. I quickly discovered, as we did previously, that there was no lightbox integration. So, I scratched my own itch, and wrote a custom file field formatter that leveraged the Colorbox module, and then shared the code with the Drupal community by creating a sandbox project.

Drupal developer community: Drupal sandbox

Although not a Drupal 7-specific feature, the ability to create a sandbox or an experimental project was introduced shortly after the release of Drupal 7. Anyone with a drupal.org account can utilize the drupal.org Git repository to share and maintain any experimental or concept type code with the Drupal community.

Drupal.org users will be able to search for your sandboxed module, enter bugs and feature requests in the drupal.org provided issue queue, and download/checkout your sandboxed code. The key differences between a sandbox project and a full project is that sandbox projects cannot have releases, or in other words, you can only download the code with Git (as you can see from the following screenshot, there are no links to directly download the project), and the code is not included in the drupal.org automated security tests. Also, sandbox projects prominently display the information stating that the code is experimental; basically 'use at your own risk'.

The really cool thing about sandbox projects is that they make it very easy to share your code, and give you the opportunity to easily explore other Drupal developers' ideas. As other users find and start using your code, you may get some feedback, which serves as a "proving grounds" for your code. This process is an integral part of the evolution of a sandbox project to becoming a full-fledged contrib project. There is an excellent documentation on sandbox projects available at `http://drupal.org/node/1011196`.

Revisit the sandbox Colorbox File module

So, I scratched my own itch and created a module that would allow displaying the Media-based fields in a lightbox. However, since last spring I have not paid as much attention to the issue queue for the module as I should have, and haven't even tested the code against the second version of the Media module. So, based on the needs at hand, I believe that it is time for us to revisit my sandbox code for the Colorbox File module.

Time for action – checking out the Colobrbox File sandbox project with Git, and testing it with the latest Media module

Now that we have installed the Colorbox module, we will install a module that integrates it with the Media module.

1. If you visit the drupal.org page for a sandbox project, you will notice a **Version control** link next to the **View** link. We will use Git to check out a copy of the **Colorbox File** module.

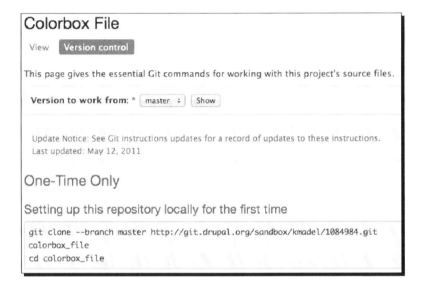

In subsequent chapters, the code of the Colorbox File module will be transformed, the module itself will be renamed, and it will become a full Drupal project. By the time you read this chapter, there will no longer be a Colorbox File sandbox project. Therefore, rather than using Git to clone the sandbox project with: `git clone --branch master http://git.drupal.org/sandbox/kmadel/1084984.git colorbox_file`, you will need to clone the current project, and switch to the last `commit` before the changes for this book.

2. Open Terminal (Mac OS X) or a Command Prompt (Windows), change to our `d7dev` `/sites/all/modules` directory, and run the following command:

```
git clone --branch master http://git.drupal.org/project/media_
colorbox.git colorbox_file
```

```
git checkout -b colorboxFile
fa74c354432310befde64c1e4e1b205c657d7c71
```

Next, we will use Drush to enable the Colorbox File module:

```
drush en colorbox_file
The following extensions will be enabled: colorbox_file
Do you really want to continue? (y/n): y
colorbox_file was enabled successfully.          [ok]
```

3. Open our d7dev site in your favorite browser, click on the **Structure** link in the **Admin** toolbar, then **Content types**, and then click on the **manage display** link for our Recipe content type.

4. Click on the **FORMAT** select for the **Media** field, and you will see that there is now an option for **Colorbox file**; select it.

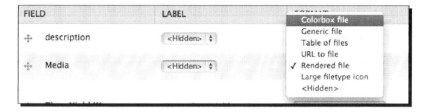

5. Now, you will see a different set of options available for the **FORMAT** configuration. Click on the **cog** button, and select **medium** for **Node image style** and **large** for **Colorbox image style**, then click on the **Update** button:

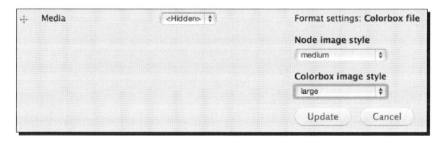

6. Next, click on the **Save** button at the bottom of the Recipe **MANAGE DISPLAY** page.

7. Now, we are ready to see if this experimental code works. Click on the **Content** link in the **Admin** toolbar, then click on the link for the Cannellini Cumin Chicken Chili recipe.

8. Click on the first Media field image for the recipe. What do you know - it works!

What just happened?

We installed the sandboxed Colorbox File, and enabled it for the Media field on our custom Recipe content type. Now, we can easily add images to our d7dev content with Colorbox support.

Drupal issue queues and enhancing the Colorbox File module

Even though the Colorbox File formatter is functional, I am not crazy about the user experience. Users have to individually click on each image to have it displayed in the Colorbox. Now, before we just go and try to figure out how to implement this new functionality for the Colorbox File module, we should check the module's issue queue at `http://drupal.org/project/issues/1084984?status=All&categories=All`. Someone may have requested the same feature, and someone may have even already implemented a fix.

If you look through all of the issues for the Colorbox File module, you will see the following issue: Image field gallery, per page/post/field options (`http://drupal.org/node/1165198`):

> *Hey maybe it's me but the option doesn't work where it takes all images on the page to click through. Is that easy to implement? Thanks in advance. Keep up the good work!*

Basically, @sanderjp is requesting the same functionality that I described previously. As you read through the individual posts for that issue, you will see that no one really has come up with something that works. Eventually, you will come across the following intriguing post from @jide (http://drupal.org/user/146088):

> Hi, I just posted #1296186: Complete rewrite of the module (http://drupal.org/node/1296186), a complete rewrite of the module, you might want to have a look at it.

@jide does not specifically state that he has a solution for the issue, but his post is intriguing enough to read through and see what his "Complete rewrite of the module" entails. If you read through the issue summary of @jide, you will see that he has added support for Colorbox galleries: "It also takes care of gallery settings." Exactly what we want for our Recipe pictures! After reading through the rest of the comments on that issue, I believe it is worth taking the time to apply the patch attached to the following issue comment: http://drupal.org/node/1296186#comment-5103976.

Time for action – applying and testing the patch for the Colorbox File module

So, now let's learn how you go about patching Drupal code.

1. First, we need to download the patch (http://drupal.org/files/colorbox_file_overhaul-2.patch) to the same directory that we checked out the Colorbox File module to: d7dev/sites/all/modules/colorbox_file.

2. Next, we will use Git to apply the patch to the Colorbox File code:

```
$ git apply -p0 colorbox_file_overhaul-2.patch
colorbox_file_overhaul-2.patch:59: trailing whitespace.

colorbox_file_overhaul-2.patch:99: trailing whitespace.

colorbox_file_overhaul-2.patch:324: trailing whitespace.

warning: 3 lines add whitespace errors.
```

Note: the trailing whitespace warnings are not a major concern, and are just a matter of some extra spaces on what are otherwise empty lines.

Applying patches to the `contrib` and `core` modules requires a certain amount of developer vigilance on your part. You must ensure that you are aware of all patches that you may have applied to a module before you apply any updates to that module. When an update becomes available for a module you should check to see if the patch that you applied has been added to the updated code. If it hasn't, then you need to test the application of the patch to the new updated code in your development environment, before using on a live site.

3. With the patch applied, we are ready to test it on our d7dev site. But, first delete the patch file from the `d7dev/sites/all/modules/colorbox_file` directory, as we wouldn't want to accidentally check that file into our Git branch.

4. Next, we have to clear our site cache by clicking on the **Performance** link in the **Shortcuts** bar, and clicking on the **Clear all caches** button.

5. Now, we will have to revisit the display settings for our Recipe content type to re-associate the Colorbox File formatter with the **Media** field. In the **Admin** toolbar, click on the **Structure** link, then click on the **Content** types link, and click on the **manage display** link for our Recipe content type.

6. Select **Colorbox file** as the **FORMAT** for the **Media** field, and you will notice that there is an updated set of FORMAT settings.

7. Now, we will configure the **FORMAT settings** for the updated Colorbox file formatter. Click on the **FORMAT settings** cog button, select **Small** for **File view mode**, **Large** for **Colorbox view mode**, and keep the defaults of `500x400` for **Dimensions** and **Per post gallery** for **Gallery (image grouping)**, and then click the **Update** button.

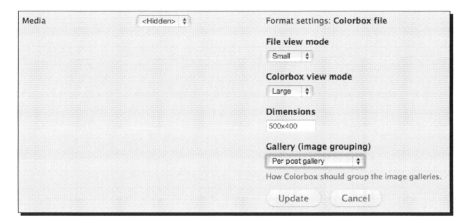

8. Finally, click on the **Save** button for the Recipe **MANAGE DISPLAY** page, and return to the page for the Cannellini Cumin Chicken Chili recipe.

9. Once again, click on the first image for our Media field, and once the Colorbox loads, you will notice that it now includes buttons to cycle through all of the images for the field.

What just happened?

We were able to add the features we desired, without writing any code. Instead, we leveraged the Drupal developer community and issue queues to add the functionality.

Summary

In this chapter, we have looked at several ways to spice up our d7dev site with multi-media, and learned some new ways of interacting with and leveraging the drupal.org developer community. In the next chapter, we will revisit the Colorbox File module with some enhancements, and we will add some features to our d7dev site that will enable visitors to our site to provide feedback and interact with our site's content.

7
How Does it Taste – Getting Feedback

Up until this point, there haven't been any compelling or interesting ways for the users to interact with our d7dev site. This chapter will show you how to add a contact form, and how to set up and integrate the Fivestar module with the custom Recipe content type to include a custom Fivestar ratings widget.

This chapter will walk through the code that adds support for HTML5 `form` elements with the **Webforms** module, and show how that code can be shared with the Drupal community as a whole (at least those that are using the HTML5 **Tools** module).

We will also revisit the Colorbox File module that we installed in the previous chapter. We will make some enhancements to the code (an advanced real world example), and we walk through the process of working with patches.

Introduction to the Drupal contact form

A very simple contact form is included with Drupal core, but not enabled by default. The core contact form provides a good starting point to introduce some interactive features to our d7dev site.

Time for action – enabling and configuring the core contact form

We will configure the core contact form, so that anonymous visitors to our site will be able to provide feedback about the site.

1. Once again, we will use Drush to enable the module, but we don't need to download it as it is a core module.

```
C:\xampp\htdocs\d7dev>drush en contact
The following extensions will be enabled: contact
Do you really want to continue? (y/n): y
contact was enabled successfully.        [ok]
```

2. Now, open up our d7dev site in your favorite browser, and click on the **Modules** link in the **Admin** toolbar. Scroll down to the module named **Contact** under the **Core** group; you will notice that it is enabled. Then, click on the **Permissions** link under the **OPERATIONS** column.

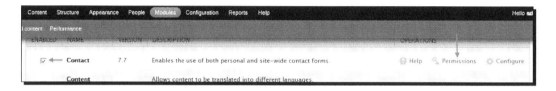

3. On the **People | Permissions** page, you will notice that the **Use the side-wide contact form** is only enabled for the **ADMINISTRATOR** role by default. Check the boxes for the **ANONYMOUS** and **AUTHENTICATED** roles, scroll to the bottom of the screen, and click on the **Save permissions** button.

4. Next, log out and navigate to `http://localhost/d7dev/contact`. You will see a simple contact form, as shown in the following screenshot:

5. Let's look at the HTML source of this form. Look for the input with id edit-mail, and you will notice that it uses the email input type because of the HTML5 Tools module that we installed in *Chapter 3, HTML5 Integration for Drupal 7 and More Module Development*.

```
<input type="email" id="edit-mail" name="mail" value="" size="60"
   maxlength="255" class="form-text form-email required">
```

What just happened?

We enabled a simple contact form to get feedback from the visitors to our d7dev site. Since we had already enabled the HTML5 Tools module in *Chapter 3, HTML5 Integration for Drupal 7 and More Module Development*, the form includes support for the HTML5 email input type.

Adding descriptive help text to our contact form

The core Contact module provides a decent out-of-the-box contact form for our site. But, what if we wanted to customize it a bit? Say, for example, that we wanted to add some help text to explain to the users why they should fill out the form. As we have seen in the previous chapters, there are usually multiple ways to accomplish customizations like this with Drupal. We are going to cover two different Drupal development recipes for creating an enhanced contact form for our d7dev site.

Using custom code to add help text to the contact form

The first approach will involve writing custom code by implementing a Drupal hook.

Time for action – adding help text to our site contact form

We will use the `dpm` function from the **Devel** module to help us get started with the first approach, then we will utilize the core `hook_form_FORM_ID_alter` hook to alter the core contact form. We will be adding this code to the `template.php` file of our custom `d7dev_theme` for the purpose of demonstrating adding code in a Drupal theme versus a custom module. If we wanted to ensure that these customizations would be available across all themes, then we would want to add the code to a custom module.

1. In Aptana Studio, open the `template.php` file in our custom theme at `/sites/all/themes/d7dev_theme`.

2. Next, switch over to the browser with the core contact form loaded, and find the ID of the `form` element.

3. Now, add the following code to the `template.php` file, and replace the `FORM_ID` portion of the hook function name with the `form id` we found in *step 2*:

```
/**
 * Implements hook_form_FORM_ID_alter ().
 */
function d7dev_theme_form_contact_site_form_alter(&$form,
  &$form_state, $form_id) {
  $form['#prefix'] = t("Please fill out the following form if you
    have any questions about the d7dev site.");
}
```

 When there are uppercase portions of a hook function name, it is an indicator that that part of the hook name needs to be substituted with a `form id` or some other identifying variable.

4. Next, reload the contact page, and you will see the descriptive text that we added.

What just happened?

We used the `hook_form_FORM_ID_alter` hook to add some descriptive test to the core contact form.

Adding contact help text with no code

For the second recipe, we are going to download and enable another contrib module, the **Webform** module (`http://drupal.org/project/webform`). The Webform module offers quite a few advanced features compared to what is available with the core contact form, to include the ability to add descriptive text without writing any code. We will use the Webform module to replace the core contact form.

Time for action – creating a contact form with help text, with the Webform module

We are going to install the Webform module, and use it to create a contact form for our d7dev site.

1. First, we need to install the Webform module. Open the Terminal (Mac OS X) or Command Prompt (Windows) application, and change to the root directory of our d7dev site.

2. Use Drush to download and enable the Webform module.

```
$ drush dl webform
Project webform (7.x-3.15) downloaded to /Applications/MAMP/
htdocs/d7dev/sites/all/modules/webform.[success]
$ drush en webform
The following extensions will be enabled: webform
Do you really want to continue? (y/n): y
webform was enabled successfully.                        [ok]
```

Now that we have installed the Webform module, we need to create a new Webform-based contact form.

3. Open up our d7dev site in your favorite browser. Click on the **Add content** link in the **Shortcuts** bar, and click the **Webform** link.

4. Enter Contact Form as the **Title**, enter the same help text from the previous approach as the **Body**: Please fill out the following form if you have any questions about the d7dev site, then click on the **Save** button.

5. After you click on the **Save** button, the Webform module will load a **Form components** configuration page for our newly created **Contact Form**.

6. We will now add all of the same fields that are part of the core contact form to our **Contact Form** Webform.

7. For the first field, enter Your name as the **LABEL**, select Textfield as the **TYPE**, check the **MANDATORY** checkbox, and click on the **Add** button.

8. Next, on the **Edit component** page for the **Your name** field, enter Please enter your first and last name. as the **Description text**, and click on the **Save component** button at the bottom of the form.

9. For the next field, enter Your e-mail address as the **LABEL**, select E-mail as the **TYPE**, check the **MANDATORY** checkbox, and click on the **Add** button.

10. Next, on the **Edit component** page for the **Your e-mail address** field, check the **User email** as default checkbox, enter Please enter your e-mail address. as the **Description text**, and then click on the **Save component** button at the bottom of the form.

11. For the first field, enter `Subject` as the **LABEL**, select `Textfield` as the **TYPE**, check the **MANDATORY** checkbox, and click on the **Add** button.

12. Next, on the **Edit component** page for the **Subject** field, leave the **Description** field empty, and click the on the **Save component** button at the bottom of the form.

13. For the first field, enter `Message` as the **LABEL**, select `Textarea` as the **TYPE**, check the **MANDATORY** checkbox, and click on the **Add** button.

14. Next, on the **Edit component** page for the **Message** field, leave the **Description** field empty, and click on the **Save component** button at the bottom of the form.

When you are done, our **Contact Form Edit components** configuration should look similar to the following screenshot:

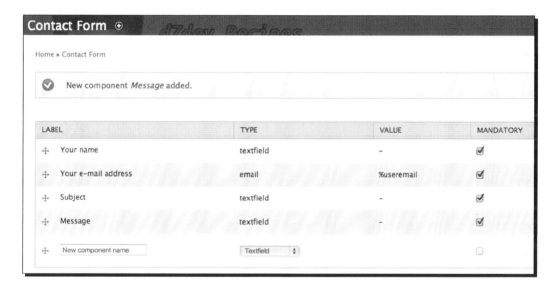

15. Now, click on the **Form settings** button, scroll down and expand the **ADVANCED SETTINGS** section, and enter **Send message** for the **Submit** button text field.

We are now ready to take a first look at our new Webform-based contact form.

16. Click on the **VIEW** tab for our new **Contact Form**, and you will see a contact form that is very similar to the one provided by the Drupal 7 core.

The Webform based contact form is not exactly the same as the contact form provided by core, and it is slightly more difficult to set up. But, it does provide a simple way to add descriptive help text without writing any custom code. Later, in this chapter, we will explore ways to make our Webform contact form match the core contact form exactly.

It is important to note that installing the Webform module may be overkill if your site's form needs do not extend beyond one simple contact form. If you need more than a couple of custom forms on your site, then installing the Webform module is highly recommended.

What just happened?

We covered two different approaches for creating a contact form, so that we could add descriptive help text to it. One approach was based on the custom code to modify the core contact module, and the other approach involved installing and configuring another contrib module. We also got an overview of the Webform module.

A more in-depth look at the Webform module

As we saw in the previous section, our Webform-based contact form is very similar to the core contact form. However, it doesn't include the checkbox to allow visitors to have a copy of the e-mail sent to them, and it doesn't live at the `/contact` path. Most importantly, especially in regards the underlying HTML5 theme of this book, the `Your e-mail address` field is of type `text`, and not of type `email` as it is with the core contact form.

```
<input class="email form-text required" type="text" id=
  "edit-submitted-your-e-mail-address" name=
  "submitted[your_e_mail_address]" value="admin@localhost.org"
  size="60" maxlength="128">
```

The HTML5 Tools module that we installed in *Chapter 3* uses `hook_form_FORM_ID_alter` to override the input type of the core contact form. Open the `/sites/all/modules/html5_tools/html5_tools.module` file, and scroll down to approximately *line 336*. The `#type` of the mail field of the contact form is changed from a core `textfield` to an `emailfield` (a non-core field provided by the **Elements** modules that we also installed in *Chapter 3*):

```
/**
 * Implements hook_form_FORM_ID_alter().
 */
function html5_tools_form_contact_site_form_alter(&$form,
  &$form_state) {
  // Modify the user registration field to use an email field.
  if (variable_get('html5_tools_override_contact_forms', 1) &&
    $form['mail']['#type'] == 'textfield') {
    $form['mail']['#type'] = 'emailfield';
  }
}
```

There is no reason why we can't do something similar for our Webform contact form's e-mail field.

Time for action – using hook_form_FORM_ID_alter to modify our Webform-based contact form

The first thing we need to do in order to use this hook is to get the `FORM_ID` of our Webform-based contact form. The `hook_form_FORM_ID_alter` core hook is executed for a specific form based on the ID of the form. To find the ID of our Webform-based contact form, we will once again turn to the trusty Devel module.

1. Open up our d7dev site in your favorite browser, click on the **Find content** link in the **Shortcuts** bar, and click on the **Contact Form** of **TYPE Webform**.

2. Once the Webform content has loaded, click on the **Devel** tab.

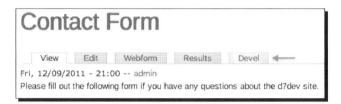

3. Next, on the **DEVEL** overlay, click on the **Render** link, and expand the top row with the text **(Array, 14 elements)**.

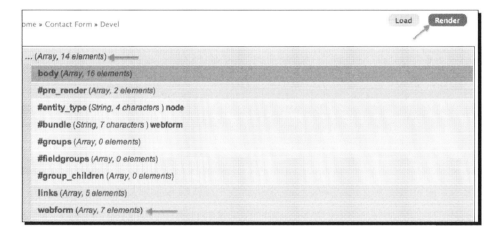

4. Now, expand the webform **(Array, 7 elements)** row, then expand the **#form** element, and find the value for the **#form_id** element:

Okay, so now that we have the form id - `webform_client_form_56`, we are ready to start writing some code.

5. In Aptana Studio, open the `d7dev.module` file located at `/sites/all/modules/d7dev/`.

6. Add the following code after the `d7dev_image_default_styles` function that we added in the previous chapter.

```
/**
 * Implements hook_form_FORM_ID_alter().
 */
function d7dev_form_webform_client_form_56_alter(&$form,
 &$form_state, $form_id) {

}
```

Note that we replaced the `FORM_ID` of the hook function name with the form ID that we retrieved previously, using the Devel module.

Before we start writing the code to convert the Webform e-mail field from a `textfield` to an `emailfield`, we are going to use the Devel module to check that our hook is being executed when we load our Webform-based contact form.

7. We are going to use the `Devel dd()` function to ensure that the hook we added is firing, and as an extra benefit, we will see the complete structure of the `$form` parameter. Add the following code to the top of the `d7dev_form_webform_client_form_56_alter` function, so that your function look similar to the following code:

```
function d7dev_form_webform_client_form_56_alter(&$form, &$form_
state, $form_id) {
  dd($form, 'd7dev_form_webform_client_form_56_alter');

}
```

> The `dd()` function is similar to the `dpm()` function that was introduced in *Chapter 2, Custom Content Types and an Introduction to Module Development*. However, the `dd()` function prints out to a file, `drupal_debug.txt`, located in the Drupal Temporary directory configured at `http://localhost/d7dev/admin/config/media/file-system`.

8. Now, in Terminal (Mac OS X) or the Command Prompt (Windows), change to the Drupal temporary directory - `/Applications/MAMP/tmp/php` for Mac OS X or `C:\XAMPP\...` for Windows, and type the following command:

```
$ tail -f drupal_debug.txt
```

9. Next, refresh the Webform contact form in your browser, then switch back to the Terminal/Command Prompt, and you should see the dump of the `$form` parameter.

```
d7dev_form_webform_client_form_56_alter: Array
(
    [#attached] => Array

...
```

So, now that we know that our hook is being fired, it is time to write the code to convert the e-mail `textfield` to an `emailfield`. We will examine the output of the `dd()` function to figure out what part of the `$form` array we need to change.

10. In the Terminal/Command Prompt, scroll down to the `[submitted]` array, and within that array, find the `[your_e_mail_address]` array.

```
[your_e_mail_address] => Array
                (
                    [#type] => textfield

...
```

11. Now, within the array, find the `[#webform_component]` array, and note the value of the `[type]` property.

```
[#webform_component] => Array
                       (
                           [nid] => 56
                           [cid] => 2
                           [pid] => 0
                           [form_key] => your_e_mail_address
                           [name] => Your e-mail address
                           [type] => email
...
```

12. In Aptana Studio, add the following code before the `dd()` function we added previously. The code will use the `['#webform']['type']` value to figure out what form fields need to be modified to use `emailfield` in place of `textfield`.

```
//loop through all of the webform fields
foreach($form['submitted'] as &$field) {
   //if the webform_component type is set and is email,
   //then this is a field we want to change
   if(isset($field['#webform_component']['type'])
      && $field['#webform_component']['type'] == 'email') {
      $field['#type']  = 'emailfield'; //set the field type to
emailfield
   }
}
```

13. Now, refresh the contact form page, switch over to the `dd()` output in the Terminal/Command Prompt, and find the updated e-mail field output.

```
[your_e_mail_address] => Array
                        (
                            [#type] => emailfield
                            [#title] => Your e-mail address
...
```

14. Sure enough, the `[#type]` is now `emailfield` instead of `textfield`, but we need to look at the actual HTML output.

```
<input class="email form-text form-email required" type="email"
   id="edit-submitted-your-e-mail-address"
   name="submitted[your_e_mail_address]"
   value="admin@localhost.org" size="60" maxlength="128">
```

15. Finally, now that we know everything is working correctly, be sure to remove the dd() function from our code. You should always be vigilant about removing any Devel functions used for testing, as you never want to deploy those types of development functions to a live site. Our final code will look similar to the following code:

```
/**
 * Implements hook_form_FORM_ID_alter().
 */
function d7dev_form_webform_client_form_56_alter(&$form,
  &$form_state, $form_id) {
  //loop through all of the webform fields
  foreach($form['submitted'] as &$field) {
    //if the webform_component type is set and is email,
    //then this is a field we want to change
    if(isset($field['#webform_component']['type'])
      && $field['#webform_component']['type'] == 'email') {
      $field['#type']  = 'emailfield'; //set the field type to
        emailfield
    }
  }
}
```

What just happened?

We used a core hook, hook_form_FORM_ID_alter, to override the input type of the e-mail field for our Webform-based contact form from text type to email type.

The reason why we added this code to our d7dev module is, because it is the type of code that is not a good candidate for re-use on other Drupal sites or sharing with the Drupal community, and all of our site-specific hook implementations and other non-theme site specific code is placed in this module. The FORM_ID that we needed to use, webform_client_form_56, is specific to this site. So, our implementation of the hook would be useless for any other site.

However, we should investigate making our code more generic, so that it will be reusable. Before we make the effort to make our Webform emailfield replacement code reusable, we should:

1. Try to understand if it will be useful to us in the short term to be able to reuse this functionality across multiple Webform-based forms or multiple Drupal sites.

2. Review the issue queue for the HTML5 Tools module to see if anyone has requested or implemented a similar solution. For the purpose of this example, we will answer yes for the first part, and if you search the HTML5 Tools issue queue (`http://drupal.org/project/issues/html5_tools`) for the word `Webform`, then you will find that there is indeed a feature request to have a Webform support added to the HTML5 Tools module: Webform module (`http://drupal.org/node/1312992`).

Hi,

is there any support with the Werbform module?

So, what can we do to make our code more generic? It turns out that Drupal 7 added a new form related hook, `hook_form_BASE_FORM_ID_alter`, that will provide a straightforward solution so that we can make our Webform emailfield enhancement work for all Webform-based forms on any site. The concept of a `BASE_FORM_ID` is what makes this possible, and to find out what `BASE_FORM_ID` to use for a given module, you just need to find and examine the module's implementation of `hook_forms`.

Time for action – using hook_form_BASE_FORM_ID_alter to make our Webform emailfield code more generic

We will introduce another Drupal form-related **hook** to enable the `emailfield` across all Webform generated forms.

1. In Aptana Studio, open the `webform.module` file found at `/sites/all/modules/webform`, and locate its `hook_forms` implementation:

```
/**
 * Implements hook_forms().
 *
 * All webform_client_form forms share the same form handler
 */
function webform_forms($form_id) {
  $forms = array();
  if (strpos($form_id, 'webform_client_form_') === 0) {
    $forms[$form_id]['callback'] = 'webform_client_form';
  }
  return $forms;
}
```

We are looking for the function being set as the callback of all Webform-based forms, and in this case, it is `webform_client_form`.

Now that we know what `BASE_FORM_ID` to use, we are ready to implement `hook_form_BASE_FORM_ID_alter`. But, we aren't going to put it in our d7dev module. Since we want to make this reusable on other sites and make it available to the Drupal community as a whole, we are going to add it to the HTML5 **Tools** module. Typically, you wouldn't add code to a core or contrib module, but in this case, we plan on contributing the code back to the Drupal community. So, it is ok to modify the `html5_tools.module` file directly.

2. This is going to be pretty simple to start. We are going to cut the `d7dev_form_webform_client_form_56_alter` function that we just added, and paste it into the `/sites/all/modules/html5_tools/html5_tools.module` file at approximately *line* 355. Then we will rename the function to `html5_tools_form_webform_client_form_alter`:

```
/**
 * Implements hook_form_FORM_ID_alter().
 */
function html5_tools_form_webform_client_form_alter(&$form,
&$form_state, $form_id) {
  //loop through all of the webform fields
  foreach($form['submitted'] as &$field) {
    //if the webform_component type is set and is email,
    //then this is a field we want to change
    if(isset($field['#webform_component']['type'])
      && $field['#webform_component']['type'] == 'email') {
      $field['#type']  = 'emailfield'; //set the field type to
emailfield
    }
  }
}
```

3. Now, refresh the Webform-based contact form in the browser, and inspect the source of the e-mail field to ensure that its input type is still set to `email`.

   Although the hook is working as expected, we aren't done yet. At least not for code that we want to share on drupal.org. If you take a look at the `html5_tools_form_contact_personal_form_alter` function right above the one we just added in the `html5_tools.module` file, you will see that the `html5_tools_override_contact_forms` variable is tested to see if it has been set to `0`. That variable is exposed as a configuration option on the HTML5 Tools configuration page (`http://localhost:d7dev/admin/config/markup/html5-tools`). We should expose a similar configuration option for Webform `email` fields.

4. Open the `html5_tools.admin.inc` file located in `/d7dev/sites/all/ module/html5_tools`, and add the following code at *line 110*:

```
if (module_exists('webform')) {
  $form['html5_tools_webform_forms'] = array(
    '#type' => 'fieldset',
    '#title' => t("Override Webform fields with their HTML5
counterparts"),
    '#collapsible' => FALSE,
  );
  $form['html5_tools_webform_forms']['html5_tools_override_
webform_email'] = array(
    '#type' => 'checkbox',
    '#default_value' => variable_get('html5_tools_override_
webform_email', 1),
    '#title' => t('E-mail field'),
    '#description' => t('Modify the Webform email textfield to an
email field.'),
  );
}
```

The code follows the pattern already used by the HTML5 Tools module, creating a variable that allows site administrators to disable/enable HTML5 e-mail input types for the Webform module, and defaults to being turned on.

5. Reload the HTML5 Tools configuration page, and you should see the following content at the bottom of the page:

6. Now that we have added a configurable variable, we need to add a check for that variable to our `html5_tools_form_webform_client_form_alter` function.

```
/**
 * Implements hook_form_FORM_ID_alter().
 */
function html5_tools_form_webform_client_form_alter(&$form,
  &$form_state, $form_id) {
  //Modify Webform email type fields ot use an email field
  if (variable_get('html5_tools_override_webform_email', 1)
    && isset($form['submitted'])) {
    //loop through all of the webform fields
```

```
foreach($form['submitted'] as &$field) {
  //if the webform_component type is set and is email,
  //then this is a field we want to change
  if(isset($field['#webform_component']['type'])
    && $field['#webform_component']['type'] == 'email') {
    $field['#type']  = 'emailfield'; //set the field type to
      emailfield
  }
}
}
}
}
```

7. Now to test that it works, uncheck the **E-mail** field checkbox for overriding the Webform e-mail `textfield`, then load our Webform contact form, and inspect the HTML for the e-mail field. It is of type `text`, so the configuration we added is working.

8. Now, go back to the HTML5 Tools configuration page, and check the **E-mail** field checkbox to re-enable our `emailfield` replacement code.

9. We now have the code that we will be usable across multiple Webform forms and across multiple Drupal sites. But, how do we get this code into the hands of other Drupal users, and better yet, have it maintained as part of the HTML5 Tools module. To share this code, we are going to create a patch.

10. Before we can create a patch the Drupal 7/Git way, we need to check out the HTML5 Tools project with Git to a new directory.

    ```
    $ git clone --branch 7.x-1.x http://git.drupal.org/project/html5_
    tools.git
    Cloning into html5_tools...
    remote: Counting objects: 232, done.
    remote: Compressing objects: 100% (153/153), done.
    remote: Total 232 (delta 149), reused 114 (delta 77)
    Receiving objects: 100% (232/232), 41.30 KiB, done.
    Resolving deltas: 100% (149/149), done.
    ```

11. Next, we need to make the same changes that we just made for our d7dev site to the code we just cloned with Git.

12. Now that we have updated the code, we are ready to create our patch. Following the drupal.org guidelines at `http://drupal.org/node/707484`, run the following command:

    ```
    $ git diff >  webform_support-1312992-8.patch
    ```

13. Next, we will comment on the issue at `http://drupal.org/node/1312992`, and upload our patch with our comments, making sure that the status of the issue is set to **needs review**.

#8 Posted by kmadel on *December 11, 2011 at 11:26pm*

Status: active » needs review

Here is an initial stab at adding HTML5 input type support for the Webform module. The initial code will only replace Webform email textfields with the Elements based emailfield.

If everyone thinks this is a good approach, it will be pretty easy to add support for other HTML5 input types.

Attachment	Size
webform_support-1312992-8.patch	2.21 KB

What just happened?

Not only did we update our code so that it will work across all Webform-based forms and any number of Drupal sites, but we also helped the Drupal community. We learned how to create a patch. We will check back in the HTML5 Tools forum in a chapter or two to see how the Drupal community responds to our patch.

Time for another recipe

Just in case you were getting hungry, we are going to add a new recipe. Let's add it now so that we have something delicious to eat as we work our way through the rest of this challenging chapter! The recipe for this chapter is Garlic Cashew Chicken with Edamame and Carrots. Enjoy!

- **name**: Garlic Cashew Chicken with Edamame and Carrots.

- **description**: A savory dish with an Asian flair. The cashews give this dish a bit of sweetness, while the edamame really helps make it filling. The carrots and onions provide a nice crunch.

- **recipeYield**: Four servings.

- **prepTime**: 20 minutes.

- **cookTime**: 20 minutes.

- **ingredients**:
  - one pound of boneless chicken breasts—sliced
  - Two tablespoons of olive oil
  - one cup of soy sauce
  - Eight cloves of garlic
  - Five lg pieces of crystallized ginger
  - One tablespoon of red pepper flakes
  - Half cup vegetable broth
  - Five carrots, sliced on the bias
  - One large sweet onion, sliced lengthwise
  - One cup of cashews, coarsely chopped
  - Two tablespoons of rice vinegar
  - Two cups of Jasmine rice

- **instructions**:
  1. Add the sliced chicken to a large bowl, and stir in half cup of soy sauce.
  2. Press the ginger and garlic through the garlic press, and mix with the chicken soy sauce mixture.
  3. Mix in the red pepper flakes with the chicken soy sauce mixture.
  4. Prepare Jasmine rice according to directions.
  5. Heat the olive oil in a large frying pan over medium heat for two minutes.
  6. Add the chicken soy sauce mixture to the pan, and increase the heat to medium high.
  7. Cook the chicken until there is no visible pinkness, and most of the liquid has reduced, for approximately 8 to 10 minutes.

8. Pour in half cup of vegetable broth, and stir to mix.

9. Reduce the heat to medium low.

10. Add the edamame and carrots, stir together, and simmer for three minutes.

11. Add the other four garlic cloves using a garlic press and the sliced onions, and simmer for three minutes.

12. Finally, add the cashews, rice vinegar, the ½ cup of soy sauce, stir to mix, and then cover. Simmer for five minutes.

13. Serve over rice.

Colorbox File enhancements

We added the Colorbox File module to our d7dev site in the previous chapter to display the images (and eventually other media types). However, one thing that I know I would like for our recipe-related media is to have customizable captions for images that will be displayed in the Colorbox overlay. Currently, the Colorbox File module displays the word **Media** as the caption for all media content displayed in the Colorbox overlay for our Recipe content type, as shown in the following screenshot:

Before we just start coding away, we will take a look at the Colorbox File issue queue (http://drupal.org/project/issues/1084984?status=All&categories=A ll), and see if there are any feature requests in the Colorbox File issue queue requesting functionality similar to what we have described. The issue at the URL http://drupal. org/node/1085174: **Image's title not displaying in Colorbox**, is definitely related to what we want to do with captions. The issue summary certainly seems clear enough:

> *I realize that the title of the images doesn't show in the Colorbox. Did I do something wrong? Or is the feature not implemented?*

Again, before we begin writing the custom code, we need to have a clear understanding of what we want the title of the media file to be, in order to begin to understand why it isn't showing up in this case, or why the caption defaults to **Media** for all the Recipe media field images on our d7dev site. If you scroll down to comment *#4* of that same issue (http:// drupal.org/node/1085174#comment-4816758), you will see that @NicolasH suggests adding a setting to the Colorbox File formatter that would allow you to select a "field to use as the colorbox title". Again, it may sound straightforward, but it really isn't that simple. It is not simple because the Media module-based fields are derived from file entities, and just as Drupal allows you to have multiple content types (node entities) with different fields, a Drupal site can have multiple file type entities, each having a different set of fields.

Drupal 7 didn't just add the ability to add fields to the nodes or content types. Drupal 7 introduced the concept of field-able entities. So, the node of the node-centric dominated development of Drupal 6 just became another entity in Drupal 7. Other entities included with Drupal 7 core include taxonomy, users, and comments, but not files. The Media module provided the initial motivation to turn the Drupal file object into a full-fledged field-able entity. Originally, the file entity code was part of the Media module itself, but has been pulled out into the separate File Entity module (http://drupal.org/project/file_entity).

The **File types** configuration page of the File Entity module illustrates the concept of field-able entities as shown in the following screenshot (http://localhost/d7dev/ admin/config/media/file-types). There is a **manage fields** link for each file (entity) type.

It would be very difficult to provide a user interface for the Colorbox file formatter settings form that would allow site administrators to select a different caption field for each of the file types. The following screenshot illustrates the limited amount of usable UI space we are working with for the field formatter settings:

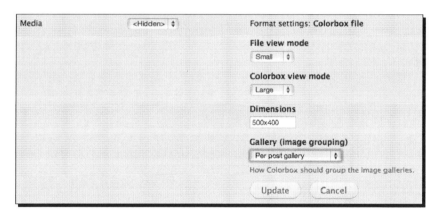

A site administrator may want to use a field called `title` for the **Image file** type, but use a field called `caption` for the **Video file** type. This illustrates how quickly something seemingly as simple as adding a caption or a title attribute to a Media field can become quite complex.

Rather than using the Colorbox File formatter settings to set the field to use as the caption for each file type, how about if we add a setting to the file types field settings configuration for all possible fields that would be used as a caption—pretty much just fields of type text, as other field types don't make much sense as a caption. Don't worry if this sounds a bit confusing at this point; it will make more sense as we walk through the code together.

Time for action – enhancing the Colorbox File module with field-based captions

So, where do we begin to implement this proposed approach and complete the associated feature request? We will start by modifying the field settings form for all file type associated text fields. This is where you will be able to configure that a field's value should be used as the value for the Colorbox caption for a given file type. We will use a hook that we used earlier in this chapter, `hook_form_FORM_ID_alter`, to modify the form used to configure text fields for all file types. In order to do that, we need to figure out what `FORM_ID` we need to use as part of the function name for that hook, and we will again turn to the Devel module to help us with this.

1. First, we will add a new text field to the Image file type. Open up our d7dev site in your favorite browser, click on the **Configuration** link in the **Admin** toolbar, and click on the **File types** under the **Media** section. Then, click on the **manage fields** link for the **Image file type**.

2. Now, enter `Caption` as the value for the **Add new field** input type. Next to `field_prefix` label in the **Name** column, type `caption`, and select **Text** from the **Select a field type** dropdown, **Text field** as the **WIDGET**, and click the **Save** button.

3. On the next screen, we are going to accept the default value of `256` for the **Maximum length**, but before we click on the **Save field settings** button, we are going to add the following code at the bottom of `colorbox_file.module` and save it:

```
function colorbox_file_form_alter(&$form, &$form_state) {
  dsm($form, 'colorbox_file_form_alter');
}
```

4. Again, we want to use `hook_form_FORM_ID_alter`, but we don't know what we need to replace `FORM_ID` with yet. So, click on the **Save field** settings button, and on the field settings page we will see the Devel `dsm` function output.

5. Expand the top row with the text **...(Array, 21 elements)**, and find the value for the **#form_id key: field_ui_field_edit_form | (Callback) field_ui_field_edit_form();**.

6. The value of the `#form_id` key is the value that we want to replace `FORM_ID` placeholder with, for our implementation of `hook_form_FORM_ID_alter`. So, we will rename the `colorbox_file_form_alter` function that we added by adding that form ID, `field_ui_field_edit_form`, in between the form and alter parts of the hook function name.

```
/**
 * Implements hook_form_FORM_ID_alter().
 */
function colorbox_file_form_field_ui_field_edit_form_alter(&$form,
&$form_state) {
```

Now that we have plugged in the correct form ID, our `form_FORM_ID_alter` hook will only be executed for forms with the `ID field_edit_form`. However, we also only want this hook to be executed for file type entities and text fields. Therefore, we need to figure out what we can use to identify a `field_edit_form` form as being for a text field on a file entity.

7. Expand the **#instance** property of the dsm output, and expand the **widget** property. You will see the value of **widget=>type** is **text_field** and the value of **entity_type** is **file**:

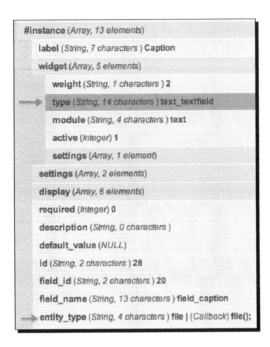

8. Next, add the following code to our colorbox_file_form_field_ui_field_ edit_form_alter function, so that we will only alter field edit forms for text fields of file type entities (we don't want this option to be available for text fields on other entity types):

```
//only want this option to appear for text fields on file
entities
    if ($form['#instance']['entity_type'] == 'file' &&
$form['#instance']['widget']['type'] == 'text_textfield') {


    }
```

9. Now, within the if block we just added, we are going to add a new checkbox to the form that will allow the site administrators to identify the current field being edited as the field to use as the Colorbox caption for the parent file type of the field. We will also add a fieldset element to wrap the checkbox, and provide some additional information:

```
// Create the fieldset tab.
$form['colorbox_file'] = array(
```

```
  '#type'    => 'fieldset',
  '#title'   => t('Colorbox Caption Field'),
  '#description' => t('Set field to be used as the Colorbox
    caption.
    Note: Selecting this text field as the Colorbox caption field
    will replace an previously checked field for this file
    type.'),
  '#tree'    => TRUE,
);

$form['colorbox_file']['caption_field'] = array(
  '#type' => 'checkbox',
  '#title' => t('Use field as Colorbox caption'),
);
```

10. Refresh the edit form for the Caption field we are adding, scroll down towards the bottom, and you should see our new `fieldset` with the checkbox we just added:

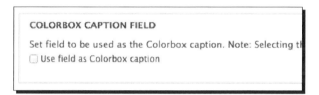

Now, we need to actually save the value of this checkbox in order to use its value when outputting a Colorbox File-formatted field. The Drupal `variable_set` function provides a straightforward and easy way to save this type of information. Basically, the `variable_set` function takes a name and value, and saves it to the variable table of our site's Drupal database. We will save the value of the Colorbox caption checkbox, but first we need to add a new `submit` function to the `field_edit_form` form, so that a custom function that we add to the `colorbox.module` code will be executed when this form is submitted.

11. Before we write the code that will save the value of the Colorbox caption checkbox, we need to associate a custom `submit` function with the `field_ui_field_edit_form` form that will allow us to act on the submitted form. Add the following code after the form array for the checkbox:

```
//additional submit function to process the caption_field checkbox
value
$form['#submit'] = array_merge($form['#submit'], array('colorbox_
file_form_field_ui_field_edit_form_submit'));
```

12. When this form is submitted, the `colorbox_file_form_field_ui_field_edit_form_submit` function will be called. We could have called that function anything that we wanted, but it makes sense to name it so that it is understood what it is being used for. So, now we need to implement the `colorbox_file_form_field_ui_field_edit_form_submit` function:

```
/**
 * Custom submit handler for the field_ui_field_edit_form altered
form.
 */
function colorbox_file_form_field_ui_field_edit_form_submit($form,
  &$form_state) {
  if ($form['colorbox_file']['caption_field']) {
    $bundle = $form['instance']['bundle']['#value'];
    variable_set('colorbox_file_' . $bundle . '_caption_field_
name', $form['#field']['field_name']);  }
}
```

Let's examine the `colorbox_file_form_field_ui_field_edit_form_submit` function above. The `if` statement will only be `true` if the Colorbox caption checkbox is checked. If it isn't checked, then we don't need to do anything. We are only going to allow one field per file type to be specified as the field to use for the Colorbox caption. So, if the checkbox is checked, we will persist the value using the `variable_set` function with a name that is unique for the current file type (we are able to extract the current file type name from `$form['instance']['bundle']['#value']` — a `bundle` is synonymous with the type of file), and in this case it will be `image`. If a new text field were later added to this file type and selected to be the Colorbox caption field, then the previous variable would just be overwritten.

Now that we have covered how the selected Colorbox caption field gets saved, we need to actually display the contents of that field in the actual Colorbox overlay. Since we know that a Colorbox caption is currently being displayed, albeit the same caption for all media items for our Recipe media field, we will start by examining how the current caption is being set. The `theme_colorbox_file` function of the `colorbox_file.theme.inc` file located at `d7dev/sites/all/modules/colorbox_file/`, sets the `title` attribute of the image that is the trigger for opening the Colorbox overlay.

```
function theme_colorbox_file($variables) {
...
  $caption = $variables['title'];

...
```

```
  return theme('link', array(
    'text' => drupal_render($variables['item']),
    'path' => $variables['path'],
    'options' => array(
      'html' => TRUE,
      'attributes' => array(
        'title' => $caption,
        'class' => 'colorbox-file',
        'rel' => $gallery_id,
      ),
    ),
  ));
}
```

The Colorbox module defaults to using the `title` attribute of the image used to trigger the Colorbox overlay as the caption in the overlay. Theme functions, such as this one, are either associated to render the array through the `#theme` property or executed directly with a call to the `theme()` function. In the case of the Colorbox File module, the `theme_colorbox_file` function is associated with the `#theme` property of the render array. The `colorbox_file_field_formatter_view` function in the `colorbox_file.module` sets the `#theme` property of the render array, as shown in the following code:

```
/**
 * Implements hook_field_formatter_view().
 */
function colorbox_file_field_formatter_view($entity_type, $entity,
$field, $instance, $langcode, $items, $display) {
....
$element[$fid] = array(
      '#theme' => 'colorbox_file',
       '#item' => $build[$fid]['file'],
       '#entity_id' => $id,
       '#field' => $field,
       '#display_settings' => $display['settings'],
       '#langcode' => $langcode,
       '#path' => 'colorbox_file/' . $fid . '/' .
         $display['settings']['colorbox_view_mode'] . '/' .
         $langcode,
       '#title' => isset($instance['label']) ? $instance['label']
         : NULL,
    );
```

You will also notice that the value being used for the `#title` property is the `$instance['label']` (as long as it is not `null`). The value of the `$instance['label']` is actually the label of the Recipe content `field_media` field, or in this case "Media". All of the properties of this render array will be available in the `$variables` parameter passed into the `theme_colorbox_file` function in `colorbox_file.theme.inc`. However, these render array properties will only be available for the function specified by `#theme` property if they have already been specified as one of the variables in the `hook_theme` implementation that registered that `theme` function. Basically, you just need to know that the variables that you want to make available in a `theme` function must be specified in a `hook_theme` function. The `colorbox_file_theme` function does just that.

```
/**
 * Implements hook_theme().
 */
function colorbox_file_theme() {
  return array(
    'colorbox_file' => array(
      'variables' => array(
        'item' => array(),
        'entity_id' => NULL,
        'field' => array(),
        'display_settings' => array(),
        'langcode' => NULL,
        'path' => NULL,
        'title' => NULL,
      ),
      'path' => drupal_get_path('module', 'colorbox_file'),
      'file' => 'colorbox_file.theme.inc',
    ),
  );
}
```

The variables array entries will be passed through to the `theme_colorbox_file` function when set on the render array in the `colorbox_file_field_formatter_view` function. In addition to the current variables being passed through to `theme_colorbox_file`, we know that we want to also pass the value of the configured Colorbox caption field through to the `theme_colorbox_file`, so that it can actually be displayed.

13. Add `'colorbox_file_caption' => NULL,` after the `'title' => NULL` entry in `colorbox_file_theme`.

14. Now, scroll down to the `colorbox_file_field_formatter_view` function, and we will add code to check if the Colorbox caption variable is set for the current file entity type. If it is set, then we will set the value of the render array caption variable to the value we will retrieve from the current file entity's caption field. Just replace the `foreach` loop in the `colorbox_file_field_formatter_view` function with the following code:

```
foreach (element_children($build) as $fid) {
  $colorbox_caption_var_name = 'colorbox_file_' .
    $build[$fid]['#bundle'] . '_caption_field_name';
//added for chapter 7

  $colorbox_caption_field_name =
    variable_get($colorbox_caption_var_name);
//added for chapter 7

  $colorbox_field_caption_value = isset($build[$fid]['#file']
    ->{$colorbox_caption_field_name}['und'][0]) ?
  $build[$fid]['#file']->
    {$colorbox_caption_field_name}['und'][0]['value'] :
    NULL;
//added for chapter 7

  $element[$fid] = array(
    '#theme' => 'colorbox_file',
    '#item' => $build[$fid]['file'],
    '#entity_id' => $id,
    '#field' => $field,
    '#display_settings' => $display['settings'],
    '#langcode' => $langcode,
    '#path' => 'colorbox_file/' . $fid . '/' .
      $display['settings']['colorbox_view_mode'] . '/' .
      $langcode,
    //chapter 7 note: this is where Media is being added as the
    //title attribute
    '#title' => isset($instances['label']) ? $instances['label'] :
      NULL,
    '#colorbox_file_caption' =>
      $colorbox_field_caption_value,//added for chapter 7
  );
}
```

You will see that if the Colorbox caption field is set - `$build[$fid]['#file']->{$colorbox_caption_field_name}['und'][0]`, then we will set the `colorbox_file_caption` render array property to the value of that field, otherwise it will be `null`. Also note that we are specifically targeting the first value of the field, `['und'][0]`, as we are not including support for displaying the text of multi-valued fields beyond the first value.

15. Next, open the `colorboxfile.theme.inc` file and replace the line: `$caption = $variables['title'];` with the following `switch` statement:

```
//added the following switch for chapter 7
 switch ($settings['colorbox_caption']) {
   case 'title':
     $caption = $variables['title'];
     break;
   case 'mediafield':
     $caption = $variables['colorbox_file_caption'];
     break;
   default:
     $caption = '';
 }
```

This code will conditionally set the `$caption` based on the value of `$settings['colorbox_caption']`, and if we look a bit further up in the function, we will see that `$settings` are being populated with the `display_settings` render array property from the `colorbox_file_field_formatter_view` function. `$settings = $variables['display_settings'];`. `display_settings` refers to the formatter settings values exposed by the `colorbox_file_field_formatter_settings_form` function, but there is no `colorbox_caption` setting, so we will add it now, otherwise the `$caption` would always be an empty string.

16. At the end of the `if ($display['type'] == 'colorbox_file') {` block in the `colorbox_file_field_formatter_settings_form` function, add the following code:

```
$caption = array(
   'title' => t('Title text'),
   'mediafield' => t('File Type text field'),
   'none' => t('None'),
);
$element['colorbox_caption'] = array(
   '#title' => t('Caption'),
```

```
    '#type' => 'select',
    '#default_value' => 'title',
    '#options' => $caption,
    '#description' => t('Title will use the label of your Media
       field and File Type text field will use the value of a
       specified text field for the file type being displayed.'),
);
```

The $caption array provides the values for the select options we will be displaying in the formatter settings form for the Colorbox File formatter. Next, similar to the way hook_theme works regarding render array properties and theme functions, we must register our colorbox_caption formatter setting with our implementation of hook_field_formatter_info.

17. In the colorbox_file_field_formatter_info function, add the following as an entry to the settings array, and we will also set the default value:

```
        'colorbox_caption' => 'title',
```

18. Next, in order to provide an accurate summary of the selected formatting options, add the following code to the colorbox_file_field_formatter_settings_summary function at the bottom of the if ($display['type'] == 'colorbox_file') { block of code:

```
    $caption = array(
      'title' => t('Title text'),
      'mediafield' => t('File Type text field'),
      'none' => t('None'),
    );
    if (isset($settings['colorbox_caption'])) {
        $summary[] = t('Colorbox caption: @type', array('@type' =>
$caption[$settings['colorbox_caption']]));
    }
```

This is not necessary to make everything work, but allows a site administrator to get a quick summary of how the formatter has been configured without opening the formatter settings form. Now, we are ready to test our field-based caption code for the Colorbox File formatter by saving the **Caption** field for the **Image file type** with the **Use field as Colorbox caption** checkbox checked. Then, we will manage the display of our Media-based imaged field on our Recipe content type, to use that field as a caption.

19. Return to the field edit form, check the **Use field as Colorbox caption** for our new **Caption** text field on the **Image file type**, and click on the **Save settings** button.

20. Next, click on the **Structure** link in the **Admin** toolbar, then click on the **Content types** link, and the **manage display** link for our Recipe content type.

Looking at the entry for our **Media** field, you will see the formatter settings summary that we just added. The **Colorbox caption** is set to **Title text** - the default we specified in our `colorbox_file_field_formatter_info` function.

21. To change the **Colorbox caption** setting, click on the **formatter settings** cog button.

The **Format settings** form now includes the **Caption select list** that we added to the `colorbox_file_field_formatter_settings_form function`.

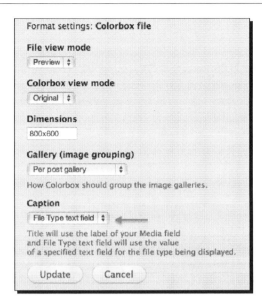

22. Select **File Type text field** from the **Caption** select list, then click on the **Update** button, and click on the **Save** button on the **Recipe MANAGE DISPLAY** page.

You will notice that the formatter summary has been updated to reflect the selection of **File Type text field** as the **Colorbox caption**. Now that we have configured this field to use the **Caption field** of the **Image file type** as the caption in the Colorbox overlay, we need to actually populate the new **Caption field** on some Image file entities.

23. Click on the **Find content** link in the **Shortcuts** bar, then click on the **Files** tab.

24. Next, click on the **Edit** link in the **OPERATIONS** column for the image titled **6808_07_white_chili_2.jpg**.

25. Enter `Spices for Cannellini Cumin Chicken Chili` as the value for the **Caption**, then click on the **Save** button.

26. Now, click on the **Content** tab of the **Find content** page, and click on the **Cannellini Cumin Chicken Chili** link.

27. Next, click on the second image in the first row of thumbnails, and you will see the new caption that we just added:

What just happened?

That may have seemed like a lot of work for a caption, and was perhaps some of the most advanced development so far in this book. However, we explored a number of important facets for Drupal 7 field-related development, and in doing so, improved a module in a way that will be useful to the Drupal community as a whole.

Rating recipes with Fivestar

Now that we have enhanced the Colorbox File module with configurable captions, we will turn our attention back to enhancing the user interaction for the site. One great way to get visitors to interact with a website is to allow them to review and rate content; in this case, recipes. The **Fivestar module** makes it easy to enable and integrate a ratings system into our d7dev site, and will allow the site visitors to rate our recipes.

Time for action – installing and configuring the Fivestar module

We will now set up the Fivestar module, so that visitors to our d7dev site will be able to rate the recipes.

1. Use Drush to download and enable the Fivestar module.

```
$ drush dl fivestar

Project fivestar (7.x-2.0-alpha1) downloaded to /Users/kurt/
htdocs/d7dev/sites/all/modules/fivestar.          [success]

$ drush en fivestar

The following projects have unmet dependencies:

fivestar requires votingapi

Would you like to download them? (y/n): y

Project votingapi (7.x-2.4) downloaded to /Users/kurt/htdocs/
d7dev/sites/all/modules/votingapi.               [success]

The following extensions will be enabled: votingapi, fivestar

Do you really want to continue? (y/n): y

fivestar was enabled successfully.      [ok]

votingapi was enabled successfully.     [ok]
```

Note that the **Voting API module** was also installed as a dependency of the Fivestar module.

2. Now, we will configure our Recipe content type to use the Fivestar module. Open up our d7dev site in your favorite browser, click on the **Structure** link in the **Admin** toolbar, then click on the **Content types** link, and click on the **manage fields** link for our Recipe content type.

3. Scroll down to the **Add new field** section to add a new field. Enter `rating` as the value for the **Add new field** input type. Next to `field_ prefix` label in the **Name** column, type `rating`, select **Fivestar Rating** from the **Select a field type** dropdown and **Stars** (`rated while viewing`) as the **widget**, and click on the **Save** button. On the next screen, click on the **Save field settings** button.

4. On the **RECIPE SETTINGS** page, enter `'If you have tried this recipe, please take the time to rate it.'` as the **Help text**. Leave 5 as the value for the **Number of stars** select list, and click on the **Save settings** button.

5. Next, load one of the recipes that we have added to our d7dev site, and you will see the following new Fivestar ratings widget:

What just happened?

We just added a compelling interactive feature to our d7dev site. Although it was a very easy process to add the Fivestar ratings to our Recipe content type, there is nothing all that compelling or unique about the appearance of the Fivestar widget. Sometimes, custom development is about aesthetics, or sometimes a good reason for custom development is as simple as creating a certain look and feel for you site. Wouldn't it be cool to have a hot pepper as the rating widget icon instead of one of the default widget icons that comes with the Fivestar module? It would give our d7dev site that extra little bit of awesomeness.

> The Fivestar module depends on the **Voting API** module. This is an excellent example of modular code reuse with Drupal. In addition to the Fivestar module, there are a number of other contrib modules that utilize the Voting API module.

Time for action – creating a custom Fivestar widget

The Fivestar module documentation provides a recipe for creating custom rating widgets. The documentation is available at `http://drupal.org/node/234391` – Creating and Contributing a Fivestar Widget Set. We are going to follow those simple instructions to create a custom Thai pepper widget for rating recipes on our d7dev site.

1. First, we are going to implement the Fivestar module `hook_fivestar_widgets` hook, so that we will be able to place our custom Fivestar widget inside our d7dev module. In Aptana Studio open the `fivestar.module` file in the `sites/all/modules/fivestar` folder.

2. Find the `fivestar_fivestar_widgets` function, and copy the entire function (including the comments).

3. Open our `d7dev.module` in the `sites/all/modules/custom/d7dev` folder, and paste the `fivestar_fivestar_widgets` function that we just copied after the `d7dev_image_default_styles` function.

4. Next, rename the function by replacing `fivestar` with `d7dev`, and modify the call to `drupal_get_path`, so that it will get the path for our d7dev module instead of the Fivestar module. When you are done, you code should look as follows:

```
function d7dev_fivestar_widgets() {
  $widgets_directory = drupal_get_path('module', 'd7dev') .'/
widgets';
  $files = file_scan_directory($widgets_directory, '/\.css$/');

  $widgets = array();
  foreach ($files as $file) {
    if (strpos($file->filename, '-rtl.css') === FALSE) {
      $widgets[$file->uri] = drupal_ucfirst(str_replace('-color',
'', $file->name));
    }
  }
  return $widgets;
}
```

5. Now create a new folder called `thaipeppers` under the `sites/all/modules/custom/d7dev/widgets` directory.

6. Next copy the `thaipepper.png` and `delete.png` images from the *Chapter 7 code download* to that folder.

7. Now, we will copy the CSS files from the `sites/all/modules/fivestar/widgets/flames` widget folder to our `thaipeppers` folder, rename them to `thaipeppers.css` and `thaipeppers-rtl.css`, and you will have a folder that looks similar to the one shown in following screenshot:

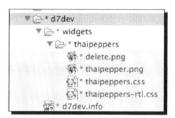

The flames rating widget is the same dimensions as our `thaipeppers` widget, so it serves as a good starting point.

8. Open the `thaipeppers.css` and `thaipeppers-rtl.css` files and replace all instances of the flames text with `thaipeppers`, and replace all instances of `flame.png` with `thaipepper.png`. The rest of the CSS will work "as is" since the flames widget is the same dimensions as our `thaipeppers` widget and our cancel image, `delete.png`, has the same name as the cancel image for the flames ratings widget.

9. Now, we will configure our Recipe content type to use our new `thaipeppers` widget. Open up our d7dev site in your favorite browser, click on the **Structure** link in the **Admin** toolbar, then click the **Content types** link, and click on the **manage display** link for our Recipe content type.

10. Next, click on the **formatter settings** cog button for the ratings field.

11. On the **Fivestar formatter settings** form expand **STAR DISPLAY OPTIONS**, and you will see our new widget. Select it and click on the **Update** button:

12. Now, while we are on the manage display page, drag the **rating** field so that it is above the **description** field, and click on the **Save** button.

13. Finally, view the Cannellini Cumin Chicken Chili recipe, and you will see our new `thaipeppers` Fivestar widget in action.

What just happened?

We created a distinctively unique `thaipeppers` Fivestar ratings widget to use for the rating recipes on our d7dev site. The process was straightforward, and shows that sometimes, adding a unique flare to a Drupal site doesn't take much development at all.

Summary

In this chapter, we have added some new features that will provide a way for visitors to interact with our d7dev site, and we enhanced some of those interactive features with HTML5. We also re-visited the Colorbox File module that was introduced in the previous chapter, and made some modifications to it that allow more control around how captions are displayed in the Colorbox overlay.

In the next chapter, we will re-visit the **Views modules** that we introduced in *Chapter 2*, and take a look at some of the more advanced programming aspects around the Views module. We will also walk through the process of sharing our changes for the Colorbox File module with the community to include learning the process for promoting Drupals sandbox projects to a full project.

8
Recipe Lists and More with Views

*This chapter will give you an in-depth introduction to the **Views module**, and introduce some of the new Views 3 plugin architecture. We will dive into some more advanced features of Views available in the Views 3 UI, and include an introduction to taxonomy-based Views. We will then develop a Views 3 style plugin to display our new Recipes view as semantic tabs.*

We also revisit the Colorbox File module as we prepare it for full project status on drupal.org.

The following topics will be covered in this chapter:

- ◆ Advanced Views configuration
- ◆ Introduction to Drupal Taxonomy
- ◆ Custom Views Style plugin
- ◆ Drupal.org project promotion

Views revisited – advanced configuration

Back in *Chapter 2, Custom Content Types and an Introduction to Module Development*, we had a quick introduction to Views 3, and saw how easy it is to create a view with the new Views wizards user interface. The new wizard-based creation for new views makes it very easy to get started with Views, but does not include many of the more advanced Views 3 configuration options. Even on the standard **Views edit** page, those advanced configuration options are hidden away, so as not to overwhelm those that are new to Views. The beginning of this chapter will explore many of those advanced configuration options available with Views 3. Views configuration can get complex pretty quickly. So, in a way, advanced Views configuration is not any less complex than some of the PHP code we have written.

Random top rated recipe block

The home page is still a bit plain and boring. We are going to use Views to create a block that will randomly showcase one of the top-rated recipes on the site. This will involve using Views filters and sort settings.

Time for action – building a random top rated recipe block with views

We are going to go beyond the basic Views wizard view creation user interface, and learn some more advanced Views features and configuration.

1. Open our d7dev site in your browser, click on the **Structure** link in the **Admin** toolbar, and click on the **Views** link.

2. Click on the **Add new** view link at the top of the **Views** page.

3. Enter `Random Top Rated Recipe` as the **View name**.

4. Select **Recipe** for the of **type** options.

5. Uncheck the **Create a page checkbox**, and check the **Create a block** checkbox.

6. Select **fields** for the **Display format** of options, and enter 1 for the **Items per page**. Your **Add a new view** form should now look similar to the following screenshot:

7. Next click on the **Continue & edit** button, as we want to configure some more advanced options that are not available as a part of the basic block creation wizard.

Now, we are going to add the Recipe content fields that we want to display in this block. Remember, this block is going to be displayed on our d7dev site's front page, so we want to make it visually appealing. Note that the **Title** field is already included by default.

8. Click on the **add** button for **FIELDS**, select **Filter by Content**, then scroll down the list, select the checkbox for **Content: image**, select the **Content: rating** field, and click on the **Add and configure fields** button. Notice that Views shows you what node or content types the fields are associated with.

9. For the **Configure field** settings for the **image** field, uncheck the **Create a label** checkbox, select `square_thumbnail` as the **Image style**, and click on the **Apply (all displays)** button.

10. For the **Configure field** settings for the **rating** field, uncheck the **Create a label** checkbox, expand the **STAR DISPLAY OPTIONS**, select our **Thaipeppers** ratings widget from last chapter, uncheck the checkbox for exposing the field for voting, and click on the **Apply (all displays)** button.

Now that we have added the fields, we are going to modify how we will filter and sort the query results for this view.

11. For sorting, we will first remove the default sort property of **Post date (desc)** by clicking on it, and then clicking on the **Remove** button.

12. Next, click on the **add** button for **SORT CRITIERIA**, select **Global** for the **Filter**, select the **Global: Random**, then click on the **Add and configure sort criteria** button.

13. All of the default values are fine on the **Configure sort criterion** form. So, just click on the **Apply (all displays)** button.

Now, we will configure the **FILTER CRITERIA**. We will leave the default criteria (only showing recipes that are published) and add an additional filter.

14. Click on the add button for **FILTER CRITERIA**, type `rating` in the **Search** input, select **Content: rating** (`field_rating:rating`), and click on the A**dd and configure filter criteria** button.

15. On the **Configure filter criterion** form, select **Is greater than** as the **Operator** and enter 3 as the **Value**, and click on the **Apply (all displays)** button. Feel free to experiment with these values, but for now, we are only going to show the recipes that have been rated 4 Thai peppers or higher.

16. When you are finished, your Views configuration should look similar to the following screenshot:

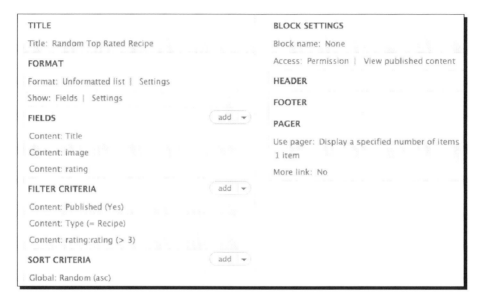

17. Next, click the **Save** button for our new **Random Top Rated Recipe** View.

Now, we need to configure this new Views-based block to show up on the front page.

18. Click on **Structure** in the **Admin** toolbar, and click on the **Blocks** link.

19. Scroll down towards the bottom of the **Blocks configuration** page, and click on the **configure** link for the **View: Random Top Rated Recipe** block that we just created.

20. Enter `Top Recipe` for **Block title**, and select **Sidebar Second** under the **REGIONS SETTINGS** for our **D7Dev Theme**.

21. Next, under the **Pages** tab, select **Only the listed pages**, enter `<front>` in the **Show block on specific pages** text area, then click on the **Save block** button.

22. Now, click on the home icon in the **Admin** toolbar, and you will see our new Views-based block.

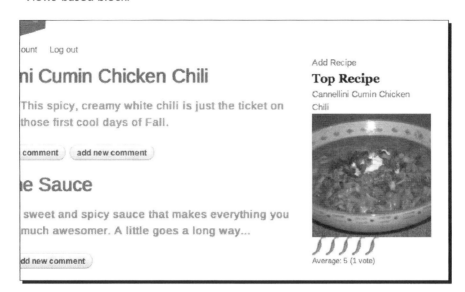

What just happened?

We used Views and leveraged some advanced configuration options to display the Fivestar module ratings field with the image and title of the top most recent recipes. Saw how easy it can be to make our d7dev site more interesting, by adding a dynamic Views-based block?

Taxonomy-based View with tabs

In this section, we are going to add another Views-based block to our front page. However, this will be a Taxonomy-based View instead of the Content-based Views that we have created so far.

Taxonomy refers to the organization of information. As we learned in the previous chapter, taxonomy is a field-able entity. The **Taxonomy module** is a core module, and it allows you to create vocabularies of terms to associate to other entity types, so that they can be organized.

So, before we can get started with the View we want to create, we need to add a new Taxonomy vocabulary with terms, and associate those terms to our recipe content. We are going to add a vocabulary for organizing recipes by type of **cuisine**.

Time for action – creating a cuisine vocabulary to organize recipes

Before we can create a Taxonomy-based view, we need to create a Drupal Taxonomy vocabulary.

1. Open our d7dev site in your browser, click on the **Structure** link in the **Admin** toolbar, and click on the **Taxonomy** link.

2. On the **Taxonomy configuration** page, click on the **Add vocabulary** link.

3. Enter `Type of Cuisine` for the **Name** input, and click on the **Save** button.

   Now, we will add some terms for our new vocabulary.

4. Click on the **add terms** link for our new **Type of Cuisine** vocabulary.

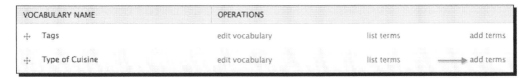

5. Enter `American` for the **Name** of our first term, and click on the **Save** button.

6. Repeat the process, and add the terms `Asian` and `Thai`.

   Now, we are going to add a taxonomy field to our Recipe content type.

7. Click on the **Structure** link in the **Admin** toolbar, click on the link for **Content types**, and click on the **manage fields** link for our Recipe content type.

8. Scroll down to the **Add new field** section. Enter `recipeCuisine` as the **LABEL**, `recipe_cuisine` for the **NAME**, select **Term reference** for the **FIELD**, select **Select list** as the **WIDGET**, and click on the **Save** button.

9. On the **FIELD SETTINGS** page, select **Types of Cuisine** as the **Vocabulary**, and click on the **Save field settings** button.

10. Once the field **EDIT** form loads, select **Unlimited** for the **Number of values** and enter `recipeCuisine` for the **Field property(s)**, which is a property of the `http://schema.org/Recipe microdata` schema that we are using for our Recipe content type, then click on the **Save settings** button.

11. Click on the **Find content** link in the **Shortcuts** bar, then click on the **edit** link for the Cannellini Cumin Chicken Chili recipe, scroll down to our new **recipeCuisine** field, select **American**, and click on the **Save** button. Repeat the process for selecting **Asian** for the `Cashew Chicken with Edamame`, **Thai** and **Asian** for the `Thai Basil Chicken`, and **Asian** for the `Awesome Sauce` recipe.

What just happened?

We got a quick introduction to Drupal Taxonomies, and created a vocabulary to organize the d7dev recipes by type of cuisine.

Now that we have added a new vocabulary for associating Recipe content to types of cuisine, we are ready to use this in a new Views-based block. We are going to create a Views-based block that displays our d7dev site's newest recipe entries by cuisine type. In addition to that, we are going to sort the list of recipes by the cuisine type with the least number of associated recipes. This will help promote cuisine types with fewer recipes. Finally, we want a tab-based user interface with a tab for each cuisine type, and the contents of that tab to be the five most recent recipes for that cuisine type. Don't worry if it sounds a bit confusing right now, we will walk through it step by step.

Time for action – creating a Recipes by cuisine type Views block

We have created a new vocabulary and associated it to our Recipe content type. Now, we will learn how to use a custom vocabulary with a view.

1. Click on the **Structure** link in the **Admin** toolbar, click on the **Views** link, and click on the **Add new view** link.

2. On the Views wizard page, enter `Recipes by Cuisine` as the **View name**, select `Taxonomy terms` for the **Show** select list, and select `Type of Cuisine` for the **of type** select list.

3. This is our first non-content (node-based) view.

4. Uncheck the **Create a page** checkbox, and check the **Create a block** checkbox.

5. Leave the remaining default settings as they are, and click on the **Continue & edit** button.

Views automatically added the Taxonomy term **Name** field, but we also want to display the most recent recipes associated to each of those cuisine terms. However, if you click on the add button for **FIELDS**, you will notice that there is no **Content** field available. We will use the Views **RELATIONSHIPS** configuration to add a relationship between the Recipe content and the taxonomy terms we are showing.

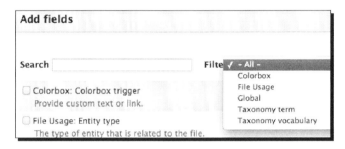

6. Click on the **add** button for **RELATIONSHIPS**, select the **Taxonomy term: Content using recipeCuisine** relationship, and click on the **Add and configure relationships** button.

7. On the next screen, the default configuration settings for this relationship are fine. So, just click on the **Apply (all displays)** button.

8. Now, click on the **FIELDS add** button and voila, there are content fields available. Type `title` into the **Search** input, select it and click on the **Add and configure fields** button.

Notice that there is a **Relationship** select list for the field configuration. All content fields on a taxonomy terms-based view require a relationship. So, this will default to the first relationship listed.

9. Uncheck the **Create a label** checkbox, as we only want to display the title itself. We will leave the **Link this field…** checkbox checked, so that users will have the ability to navigate to the full recipe. Click on the **Apply (all displays)** button.

Now, if you scroll down to the bottom of the Views configuration page, you will see a preview of this Views output, and you will see that we are displaying cuisine type term names and recipe titles, but we want to group the recipe titles by term names.

10. Next, under the **FORMAT** section, click on the **Settings** link for **Format** (as shown in the following screenshot), then select **Taxonomy term: Name** for the **Grouping** field.

11. Now, our recipes are grouped by cuisine type term name. Therefore, listing the term name in each result under the group heading is a bit redundant, so click on the **FIELDS Taxonomy term: Name** link, check the **Exclude from display** checkbox and uncheck the **Link this field…** checkbox, then click on the **Apply (add displays)** button.

12. Now, we will add a sort criterion to display the grouped terms with the most recent recipes first. Click on the **add** button for **SORT CRITERIA**, type `date` in the **Search** field, select the **Content: Post date** field, then click on the **Add and configure sort criteria** button.

13. Select **Sort descending** on the criterion configuration screen, and click on the **Apply (all displays)** button.

The preview for this View should now look similar to the following screenshot:

14. Next, click on the **Save** button for this View.

What just happened?

We have created a Views-based block of recipes displayed by the cuisine type name.

Although everything appears ok on the surface, there is a problem with the groupings and the limits for our new view. We wanted to display three cuisine types and five recipes per cuisine type, but the view we created is only limiting the total number of rows being returned. If we were to add one more recipe, then that recipe would be displayed. However, the sixth-oldest recipe would drop off, and if the newly added recipe happened to be of type `Thai` or `Asian`, then the `American` grouping would disappear. So, we would only be left with two groups of cuisine types. It turns out that this is a rather complex problem to solve with SQL, but there is a contrib module that will allow us to get the exact results that we want. The Views Field View module (`http://drupal.org/project/views_field_view`) enables a **Global Views** field that allows you to embed another View as a field of a parent view, sort of like a set of Russian Dolls. For actual production use, however, do note that there are some pretty serious performance implications for using this approach, as there will be a total of four SQL queries instead of one. So, you will definitely want to make sure you understand Views caching and Drupal caching in general before you use an approach like this on a production site.

 There is a good summary of why Views caching is beneficial to your Drupal site available at `http://2bits.com/caching/overcoming-long-views-rendering-time-drupal-sites.html`. By default, Views caching is enabled, but you should disable it when doing active Views development (and remember to re-enable it for your live site). To disable Views caching, click on the **Structure** link in the **Admin** Toolbar, click on the **Views** link, then click on the **Settings** tab, as shown in the following screenshot. On the **Views Settings** page, click on the **Advanced** link, check the **Disable views data caching** check box, and click on the **Save configuration** button at the bottom of the screen.

Time for action – installing and using the Views Field View module for our Recipe by Cuisine Type View

By installing and using the Views Field View module, we will learn how there are a number of Views related contrib modules that extend the features and capabilities of the Views module.

1. First, we need to install the **View Field View** module. Open the Terminal (Mac OS X) or Command Prompt (Windows) application, and change to the root directory of our d7dev site.

2. Use Drush to download and enable the Views Field View module:

```
$ drush dl views_field_view
Project views_field_view (7.x-1.0-rc1) downloaded to /Users/kurt/
htdocs/d7dev/sites/all/modules/views_field_view.   [success]
$ drush en views_field_view
The following extensions will be enabled: views_field_view
Do you really want to continue? (y/n): y
views_field_view was enabled successfully. [ok]
```

   Now, before we can modify our Recipes by Cuisine view, you need to understand how the Views Field View functionality is going to work. Basically, we will remove the recipe title field and add a **Global: View** field. The **Global: View** field will allow us to specify another view to use as the contents of the field, rather than a field on our Recipe content type. It will also allows us to pass any other field available for our view as an argument to pass as a contextual filter to the other view being used as the contents of the field. I know it sounds pretty complicated, and that is why we are going to walk through it together, nice and slow. To start with, we will need to add a new view to use as the Views Field View. Basically, we want a list of recipes ordered by descending post date, so we will use the **Views Field View** field to display the contents of our Recipe List view inside the rows of our Recipes by Cuisine view.

3. Click on the **Structure** link in the **Admin** toolbar, then click on the **Views** link, and click on the **edit** button for our Recipe List View.

4. At the top of the next page, click on the **Add** button, then click on the **Page** link.

5. Next, click on the **Page 2** link for the **Display name**, enter `Recipe Cuisine Page` for the **Name**, and click on the **Apply** button.

Also, the content for this view is a bit on the light side, so we will add a few fields and choose a different image style for the recipe image being displayed.

6. Click on the **add** button for **FIELDS**, select **Content** for the **Filter**, scroll down and the select the **Content: rating** and **Content: description** fields, then click on the **Add and configure** fields button.

7. For both the new fields, uncheck the **Create a label** checkbox, and set the **For** select to **All displays (except overridden)**. For the rating field, be sure to expand the **STAR DISPLAY OPTIONS**, select our **Thaipeppers** widget, and uncheck the **Expose this Fivestar field...** checkbox.

8. Now that we have added some new fields, we want to rearrange them. Click on the drop-down arrow of the **FIELDS add** button, and select **rearrange**.

9. Next, on the **Rearrange fields** screen, move the **Content: rating** field above the **Content: description** field, and click on the **Apply (all displays)** button.

10. Now, click on the **Content: image** field link under the **FIELDS** section, select **small** from the **Image style** select list, and click on the **Apply (all displays)** button.

Next, we need to adjust the pager settings for this view.

11. Under the **PAGER** options, click on the **Full** link, select **This page (override)** for the **For** select, select **Display a specified number of items**, and click on the **Apply (this display)** button.

> You may have noticed that when saving the Views settings, the button to save your settings is typically labeled **Apply (all displays)**. However, in the last step (*step 11*) the button is labeled **Apply (this display)**. As we have already seen, Views allows multiple displays for any given view and our Recipe List view has three displays: one Block display and two Page displays. As you can see in the following screenshot, Views allows you to share the configuration for certain settings for all the displays of the view or to override the settings for the current display being modified.

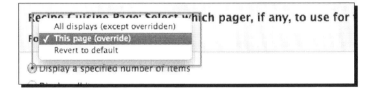

12. On the **Pager** options form, enter 2 for **Items per page**, and click on the **Apply (this display)** button.

Now, only two recipes will be displayed with no pager. This will allow us to test that only two of the three Asian recipes show up under the **Asian Cuisine Type** grouping. We can set it back to five after we test that it is working for two.

13. Now, since we are using a **Page display** type for this View, we have to set the **Path**. Under **PAGE SETTINGS** click on the link next to **Path:**, enter `recipes/%`, and click on the **Apply** button.

The % is a placeholder for the cuisine type term argument that will be passed in by our Recipes by Cuisine view to this view. So, we are now ready to add a contextual filter that will limit the results to those with same term as being passed in for the Recipe by Cuisine view. Basically, this view will only be executed if an argument is passed to it, and the **Views Field** View field that we will add to our Recipes by Cuisine view will allow us to configure what field gets passed as an argument.

14. Expand the **Advanced** section on the right side of the page, and click on the add button for the **CONTEXTUAL FILTERS**.

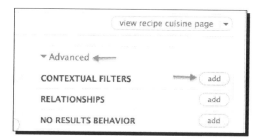

15. Enter **recipeCuisine** in the **Search** field, select **Content: recipeCuisine (field_recipe_cuisine)**, and click on the **Add and configure contextual filters** button.

16. On the next screen, it is very important that we only apply this contextual filter for **This page (override)**. Then, select **Provide default value** for the **WHEN THE FILTER VALUE IS NOT IN THE URL** select list, select **Taxonomy term ID from URL** as the **Type**, check the **Load default filter from node page, that's good for related taxonomy blocks** checkbox, and click on the **Apply (this display)** button.

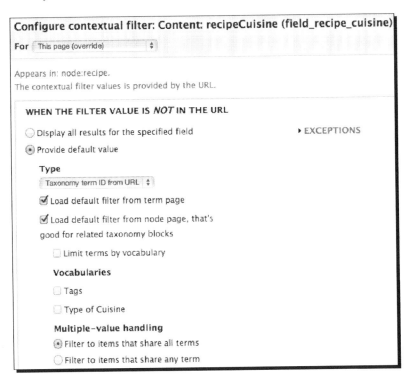

17. Save the view, and return to the **Views list** page.

18. Now click on the **edit** link for our Recipes by Cuisine view.

19. Next, click on the **(field_recipe_cuisine) Content: Title** link in the **FIELDS** section, and click on the **Remove** button.

This field will no longer be needed as it is going to be replaced with the output of the Views Field View-based field. Now, we will add the **Term ID** field that we will use to pass as an argument to Recipe List View.

20. Click on the **FIELDS** add button, filter by **Taxonomy term**, select **Taxonomy term: Term ID**, and click on the **Add and configure field** button.

21. Configure the field by checking the **Exclude from display** checkbox, then click on the **Apply (all displays)** button.

We exclude this field from being displayed, as we only need it to pass as an argument. It does not need to be displayed.

22. Once again, click on the **FIELDS add** button, filter by **Global**, select **Global: View**, and click on the **Add and configure fields** button.

23. Uncheck the **Create a label** checkbox. Then, under **VIEW SETTINGS**, select **recipe_list** as the **View**, **Recipe Cuisine Page** as the **Display**, and click on the **Apply (all displays)** button.

Now, we need to set what field to use from this view to pass as an argument to the contextual filter that we created on the **Recipe Cuisine Page** display of the **Recipe List** view.

24. Expand **REPLACEMENT PATTERNS**, copy the [tid] pattern, paste it into the **Arguments** input, and click on the **Apply (all displays)** button.

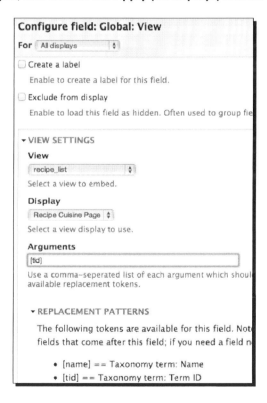

Now our Recipes by Cuisine view preview will look something similar to the following sceenshot:

We are getting close, but this is still not quite what we are looking for, because the Asian recipes are being duplicated. Basically, the way that Grouping works for Views is that a query is run to get all of results based on the filters and sort criteria, and then the Views uses the PHP code to do the grouping as opposed to using the SQL GROUP BY clause.

25. Under the **Advanced** section, click on the **Use aggregation** link, check the **Aggregate** checkbox, and click on the **Apply (all displays)** button.

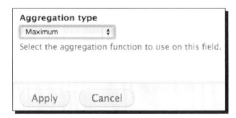

26. Now, if you look at the **(field_recipe_cuisine) Content: Post date (desc)** sort criterion that we added, you will notice a new **Aggregation** settings links. Click on that link, select **Maximum** for the **Aggregation type**, and click on the **Apply** button.

Now we are really close, but the Asian recipes come before the Thai recipe, even though Thai Basil Chicken is the newest recipe for my local d7dev site. Remember, when cuisine types share a recipe that is the most recent recipe, we want to show the cuisine type that has the least total number of recipes before the cuisine type with more recipes. To do that, we will need to add another sort criterion.

27. Click on the **SORT CRITERIA add** button, enter `nid` as the **Search** input text, select the **Content: Nid** field, and click on the **Add and configure sort criteria** button.

28. Select **Count** as the **Aggregation type**, and click on the **Apply and continue** button.

29. The sort criterion configuration is good as is, so just click on the **Apply (add displays)** button.

30. Now, scroll down to the View preview, and you will see that the Thai cuisine type is listed first.

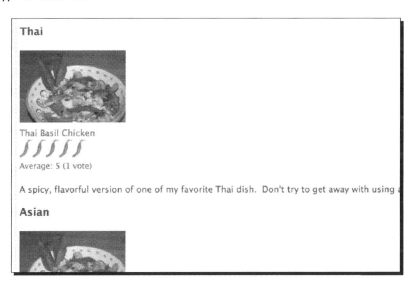

31. Finally, click on the **Save** button.

Now that our Recipes by Cuisine view is displaying the information the way we want, it is time to add the new block to the front page.

32. Click on the **Structure** link in the **Admin** toolbar, and click on the **Blocks** link.

33. Scroll down until you see the **View: Recipes by Cuisine** block, and click on the **configure** link for it.

34. Select **Sidebar Second** for our **D7Dev** theme, select to display it only on listed pages, enter `<front>` as the only path to display it for, and click on the **Save block** button.

35. Next, click on the **home** icon in the **Admin** toolbar, and you will see our new **Recipe by Cuisine** block on the right side of the page.

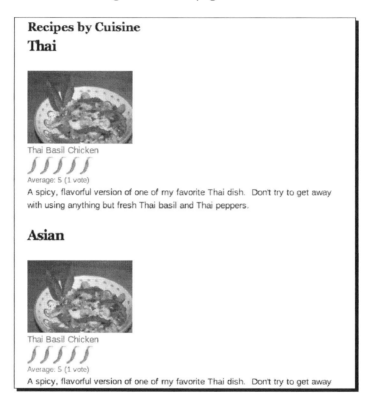

What just happened?

With the help of the Views Field View module, we have created a view that displays the information we want to display. However, the groups are still not displayed as tabs.

Tabbed Views display

In order to make the **Recipes by Cuisine** block more visually appealing, and to more efficiently utilize the viewable area of our d7dev front page, we want to display each cuisine type as a tab, and have only the recipes for the active tab be visible. We are going to use a JavaScript-based approach for displaying our groups of recipes by cuisine in a tabbed interface. Take a look at the jQuery UI tabs page (`http://jqueryui.com/demos/tabs/`), and you will see an example of how we would like Recipe by Cuisine block to look.

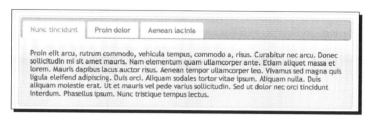

The reason I am pointing out jQuery UI tabs is because Drupal 7 includes the jQuery UI JavaScript library (Drupal 7 includes version 1.8.7 of the jQuery UI library along with version 1.4.4 of the jQuery library). So, it makes a lot of sense to use a JavaScript widget for tabs that is already available to us as part of the core Drupal 7 install. However, the markup that is currently being generated for our Recipe by Cuisine View will be fairly difficult to integrate with the JavaScript of jQuery UI tabs, because jQuery UI tabs is set up to handle the tabs and the tab content in separate HTML containers. Take a look at the example markup from the jQuery UI tabs page in the previous screenshot to see what I mean.

```
<div id="tabs">
  <ul>
    <li><a href="#tabs-1">Tab 1</a></li>
    <li><a href="#tabs-2">Tab 2</a></li>
    <li><a href="#tabs-3">Tab 3</a></li>
  </ul>
  <div id="tabs-1">
    Tab Content 1
  </div>
  <div id="tabs-2">
    Tab Content 2
  </div>
  <div id="tabs-3">
    Tab Content 3
  </div>
</div>
```

The markup that Views is generating for our Recipes by Cuisine View is more semantic. In that, it keeps the group titles with the associated content (Views actually generates a lot more markup than this, so please take a look at the source output for our Recipes by Cuisine View in your browser). Basically, a simplified version of what Views generates for the default format of **Unformatted** list is closer to the following:

```
<div>
  <h3>Tab 1</h3>
  <div>
    Tab Content 1
  </div>
  <h3>Tab 2</h3>
  <div>
    Tab Content 2
  </div>
  <h3>Tab 3</h3>
  <div>
    Tab Content 3
  </div>
</div>
```

Therefore, if we want to use jQuery UI tabs, then we would have to modify the markup that Views is generating for our Recipes by Cuisine View. Views has a plugin architecture based on the CTools module, and one type of plugin that Views supports is a style plugin.

> Views offers a number of extension points for other modules. Other Views plugin types include display, row, argument default, argument validator, access, query, cache, exposed form, pager, and localization. It would take an entire book to offer documented examples for these plugins, and examples for the other extension points of Views – handlers and lifecycle hooks. However, this example of creating a custom style plugin will provide a good introduction to Views development.

A Views style plugin would allow us to generate exactly the type of markup that is typically used with jQuery UI tabs. However, since we are going to write a custom plugin for Views anyways, why write one for creating tabs that aren't very semantic and are limited in regards to progressive enhancement. For example, if someone viewed the Recipes by Cuisine block on our d7dev site with JavaScript turned off in their browser, then the cuisine type group titles would be listed separately from the recipe content being grouped by them. I am not going to go on a semantic HTML rant or anything like that, however, the idea of better semantics and progressive enhancement fits nicely with the HTML5 sub-theme of this book.

Although HTML5 is not necessarily synonymous with progressive enhancement, the two are often used together quite effectively (similar to how JSON is not synonymous with AJAX, but often used together). Another good reason to build a semantic tabs style plugin for Views is because there are already a number of jQuery UI tab-based style plugins for Views to include **Quick Tabs** (`http://drupal.org/project/quicktabs`) and **Views UI Tabs** (`http://drupal.org/sandbox/recrit/1236298`).

Time for action – developing a Views style plugin for Semantic tabs

We are going to create a new module for our introduction to plugins for Views 3. Who knows, maybe someday we will contribute it to drupal.org.

1. Open Aptana Studio, and navigate to the `sites/all/modules/custom` folder in our d7dev project.

2. Right-click on the `custom` folder ,and create a new folder named `views_ semantic_tabs` – the name of our new module.

3. Now, right-click on that folder, create a new file name `views_semantic_tabs. info`, and enter the following information:

    ```
    name = Views Semantic Tabs
    description = Provides a Views style plugin for displaying grouped
    fields in semantic tabs.
    core = 7.x
    package = Views

    files[] = views_semantic_tabs_style_plugin.inc

    ; Module dependencies
    dependencies[] = views
    ```

    All Views development starts with the `hook_views_api` hook that is required so that Views knows what version of the Views API the module is using. Although there is only one version of Views for Drupal 7, version 3, this is still required. Also notice that we specify the location of the `views_semantic_tabs_style_plugin. inc` file. This is because modules must declare any code files that contain class or interface declarations, and as we will find out shortly that file will contains a class.

4. Right-click on the `views_semantic_tabs` folder we just created, create a new file named `views_semantic_tabs.module`, and then add the following code to that file:

```php
<?php

/**
 * Implementation of hook_views_api().
 */
function views_semantic_tabs_views_api() {
  return array(
    'api' => 3,
  );
}
```

Now, we are going to implement `hook_views_plugins`. This hook will register our custom plugin with Views. However, Views uses convention over configuration regarding this special hook, and requires that this hook be placed in a specifically named file: `MODULENAME.views.inc`.

5. Right-click on the `views_semantic_tabs` folder, create a file named `views_semantic_tabs.views.inc`, and add the following code:

```php
<?php

/**
 * Implements hook_views_plugins
 */
function views_semantic_tabs_views_plugins() {
  $module_path = drupal_get_path('module', 'views_semantic_tabs');
  return array(
    'style' => array(
      // Views style plugin for semantic tabs.
      'views_semantic_tabs' => array(
        'title' => t('Semantic Tabs'),
        'help' => t('Displays grouped rows as semantic tabs with jQuery.'),
        'handler' => 'views_semantic_tabs_style_plugin',
        'uses row plugin' => TRUE,
        'uses grouping' => TRUE,
        'uses options' => TRUE,
        'type' => 'normal',
        'theme' => 'views_semantic_tabs',        ),
    ),
  );
}
```

Our implementation of `hook_views_plugins` provides the display name or title of our plugin, along with some descriptive help text. It also provides several other properties that tell Views what features our plugin is going to implement, and the file that contains the implementations. The `handler` property specifies the name of the file that will actually implement the Views plugin; in this case, a `style` plugin, and the `uses...` properties lets Views know exactly what our handler will implement.

6. Right-click on our `views_semantic_tabs` folder, and create a file named `views_semantic_tabs_style_plugin.inc`.

   We are going to start with some code from the Views module to give us a head start on the code for our handler.

7. In Aptana Studio, navigate to the `sites/all/modules/views/plugins` folder, open and copy the contents of the `views_plugin_style_default.inc` file, and paste them into our `views_semantic_tabs_style_plugin.inc` file. Then, modify the code so that it looks similar to the following code:

```php
<?php
/**
 * @file
 * Contains the semantic tabs style plugin.
 */

/**
 * Semantic tabs style plugin to render rows decorated as tabs and
 * using the grouping field as the tab title.
 *
 * @ingroup views_style_plugins
 */
class views_semantic_tabs_style_plugin extends views_plugin_style
{

  /**
   * Options form
   */
  function options_form(&$form, &$form_state) {
    parent::options_form($form, $form_state);
    $form['grouping']['#required'] = TRUE;
    $form['grouping']['#description'] = t('Grouping is required
for this style.');
  }
}
```

The first thing that might jump out to you is that this code looks a bit different than all of the code that we have written so far. Notice that this is a PHP class that extends the `views_plugin_style` class.

This example provides a good introduction to **Object-Oriented Programming (OOP)** with PHP and Drupal. Views leverages a number of PHP's OOP constructs to include the `class` and `extend` constructs. View's use of OOP provides a striking contrast to the procedural hook-based approach, typically seen with Drupal development (although that is slowly changing, just look at the new database abstraction layer for Drupal 7, `http://api.drupal.org/api/drupal/includes- -database--database.inc/group/database/7`), based on PHP Data Objects. A short and simple summary of the difference between the two approaches is that a child class has the ability to extend and override its parent class, while with a procedural hook the parent hook has the control and is able to override and extend the output of its children hooks.

Basically, by extending the `views_plugin_style` class, our class only has to implement the methods where we need to modify the functionality of the base plugin style class. Also notice the use of `parent:: construct:` `parent::options_form($form, $form_state)`. The `parent:: construct` allows us to access the output of the class we are extending, and manipulate that output. In this case, we are making the `$form['grouping']` field `required`, and modifying its description. Note: We know that grouping will be available because we configured it in our `views_semantic_tabs_views_plugin` hook implementation

Now, we want take a look back at the `views_plugin_style` class that we are extending and look at its `render` method. Remember, we don't want to rearrange the output of the group headings and the grouped content.

8. Enter the following code after our `options_form` method:

```
/**
 * Render the display in this style.
 */
function render() {
  $output = parent::render();

  /*  set up JavaScript and CSS for tabs */
  drupal_add_js(drupal_get_path('module', 'views_semantic_tabs')
    .'/js/jquery.tabs.js');

  drupal_add_js(drupal_get_path('module', 'views_semantic_tabs')
    .'/js/views-semantic-tabs.js');
```

```
    drupal_add_css(drupal_get_path('module', 'views_semantic_tabs')
      .'/css/tabs.css');

    $view_settings['display'] =  $this->view->current_display;
    $view_settings['viewname'] = $this->view->name;

    $views_semantic_tabs_id = 'views-semantic-tabs-'. $this->view->
      name .'-'. $this->view->current_display;

    drupal_add_js(array('views_semantic_tabs' => array
      ($views_semantic_tabs_id  => $view_settings)), 'setting');

$output = '<dl>' . $output . '</dl>';
  return $output;
}
```

Notice that, at the very top of our `render` method, we get the output of the parent class, and the rest of the code is for setting up the necessary JavaScript and CSS that will turn our markup into beautiful semantic tabs. We will write the `views-semantic-tabs.js` ourselves, but the `jquery.tabs.js` and `tabs.css` will come from a jQuery plugin that I found on github and forked, and can be downloaded from `https://github.com/kmadel/lightweight-semantic-jquery-tabs/downloads`. The `jquery.tabs.js` plugin does require a specific markup structure, but it is more semantic and does not require manipulating the order of the output, rather only the markup that wraps the output. Here is a simplified example of the type of markup we want our Views style plugin to generate:

```
<dl>
  <dt>Tab 1</dt>
  <dd>
    Tab Content 1
  </dd>
  <dt>Tab 2</dt>
  <dd>
    Tab Content 2
  </dd>
  <dt>Tab 3</dt>
  <dd>
    Tab Content 3
  </dd>
</dl>
```

The semantic nature of the definition list element is discussed in several excellent articles to include `http://www.maxdesign.com.au/articles/definition/` and `http://arcnerva.com/blog/web-development/semantic-html-definition-lists-dl-dt-dd/`.

9. Download the `lightweight-semantic-jquery-tabs` project from github, unzip it, copy the `jquery.tabs.js` file to a new `js` folder, and copy the `tabs.css` file to a new `css` folder, both in our `views_semantic_tabs` folder.

    Before we create the `views-semantic-tabs.js` file, we will look at the theming of the `$output` in our `render` method. The `$output` in our extension to the render method is actually the rendered markup that is generated by the theme that we specified in the `views_semantic_tabs_views_plugins`. When the `views_plugin_styles` parent executes its `render` method, it includes the following code for each grouped set of results:

    ```
    $output .= theme($this->theme_functions(),
      array(
        'view' => $this->view,
        'options' => $this->options,
        'rows' => $rows,
        'title' => $title)
    );
    ```

    `$this->theme_functions()` returns an array of theme functions/templates to process the array, and this includes the `theme` template that we specified in our `views_semantic_tabs_views_plugins`. The only additional output we need to add to extending the `render` method is to wrap the entire output in a `dl` element.

10. Right-click on the `views_semantic_tabs` folder, and create a new folder named `theme` to match the theme path property in `views_semantic_tabs_views_plugins`.

11. Next, right-click on the new `theme` folder, create a new file named `views-semantic-tabs.tpl.php`, and add the following code to that file:

    ```php
    <?php
    /**
     * @file views-semantic-tabs.tpl.php
     * Default simple view template to display a list of rows as
    semantic tabs.
     *
     * @ingroup views_templates
     */
    ```

```
?>
<?php if (!empty($title)): ?>
  <dt><a href="#"><?php print $title; ?></a></dt>
<?php endif; ?>
  <dd>
  <?php foreach ($rows as $id => $row): ?>
      <?php print $row; ?>
  <?php endforeach; ?>
  </dd>
```

First, you need to understand that this template will be used for each tab. This is why we had to wrap the final `$output` with the `dl` element in the `render` method of our style plugin class. We are wrapping `$title` (which is the output for field we specified to use for grouping) with the `dt` element, and the `$rows` output (which is the content for the tab) is wrapped with the `dd` element, as required by the `jquery.tabs.js` jQuery plugin we are using to generate the tabs.

Now, we are ready to create the `views-semantic-tabs.js` file.

12. Right-click on the `js` folder we created, create a new file named `views-semantic-tabs.js`, and add the following JavaScript code to that file:

```
(function ($) {

  Drupal.behaviors.views_semantic_tabs =  {
    attach: function(context, settings) {
      $.each(settings.views_semantic_tabs, function(id) {
        var viewname = this.viewname;
        var display = this.display;

/* the selectors we have to play with, will be unique per
  View instance*/
        var displaySelector = '.view-id-'+ viewname +'
          .view-display-id-'+ display +' .view-content dl';

        $(displaySelector, context)
          .once('views_semantic_tabs').tabs();
      });
    }
  };

})(jQuery);
```

Now, this isn't a full introduction to JavaScript and jQuery, but we will walk through this code and explain some Drupal 7-specific JavaScript concepts.

First, notice how the entire block of JavaScript code is wrapped with `(function ($) { ... })(jQuery);`. This is a new JavaScript namespacing feature of Drupal 7, and allows other JavaScript libraries to be used with Drupal with less likelihood of conflicts.

Next, we will look at the `Drupal.behaviors` object. It provides a mechanism for attaching JavaScript functionality or behaviors to page elements. It also ensures that the **Document Object Model (DOM)** is ready for manipulation, similar to the `jQuery .ready()` method, but the `Drupal.behaviors` approach is more useful for AJAX-related JavaScript, because behaviors can be fired whenever new DOM elements are added to the document. Also, a new `settings` parameter was added, so that the settings that we added with the `drupal_add_js` function in our Views style plugin will be passed in directly to our JavaScript rather than being accessed through the global `Drupal.settings` object, as was the case for Drupal 6.

Finally, look at the code where we are actually applying the `tabs()` method to the rendered output of our Views style plugin. Drupal 7 adds a built in support for jQuery once the plugin that ensures that the tabs will only be applied to an element once. In Drupal 6, the additional custom JavaScript would have to written to manage this – usually something along the lines of checking for a CSS class that would be dynamically applied to elements as they are processed.

Now that we have completed all of the code, our `views_semantic_tabs` folder should look similar to the following screenshot:

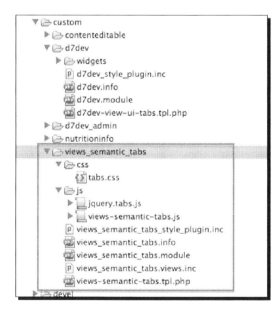

Now, we are ready to test our new Views style plugin by applying it to our Recipes by Cuisine view, but first we will need to enable our new module. We could use Drush for this, but I would like to enable custom modules in the browser so that I see my new module.

13. Open our d7dev site in your browser, click on the **Modules** link in the **Admin** toolbar, and scroll down to the **Views** section of the modules.

14. You should see our new **Views Semantic Tabs** module listed along with the other **Views** modules that we have installed.

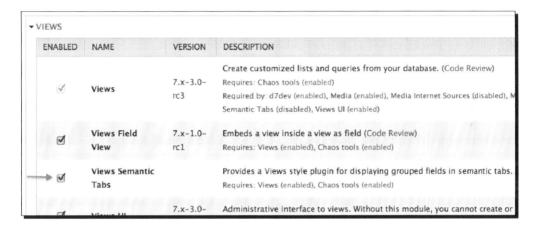

15. Check the checkbox to enable our new module, and click on the **Save** configuration button.

16. Next, click on the **home** link in the **Admin** toolbar, then click on the **contextual links** button for our **Recipes by Cuisine** view, and click on the **Edit view** link.

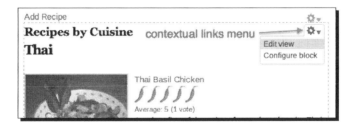

17. Scroll down to our **Recipes by Cuisine** view, and click on its **edit** link.

18. Under **FORMAT**, click on the **Unformatted list** link.

The view style settings form now includes our new Views style plugin: **Semantic Tabs**.

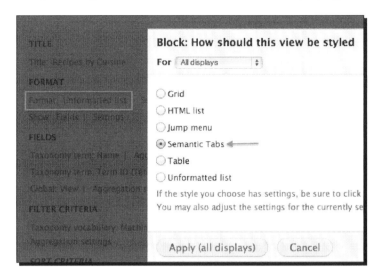

19. Select our **Semantic Tabs** style, and click on the **Apply (all displays)** button.

20. Next, on the **Style options** screen, select **Taxonomy term: Name** as **Grouping field**, and click on the **Apply (all displays)** button. Notice that **Grouping field** is required as we specified in our plugin class.

21. Now, click on the **Save** button to save our changes to the view.

You should now have a Recipe by Cuisine view block that looks similar to the following screenshot:

What just happened?

Although this example was fairly complex, the actual code is pretty straightforward once you get your head wrapped around some of the development concepts for Views 3 plugins. Not only were we able to create a custom Views style plugin that will enhance the display of content on our d7dev site, but we also learned some OOP PHP, and wrote some code that may be useful to others.

Time for another Recipe

Here is a little bit of spicy Americana for you – Kurt's Classic Chili. Add it to the d7dev site, and checkout the **Recipes by Cuisine** view from the previous section (the secret ingredient is the bay leaves).

- name: Kurt's Classic Chili.

- description: There is nothing like a warm bowl of chili on a cold winter day. The homemade chili powder really gives this dish a distinct and delicious flavor.

- recipeYield: Eight servings

- prepTime: 30 minutes

- cookTime: 60 minutes

- ingredients:

  - One pound of ground beef

  - Two tablespoon of olive oil

  - One large sweet onion, chopped

  - Six cloves garlic, crushed

  - Eight ancho peppers, dried

  - Eight guajillo peppers, dried

  - Two tablespoon of molasses

  - One tablespoon of cocoa powder

  - Six oz lager beer

  - Three tablespoon of cumin

  - Half cup beef broth

  - Two cups tomato sauce

  - One large yellow bell pepper, diced

  - One large jalapeno pepper, diced

  - One cup light kidney beans

  - One cup dark kidney beans

  - Three Bay leaves

- instructions:

  1. Combine dried peppers in a food processor, and process for two minutes.

  2. Add crushed garlic, molasses, and cocoa powder, and process for two minutes.

  3. Add oil to a large Dutch oven over medium low heat, and heat up for three to four minutes.

  4. Turn the heat to medium, add onions and cook, stirring frequently, until it just starts to caramelize for about four to eight minutes.

5. Add ground beef to onions, stirring frequently until meat is browned for about eight minutes.

6. Combine the dried chilies mixture with ground beef and onions, and sauté for three to four minutes.

7. Add beer and stir to loosen any browned bits from bottom of Dutch oven, and simmer over medium heat for five minutes.

8. Add tomato sauce and cumin, and stir until combined. Simmer for five minutes.

9. Add diced pepper, kidney beans, and bay leaves. Reduce heat to low and simmer, stirring occasionally, for 30 minutes

Promoting the Colorbox File module as a full project

Over the last few chapters, we have put a lot of effort into the Colorbox File project. It seems that it would make a lot of sense to make these enhancements available to the Drupal community as a whole. But, before we do that, there are a few things we need to do to ensure so that the module is as useful as possible for the Drupal community.

Drupal has coding standards that are strictly enforced when promoting any code for the first time. A good overview of coding standards for Drupal is available at `http://drupal.org/coding-standards`. Before any code is contributed to drupal.org, it should be checked to make sure that it conforms to Drupal's coding standards. Thankfully this is pretty easy, because as pointed out on the page mentioned previously, there is a **Coder** module that provides an automated process for checking standards compliance of your code.

Introduction to the Coder module

The Coder module is a very useful module for Drupal developers. It basically scans your custom Drupal code, and will tell you if anything is not formatted correctly, according to Drupal coding standards.

Time for action – installing and using the Coder module

As we have seen in previous chapters, with our use of the Devel module, there are Drupal contrib modules that assist with development. Now, we will install and learn about another such module.

1. First, we need to install the Coder module. Open the Terminal (Mac OS X) or Command Prompt (Windows) application, and change to the root directory of our d7dev site.

2. Use Drush to download and enable the Coder module.

```
$ drush dl coder

Project coder (7.x-1.0) downloaded to /Users/kurt/htdocs/d7dev/
sites/all/modules/coder.    [success]

Project coder contains 3 modules: coder_upgrade, coder_review,
coder.

$ drush en coder_review

The following extensions will be enabled: coder, coder_review

Do you really want to continue? (y/n): y

coder was enabled successfully.            [ok]

coder_review was enabled successfully.     [ok]
```

Note that there are three modules that are part of the Coder project. At this point, we are only interested in the **Code Review** (code_review) module, so we will enable that one and its dependencies. Remember, Drush will handle enabling any dependencies for a module; in this case the main coder module. So, we can save a little bit of time by specifically enabling the coder_review module with Drush.

3. Open up our d7dev site in your favorite browser, click on the **Configuration** link in the **Admin** toolbar, then click on the **Coder** link in the **DEVELOPMENT** section.

4. Most of the default settings for **REVIEWS** are good, but we want to select **minor (most)** for the **show warnings at or above the severity warning level** setting.

5. We also only want to run a Coder review against the Colorbox File module. So, scroll down and expand the **SELECT SPECIFIC MODULES** section, and select the checkbox for the `colorbox_file` module, then click on the **Run reviews** button.

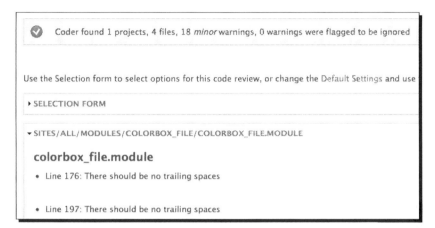

6. Next, in Aptana Studio, open the `colorbox_file.module` and `colorbox_file.theme.inc` files, make all of the changes identified by the Code Review module, and save the files.

7. Now, back in the browser, expand the **SELECTION FORM** section and click on the **Run reviews** button again.

This time, the Coder Review module did not find any warnings.

What just happened?

We learned how to use the Coder Review module to simplify the process of making sure our code adheres to the Drupal coding standards, and in doing so, we added a new tool to our Drupal development tool box. You should always check your code with the Coder Review before sharing it on drupal.org.

Commit changes to Colorbox File sandbox

Now that we have cleaned up the code for the Colorbox File module, it is time to make those changes available for all of the Drupal community.

Please note that you will not be able to follow along in this section, as the code will have already been committed, and you don't actually have the permission to commit the code to someone else's sandbox repository.

Time for action – committing Colorbox File module changes to Drupal Git Repository

In order to make the changes we made to the Colorbox File module available on Drupal.org, we need to commit our changes to the existing Colorbox File sandbox repository.

1. First, I will open the Terminal (Mac OS X) application, and change to my `colorbox_file` directory with the changes we made.

   If you ran the `git status` command in that directory before I committed the changes here, you would see the following output:

   ```
   $ git status
   # On branch master
   # Changes not staged for commit:
   #   (use "git add <file>..." to update what will be committed)
   #   (use "git checkout -- <file>..." to discard changes in working
   directory)
   #
   #       modified:   colorbox_file.info
   #       modified:   colorbox_file.module
   #
   # Untracked files:
   #   (use "git add <file>..." to include in what will be committed)
   #
   #       README.txt
   #       colorbox_file.js
   #       colorbox_file.pages.inc
   #       colorbox_file.theme.inc
   no changes added to commit (use "git add" and/or "git commit -a")
   ```

   The `git status` command tells us that we have two files that have changed, and four files that are untracked or new.

2. Now, I will add and commit the new and updated files to my local repository.

   ```
   $ git add -A
   You have new mail in /var/mail/kurt
   Kurt-MacBook-Pro:colorbox_file kurt$ git commit -m "Issue #1296186
   by jide, 1291618 by oxyc, and changed and enhancements by kmadel:
   Changes include support for all entity types, entity based fields
   as colorbox caption."
   ```

```
[master ecd0b10] Issue #1296186 by jide, 1291618 by oxyc, and
changed and enhancements by kmadel: Changes include support for
all entity types, entity based fields as colorbox caption.
 6 files changed, 486 insertions(+), 183 deletions(-)
 create mode 100644 README.txt
 create mode 100644 colorbox_file.js
 rewrite colorbox_file.module (79%)
 create mode 100644 colorbox_file.pages.inc
 create mode 100644 colorbox_file.theme.inc
```

3. Next, I will push the committed changes to the repository on drupal.org.

```
$ git push -u origin master
...
To kmadel@git.drupal.org:sandbox/kmadel/1084984.git
   fa74c35..ecd0b10  master -> master
Branch master set up to track remote branch master from origin.
```

What just happened?

This is all it took to make all of the new Colorbox File code available on drupal.org (through git only). If you visit the repository viewer page for that sandbox (`http://drupalcode.org/sandbox/kmadel/1084984.git`), you will see the push that I just made.

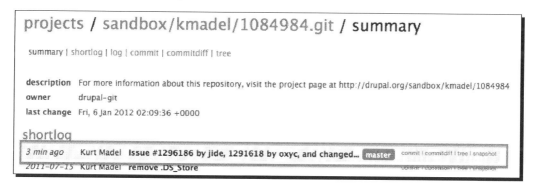

Now, all I need to do is update the issues mentioned in my commit message (the `-m` argument for the `commit` command), and everyone who is interested in the Colorbox File module will know that the changes are available.

Summary

In this chapter, we have learned a lot about Views and have seen how Views allows you to add interesting components to your site through a web-based user interface. We also learned that Views offers a powerful development platform for custom extensions.

We were introduced to the Coder module, and we used it to clean up the code for the Colorbox File module. We then pushed those changes to the Colorbox File sandbox Drupal repository for others to use.

In the next chapter, we are going to add some visually-striking banner components that will leverage the Views development from this chapter, and show off all the beautiful photos of the recipes on the d7dev site. We will also revisit the Colorbox File module, and walk through the process of promoting sandbox projects to full projects on drupal.org.

9
Rotating Banners and Project Promotion

In this chapter we are going to enhance the appearance of our d7dev site's front page with a rotating banner. We are going to introduce another Views style plugin that will provide an interactive rotating banner, so that we can highlight the images of the recipes on our d7dev site.

We are also going to revisit the Colorbox File module, and walk through the process of promoting a sandbox project to a full project on Drupal.org.

The following topics will be covered in this chapter:

- Creating and styling a rotating banner with the Views Slideshow module
- Creating a custom Drush command
- Creating a `.install` file for the Colorbox File module
- Promoting the Colorbox File module from a sandbox project to a full project

Rotating banner with Views Slideshow

We will examine an approach that is based on a Views plugin and predominantly consists of Views configuration. Customization of the Views plugin output will be handled with custom CSS.

The **Views Slideshow module** is an excellent example of a Views style plugin, and it provides much more functionality than just rotating banners. Basically, the Views Slideshow module wraps the jQuery Cycle plugin as a Views style plugin, but it does so with a sub-module, which is the `views_slideshow_cycle` module. The `views_slideshow` module is more than a Views style plugin. It is itself a plugin framework for integrating different jQuery slideshow plugins with Views, and also provides a default implementation based on the jQuery Cycle plugin.

Time for action – installing the Views Slideshow module

Before we build a rotating banner with Views, we need to install the Views Slideshow module.

1. Open the Terminal (Mac OS X) or Command Prompt (Windows) application, and change to the root directory of our d7dev site.

2. Use Drush to download and enable the Views Slideshow module.

    ```
    $ drush dl views_slideshow

    Project views_slideshow (7.x-3.0) downloaded to /Users/kurt/
    htdocs/d7dev/sites/all/modules/views_slideshow.
      [success]

    Project views_slideshow contains 2 modules: views_slideshow_cycle,
    views_slideshow.

    $ drush en views_slideshow_cycle

    The following projects have unmet dependencies:

    views_slideshow_cycle requires libraries

    Would you like to download them? (y/n): y

    Project libraries (7.x-1.0) downloaded to /Users/kurt/htdocs/
    d7dev/sites/all/modules/libraries.    [success]

    The following extensions will be enabled: libraries, views_
    slideshow, views_slideshow_cycle

    Do you really want to continue? (y/n): y

    libraries was enabled successfully.                  [ok]

    views_slideshow was enabled successfully.            [ok]

    views_slideshow_cycle was enabled successfully.      [ok]
    ```

What just happened?

Views Slideshow consists of two modules: the base `views_slideshow` module and the `views_slideshow_cycle` module. We only need to tell Drush to install the `views_slideshow_cycle` module, because Drush will automatically install any dependencies belonging to the same parent module; in this case, the `views_slideshow` module will automatically be enabled by Drush. Also, notice how Drush prompted us to download other unmet dependencies; in this case, the `libraries` module. The **Libraries API module** (`http://drupal.org/project/libraries`) provides a common repository for sharing things, such as jQuery plugins, across modules, so that each module that may need something like the jQuery Cycle plugin doesn't need to install its own copy.

Custom Drush commands

We are not quite ready to begin using the Views Slideshow module because, as mentioned above, it requires the jQuery Cycle plugin. You may recall from *Chapter 6, Adding Media to our Site*, that the Colorbox module included a Drush task that downloaded the Colorbox JavaScript plugin to the `sites/all/libraries/colorbox` folder. We are going to use code from the Colorbox module as a starting point to create a similar Drush task to download the Views Slideshow required jQuery Cycle plugin to the `sites/all/libraries/jquery.cycle` folder. You will find that there is a lot of existing code that can serve as a good starting point for your own custom code.

Time for action – creating a custom Drush command to install the jQuery Cycle plugin

Now, let's learn how you can integrate Drush with a Drupal module to make certain install tasks easier.

1. In Aptana Studio, create a new folder named `drush` in the `d7dev/sites/all/modules/views_slideshow` folder.

2. Next, copy the `colorbox.drush.inc` file from the `modules/colorbox` folder to the `drush` folder we just created, and rename it to `views_slideshow.drush.inc`.

3. Open the `views_slideshow.drush.inc` file in Aptana Studio, and modify the first eleven lines so they look as follows:

```php
<?php

/**
 * @file
 *    drush integration for views_slideshow.
 */

/**
 * The jQuery Cycle plugin URI.
 */
define('JQUERY_CYCLE_DOWNLOAD_URI',
  'https://github.com/downloads/malsup/cycle/jquery
  .cycle.all.latest.js');
```

We are updating some of the comments to reflect that this is for the Views Slideshow module, and changing the name of the constant and location for downloading the jQuery Cycle plugin.

4. Next, we are going to rename the `hook_drush_command` to `views_slideshow_drush_command`, and update the `$items` array. The final function should look similar to the following code:

```php
function views_slideshow_drush_command() {
  $items = array();

  // the key in the $items array is the name of the command.
  $items['jquery-cycle-plugin'] = array(
    'callback' => 'drush_jquery_cycle_plugin',
    'description' => dt("Downloads the jQuery Cycle plugin."),
    'bootstrap' => DRUSH_BOOTSTRAP_DRUSH, // No bootstrap.
    'arguments' => array(
      'path' => dt('Optional. A path where to install the jQuery
        Cycle plugin. If omitted Drush will use the default
        location.'),
    ),
    'aliases' => array('jcycle'),
  );

  return $items;
}
```

5. Now, we will update `hook_drush_help`.

```
function views_slideshow_drush_help($section) {
  switch ($section) {
    case 'drush:jquery-cycle-plugin':
      return dt("Downloads the jQuery Cycle plugin from https://
github.com/downloads/malsup/cycle, default location is sites/all/
libraries.");
  }
}
```

6. Next, delete the commented out `drush_colorbox_post_pm_enable` function.

7. Now, add the following code after the `JQUERY_CYCLE_DOWNLOAD_URI` constant to create another PHP constant that we will use in the next step.

```
define('JQUERY_CYCLE_FILE_NAME', 'jquery.cycle.all.js');
```

8. Rename the `drush_colorbox_plugin` function to `drush_jquery_cycle_plugin`, and update the code:

```
/**
 * Command to download the jQuery Cycle plugin.
 */
function drush_jquery_cycle_plugin() {
  $args = func_get_args();
  if (!empty($args[0])) {
    $path = $args[0];
  }
  else {
    $path = 'sites/all/libraries/jquery.cycle';
  }

  // Create the path if it does not exist.
  if (!is_dir($path)) {
    drush_op('mkdir', $path);
    drush_log(dt('Directory @path was created', array('@path' =>
      $path)), 'notice');
  }

  // Set the directory to the download location.
  $olddir = getcwd();
  chdir($path);
```

```
$filename = basename(JQUERY_CYCLE_DOWNLOAD_URI);

// Remove any existing jQuery Cycle plugin file
if (is_file(JQUERY_CYCLE_FILE_NAME)) {
  drush_op('unlink', JQUERY_CYCLE_FILE_NAME);
  drush_log(dt('An existing jQuery Cycle plugin was overwritten
    at @path', array('@path' => $path)), 'notice');
}

// Download the jQuery Cycle JavaScript file
if (!drush_shell_exec('wget ' . JQUERY_CYCLE_DOWNLOAD_URI)) {
  drush_shell_exec('curl -O ' . JQUERY_CYCLE_DOWNLOAD_URI);
}

//rename the jQuery Cycle JavaScript file to jquery.cycle.all.js
drush_op('rename', $filename, JQUERY_CYCLE_FILE_NAME);

// Set working directory back to the previous working directory.
chdir($olddir);

if (is_dir($path)) {
  drush_log(dt('jQuery Cycle plugin has been downloaded to @
path', array('@path' => $path)), 'success');
  }
  else {
    drush_log(dt('Drush was unable to download the jQuery Cycle
      plugin to @path', array('@path' => $path)), 'error');
  }
}
```

We modified the $path variable to include the name of the folder where the Views Slideshow module looks for the jQuery Cycle plugin. Next, we removed the check for the **unzip** dependency and all of the unzip-related code, because the jQuery Cycle plugin that we are downloading is not zipped. Then, we replaced the COLORBOX_ DOWNLOAD_URI constant with the constant that we created for the jQuery Cycle plugin URI. Finally, we added some code to rename the downloaded file to the name that the Views Slideshow uses.

9. Open the Terminal (Mac OS X) or Command Prompt (Windows) application, change to the root directory of our d7dev site, type `drush`, and in the resulting list of Drush commands you should see our new `jquery_cycle_plugin` command under other commands.

10. Now, use Drush to download the jQuery Cycle plugin for the Views Slideshow module.

```
$ drush jquery-cycle-plugin

jQuery Cycle plugin has been downloaded to sites/all/libraries/
jquery.cycle    [success]
```

What just happened?

We created a custom Drush command to make it super-easy to download the jQuery Cycle plugin, a required JavaScript library for the Views Slideshow module.

Creating a rotating banner with Views Slideshow

Again, the Views Slideshow module is a Views style plugin. We are going to create a block-based view that will use this style plugin to turn our recipe images into a rotating banner that we will be able to display on the front page of our d7dev site.

Time for action – creating a banner using the Views Slideshow module

Now that we have installed and set up the Views Slideshow module, it is time for us to build a Views-based rotating banner.

1. Open our d7dev site in your browser, click on the **Structure** link in the **Admin** toolbar, and click on the **Views** link.

2. We are creating a new view. So, click on the **Add new view** link at the top of the **Views** List page.

3. Enter `Front Banner` as the **View name**, and select **Recipe** for the of type. We are going to create our rotating banner as a block, so uncheck the **Create a page** checkbox and check the **Create a block** checkbox.

4. Next, select **Slideshow of fields** for the **Display format**. Check that the **Add new view** form looks similar to the following screenshot, and click on the **Continue & edit** button:

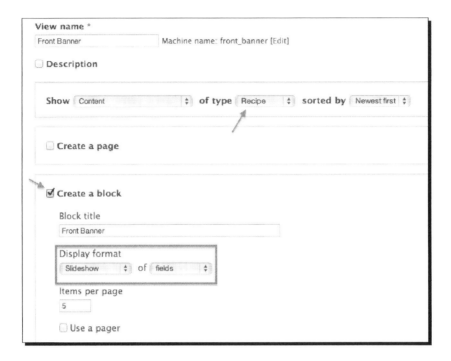

Now, we need to decide what fields we want to display in the banner. The **Content: Title** field has been added by default. But, we obviously want to display an image in the rotating banner.

5. Click on the **add** button for **FIELDS**, select **Content: image**, and click on the **Add and configure fields** button.

6. Next, in the **Configure field** form, uncheck the **Create a label** checkbox, select **large** as the **Image style**, and click on the **Apply (all displays)** button.

    Now, if you scroll down to the **Auto preview** area of the **Views edit** page, you will see a working slideshow that looks something similar to the following screenshot:

Content ✿▾

Thai Basil Chicken

Also, if you wait, you will see that the Awesome Sauce recipe is displayed even though it doesn't have an image associated with it. We will add a filter to our view, so that only recipes with a **Content: image** field will be displayed in the rotating banner.

7. Click on the **add** button for **FILTER CRITERIA**, select the first **Content: image (field_image:fid)** filter, and click on the **Add and configure filter criteria** button.

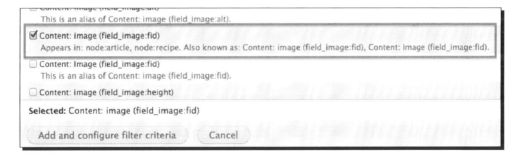

8. On the **Filter criteria** form, select **Is not empty (NOT NULL)** from the **Operator** select list, and click on the **Apply (all displays)** button.

Now, if you look at the preview, you should no longer see the Awesome Sauce recipe. You will notice that the **Content: Title** field is above the image, but I think it would look better underneath the image. We will rearrange the fields to place the **Content: Title** field under the **Content: image** field.

9. Click on the drop-down for the **FIELDS add** button, and select **rearrange**.

10. Now, just drag the **Content: Title** field under the **Content: image** field, and click on the **Apply (all displays)** button.

Now, we are ready to see how our new Views Slideshow banner looks on the front page.

11. Click on the **Save** button for our new view, click on the **Structure** link in the **Admin** toolbar, and click on the **Blocks** link.

12. Scroll down until you find the **View: Front Banner** block that we just created, and click on its **configure** link.

13. Next, in the block configuration form, type in `<none>` as the **Block title**, select **Content** as the **region to display the block for our D7Dev Theme**, select **Only the listed pages**, and enter `<front>` as the only page to display it on:

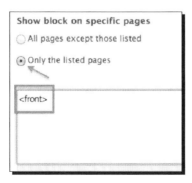

14. Click on the **Save block** button. On the **Blocks configuration** page, drag the **View: Front Banner** block above the **Main page content** block in the **Content** regions, and click on the **Save blocks** button at the bottom of the screen.

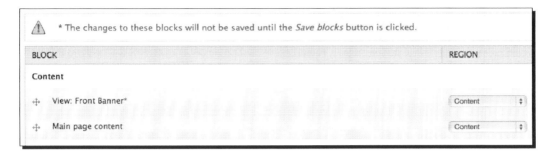

15. Now, navigate to the front page of our d7dev site to see what our new Views Slideshow rotating banner looks like.

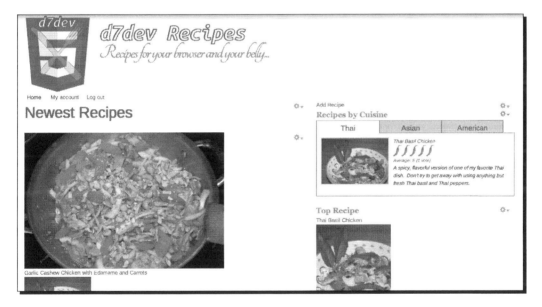

What just happened?

We created a rotating banner block with the Views Slideshow style plugin, and added the block to the front page of our d7dev site.

Have a go hero – creating a new image style for the images in our rotating recipe banner

In *Chapter 6*, we were introduced to image styles for Drupal 7. Add a new image style named `front_banner` that will scale our recipe images to be no wider than 680 pixels and cropped to 410 pixels in height, and apply it to the **Content: image** field of our **Front Banner** view. This will create a more consistent look for our rotating banner as it won't change the size from slide to slide. When you are done, the Front Banner should look similar to the following screenshot:

Enhance the appearance of our rotating banner with a pager and CSS

Our new rotating banner works fine, but we can easily improve its appearance with some custom CSS. We are going to add custom CSS to our theme to tweak the appearance of the rotating banner, but first, we are going to add a pager that will show how many slides there are and the current slide.

Time for action – updating the front banner view to include a slideshow pager

We are going to enhance our Views rotating banner with a pager.

1. Open our d7dev site in your browser, mouse over our new rotating banner, click on the contextual links widget, and click on the **Edit view** link.

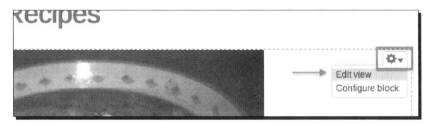

2. Next, we need to add a field to our view for the Views Slideshow plugin to use as a pager. Click on the **FIELDS add** button, then type `global` in the **Search** input, select the **Global: View result counter** field, and click on the **Add and configure fields** button.

3. Now, on the **Configure field** form, uncheck the **Create a label** checkbox, check the **Exclude from display** checkbox, and click on the **Apply (all displays)** button.

Views will now add a field consisting of an integer starting with `1`, incremented for each result, and included with each result as a hidden field that won't be displayed. Now, we will take our first look at the format settings for the Slideshow format that we have been using for this view. We didn't need to look at this until now, because up until now, we have only been using the default settings.

4. Click on the **Settings** slink for the **Slideshow** format.

The first thing you will notice about the **Style options** form for the Slideshow plugin is that it has a lot more configurable settings than our Views Semantic Tabs module from the previous chapter.

5. Scroll down to the **Bottom Widgets** settings, check the **Pager** checkbox, under the **Pager** fields select the **Global: View result counter** field that we just added, and click on the **Apply (all displays)** button.

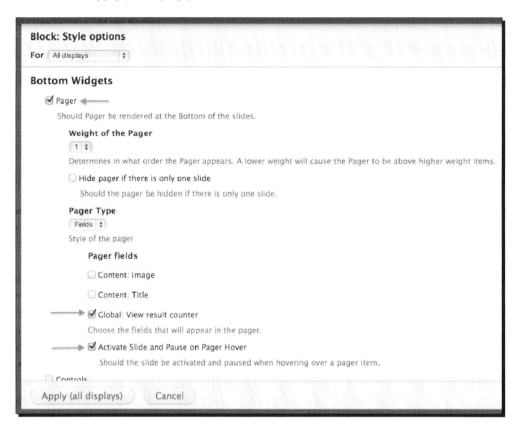

6. Now, click on the **Save** button for the view, and take a look at the updated rotating recipe banner.

Cannellini Cumin Chicken Chili

1
2
3

Not quite the visually striking pager we were looking for, but if you click any of the numbers, you will notice that the slide will change to that paged item. So, although the pager works, it doesn't look all that great. Let us see what we can do about the way it looks by adding some custom CSS to our d7dev theme.

We are going to use the Google Chrome browser for the next few steps of this recipe. I know that there are a number of browsers to choose from, but the Chrome browser offers one of the best DOM inspectors of any browser, the inspector, and other development tools are built-in to the browser (no extra plugin to install, such as Firebug on Firefox), and it is my opinion that Chrome has the best browser-integrated developer tools. Better yet, Chrome is available for Windows and Mac OS X. Download Chrome from http://www.google.com/chrome. Of course, you are welcome to use another browser, but the following steps were written with Chrome in mind.

7. Open the front page of our d7dev site in Chrome, right-click on our rotating banner, and select **Inspect Element** from the contextual menu that pops up.

8. In the **Elements** inspector, find the `div` with the class `views-slideshow-controls-bottom`, and expand it.

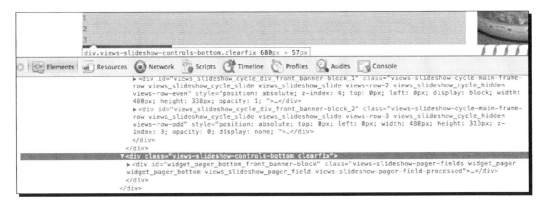

 The purpose of using the browser DOM inspector to make these changes is to expedite CSS code changes. You will see the outcome of these changes instantly in your browser, and when you are done, you will be able to copy those changes to the appropriate CSS file to make them permanent.

9. Select `div` with the `class views-slideshow-pager-fields`, so that it is highlighted, then click inside the `element.style` curly brackets in the **Styles** inspector, and type in `float: right;`.

10. Now, enter the following CSS below the `float: right` style that we just added:

```
position: relative;
bottom: 40px;
```

11. Next, in Aptana Studio, open our `global.css` file located at `d7dev/sites/all/ themes/d7dev_theme/css`.

12. Scroll to the bottom of the file, and add the following style:

```
/* Front Banner styels */
div.views-slideshow-pager-fields{
   float: right;
   position: relative;
   bottom: 44px;
   width: 300px;
   text-align: right;
   z-index: 100;
}
```

13. Now, back in Chrome, expand the `views-slideshow-pager-fields` div, find div with the class `views-slideshow-pager-field-item`, add the following styles to the `global.css` file for the `div.views-slideshow-pager-field-item` selector, and refresh the front page in Chrome:

```css
div.views-slideshow-pager-field-item{
   display: inline-block;
   background-color: #999;
   width: 10px;
   height: 10px;
   text-indent: -9999px;
   border: 2px solid #CCC;
   -moz-border-radius: 4px;
   border-radius: 8px;
   margin-left: 4px;
   cursor: pointer;
}

div.views-slideshow-pager-field-item:hover,
div.views-slideshow-pager-field-item.active{
   background-color: #BF0000;
}
```

Now, you should have a pager that looks similar to the following screenshot (outlined in white just to highlight it):

Thai Basil Chicken

Now, we need to do something about the recipe title. It gets a bit lost underneath the recipe image on the left side. We are going to increase the font size and position it above the pager, but on the left side of the image, and add a background that is slightly transparent.

14. Right-click on a recipe title, and select **Inspect Element**.

15. Highlight the `div` above the `anchor` element with the class `views-field-title`. In Aptana Studio, create a new style in the `global.css` file for `div.views-field-title`, refresh the page in Chrome, and add the following CSS to the `div.views-field-title` selector under the **Matched CSS Rules**:

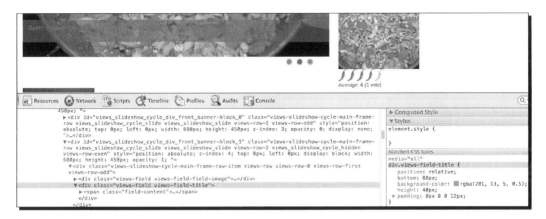

16. Add the following CSS (as seen in Chrome) to the `div.views-field-title` selector in Aptana Studio:

```
position: relative;
bottom: 80px;
background-color: rgba(201,13,5,0.5);
height: 40px;
padding: 8px 0 0 12px;
margin: 0 4px;
```

Now the background looks good, but the red title text gets lost in it.

17. Add the following CSS to our `global.css` file after the `div.views-field-title` style:

```
div.views-field-field-image{
  border: 4px solid #CCC;
}

div.views-field-title {
  position: relative;
```

```
    bottom: 80px;
    background-color: rgba(201,13,5,0.5);
    height: 40px;
    padding: 8px 0 0 12px;
}

div.views-field-title a{
    font-size: 26px;
    color: #CCC;
    -webkit-text-fill-color: #CCC;
    -webkit-text-stroke-width: 1px;
    -webkit-text-stroke-color: #FFF;
}

div.views-field-title a:hover{
    color: #FFF;
    -webkit-text-fill-color: #FFF;
    text-decoration: none;
}
```

18. Refresh the front page in Chrome, and you will see that the recipe titles are much easier to read. However, notice that the pager has been pushed down off the image.

19. In Aptana Studio, modify the `bottom` property of the `div.views-slideshow-pager-fields` selector from `44px` to `70px`.

    Refresh the front page in Chrome again, and you will notice that our rotating banner is looking pretty good. However, the CSS that we have added to `global.css` has affected other recipe title fields on the page. We need to find a parent selector for our rotating banner, so that the CSS we have just added will only affect the recipe titles for our rotating banner.

20. In Chrome, right-click on the recipe image in our rotating banner, select **Inspect Element**, and scroll up in the **Elements** inspector until you find a `div` with the class `view-id-front_banner`. Copy that class name and append it, along with a `.` prefix, to all of the CSS selectors that we have added for our rotating banner in the `global.css` file. So, for example, `div.views-field-title` will become `.view-id-front_banner div.views-field-title`.

21. Once you have appended that class to all of the front banner styles, refresh the front page in Chrome.

    Our rotating banner should look the same as it did before. But now, all of the other recipe titles on the front page should look as they did before we added the front banner styles to the `global.css` file.

What just happened?

We added a pager to our rotating banners, and although we did not write much custom PHP code, we saw how a little bit of Views configuration with the right contrib module, Views Slideshow, and how some creative CSS can be combined to great effect.

Time for another recipe

Here is a hearty and tasty soup for a cold winter day. Just about anyone, with just about any dietary restrictions, should be able to enjoy this healthy and delicious soup.

- name: Potato Leek Soup (Vegan)
- cuisineType: European
- description: This healthy yet still creamy soup will really stick to your ribs and warm you up on a cold day.
- recipeYield: Ten servings
- prepTime: 30 minutes
- cookTime: 45 minutes
- ingredients:
    - Five to six large russet potatoes, peeled and quartered
    - Four leeks, cleaned and thinly sliced
    - One large sweet onion, diced
    - Four tablespoon vegan butter
    - One tablespoon olive oil
    - Six cups vegetable broth
    - One cup plain soy milk
    - Sea salt
    - Freshly ground black pepper
    - One tablespoon rice vinegar
    - Two teaspoon crushed red pepper
    - One-fourth cup parsley, finely chopped
- instructions:
    1. Melt vegan butter in a large Dutch oven over medium heat.
    2. Once the butter melts, add diced onion and sauté until it just starts to caramelize.
    3. Add the finely sliced leeks and sauté over medium heat for ten minutes, stirring every minute or so.
    4. Add diced potatoes and sauté with leeks and onions for ten minutes.
    5. Add the olive oil and stir to combine.

6. Add vegetable broth and plain soy milk, stir to combine, bring to a boil over medium-high heat, and reduce the heat to low.

7. Simmer over low heat for 15 minutes.

8. Using an emersion hand blender, blend the soup into a smooth puree.

9. Stir in vinegar and crushed red pepper.

10. Stir in sea salt and freshly ground black pepper to taste.

11. Stir in fresh parsley and enjoy.

Promoting a sandbox project to a full project

Although we committed our Colorbox File changes to the sandbox Git repository, and in doing so made the code available to anyone who wants to use it, using Git is a barrier for many people who aren't developers, and just want to download a module, configure it, and use it. A sandboxed module will also deter people from trying your module, because they may not trust a module that is not a full project (and Drupal includes a big warning at the top of all sandboxed module pages). I will walk you through the process to promote the Colorbox File module to a full Drupal.org project, and then, I will create a release that can be easily downloaded without Git.

 You won't actually be able to execute the following instructions as a project can only be promoted to a full project once. If you don't already have the ability to promote to full projects, it is a fairly lengthy process to get the initial permission to promote projects on drupal. org. The process for your first full project promotion is quite different than the process to promote successive projects to full projects. The process for gaining the ability to promote projects is documented at `http://drupal.org/node/1011698`.

At this point, I will only create a dev release until the community has had an opportunity to test it. Once there has been some feedback, I will create a full release. Before we begin, I have decided to rename the module from Colorbox File to Media Colorbox, and there is some work involved with making that happen. Although the module is not dependent on the Media module, it is more aligned with the concepts of the Media module, and will probably be more easily discovered if it is clearly associated with the Media module.

To rename the module, we have to disable and uninstall the module, and before we uninstall the module, we need to write some "house keeping" code to do a little bit of Drupal clean up. You may recall from *Chapter 6*, that we used the `variable_set` function to store the Colorbox caption field settings in the Drupal variable table.

			name The name of the variable.	
☐	✎	✗	additional_settings__active_tab_recipe	s:14:"edit-microdata";
☐	✎	✗	admin_theme	s:5:"seven";
☐	✎	✗	backup_migrate_destination_id	s:8:"download";
☐	✎	✗	backup_migrate_profile_id	s:7:"default";
☐	✎	✗	backup_migrate_source_id	s:2:"db";
☐	✎	✗	clean_url	s:1:"1";
☑	✎	✗	colorbox_file_image_caption_field_name	s:13:"field_caption";
☐	✎	✗	comment_anonymous_recipe	i:0;
☐	✎	✗	comment_default_mode_recipe	i:1;

When someone uninstalls this module, for whatever reason, we don't want to leave the unneeded data in the variable table because there is no reason to keep the data and it is bad practice. Drupal core provides a hook that is specifically for this type of clean up: `hook_uninstall`.

Time for action – implementing hook_uninstall for the Colorbox File module

The `hook_uninstall` function must be implemented in a module's `.install` file per the documentation available at `http://api.drupal.org/api/drupal/modules--system--system.api.php/function/hook_uninstall/7`.

1. In Aptana Studio, right-click on the `colorbox_file` folder at `d7dev/sites/all/modules`, and create a new file named `colorbox_file.install`.

2. Open the `colorbox_file.install` file, and add the following code:

```php
<?php

/**
 * @file
 * Uninstall function for the colorbox file module.
 */
```

```
/**
 * Implements hook_uninstall().
 */
function colorbox_file_uninstall() {
  //Remove all colorbox_file varialbes
  db_delete('variable')->condition('name', 'colorbox_file_%',
    'LIKE')->execute();
}
```

We know that we prefixed all of the variables for the `colorbox_file` module with that same name: `colorbox_file`. The `db_delete` function will delete all the rows in the variable table where the name column value begins with `colorbox_file_`.

The `db_delete` function (`http://api.drupal.org/api/drupal/includes--database--database.inc/function/db_delete/7`) is a new function for Drupal 7 core. It is part of the completely rewritten database API for Drupal 7. Previously with Drupal 6, this code would have had to be written in a manner similar to the following:

```
db_query("DELETE FROM {variable} WHERE name
LIKE %s", "colorbox_file_%");
```

In Drupal 6, you actually wrote the SQL that was going to be executed. The new database API for Drupal 7 abstracts the grammar of queries, and makes it a bit easier to create Drupal database drivers for other databases, besides the MySQL database. There are contrib modules that provide drivers for Microsoft SQL Server - `http://drupal.org/project/sqlsrv`, and the Oracle Database - `http://drupal.org/project/oracle`.

What just happened?

With a modest level of effort, we improved the Colorbox File module by removing unneeded records from the variable table when it was uninstalled, and we made the module more compliant with the accepted Drupal coding standards.

Time for action – uninstalling and renaming the Colorbox File module

Now that we have implemented the `hook_uninstall` function for the Colorbox File module, we are ready to test that it works and then move forward with renaming the module to Media Colorbox.

1. Open the Terminal (Mac OS X) or Command Prompt (Windows) application, change to the root directory of our d7dev site, and type the following command:

```
$ drush dis colorbox_file
The following extensions will be disabled: colorbox_file
Do you really want to continue? (y/n): y
colorbox_file was disabled successfully.     [ok]
$ drush pm-uninstall colorbox_file
The following modules will be uninstalled: colorbox_file
Do you really want to continue? (y/n): y
colorbox_file was successfully uninstalled.    [ok]
```

First, we disabled the `colorbox_file` module with the `dis` command, and uninstalled the module with the `pm-uninstall` command. The code we added to the new `colorbox_file_uninstall` function will get called when that command is executed. If you refresh the contents of the variable table, you will see that there are no longer any `colorbox_file_` variables:

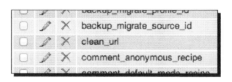

2. Now, in Aptana Studio, rename the `colorbox_file` folder to `media_colorbox`, and rename all of the files in the folder to begin with `media_colorbox` instead of `colorbox_file`. When we are done, the folder and contained files should look similar to the following:

3. Next, we need to rename all the function names and all references to Colorobox File and `colorbox_file` in the code. Rather than walking through each instance of renaming the function names, variable names, and documentation, replace the existing files with the `media_colorbox` files from the code download for this chapter.

4. Now that we have renamed everything, we need to test that everything still works. We will enable the newly named `media_colorbox` module with Drush:

```
$ drush en media_colorbox

The following extensions will be enabled: media_colorbox

Do you really want to continue? (y/n): y

media_colorbox was enabled successfully.     [ok]
```

5. Now, we need to test the changes that were made. In your favorite browser, click on the **Configuration** link in the **Admin** toolbar, then click on the **File types** link under the **Media** section, and click on the **manage fields** link for the **Image file** type.

6. On the **MANAGE FIELDS** page for the **Image file** type, click on the **edit** link for the **Caption** field.

7. On the **Caption field edit** page, scroll down to the **COLORBOX CAPTION FIELD** setting, check the **Use field as Colorbox caption** checkbox, and click on the **Save settings** button.

8. Now, click on the **Structure** link in the **Admin** toolbar, then click on the **Content types** link, and click on the **manage display** link for our Recipe content type.

9. On the **MANAGE DISPLAY** page for our Recipe content type, select the **Media Colorbox FORMAT** for the **Media** field, and click on the **format settings** button.

10. Configure the **Media Colorbox Format** settings, so that they match the following screen shot. Click on the **Update** button, and click on the **Save** button.

11. Now, we need to make sure that it works. Click on the **Find content** link in the **Shortcuts** bar, click on the link for the Cannellini Cumin Chicken Chili recipe, and click on the image of the spices for the **media** field (the second image in the first row), and you should see something similar to the following screenshot:

What just happened?

We renamed the Colorbox File module to the Media Colorbox module, and we tested the module to make sure that it still works after the non-trivial amount of files, functions and variables that were renamed.

Time for action – promoting the Media Colorbox module to be a full project on Drupal.org

Now that we have finished renaming the Colorbox File module to Media Colorbox, we are ready to promote it to full project status on Drupal.org.

1. First, we need to push the updated code to the sandbox repository. Executing the `git status` command at the command line in the `media_colorbox` directory (`d7dev/sites/all/modules/media_colorbox`), will return the following status information:

```
# On branch master

# Changes not staged for commit:

#    (use "git add/rm <file>..." to update what will be committed)

#    (use "git checkout -- <file>..." to discard changes in working
directory)

#

# modified:    README.txt

# deleted:     colorbox_file.info

# deleted:     colorbox_file.js

# deleted:     colorbox_file.module

# deleted:     colorbox_file.pages.inc

# deleted:     colorbox_file.theme.inc

#

# Untracked files:

#    (use "git add <file>..." to include in what will be committed)

#

# media_colorbox.info

# media_colorbox.install

# media_colorbox.js

# media_colorbox.module

# media_colorbox.pages.inc

# media_colorbox.theme.inc
```

2. Next, execute the following `git` commands to remove the old files, add the new files, commit the changes, and push the committed changes to the sandbox repository:

```
$ git add -A
$ git commit -m "renamed"
[master 99fc324] renamed
 9 files changed, 114 insertions(+), 93 deletions(-)
 delete mode 100644 colorbox_file.info
 delete mode 100644 colorbox_file.js
 create mode 100644 media_colorbox.info
 create mode 100644 media_colorbox.install
 create mode 100644 media_colorbox.js
 rename colorbox_file.module => media_colorbox.module (72%)
 rename colorbox_file.pages.inc => media_colorbox.pages.inc (73%)
 rename colorbox_file.theme.inc => media_colorbox.theme.inc (82%)
$ git push -u origin master
Counting objects: 11, done.
Delta compression using up to 2 threads.
Compressing objects: 100% (9/9), done.
Writing objects: 100% (9/9), 5.04 KiB, done.
Total 9 (delta 1), reused 0 (delta 0)
To kmadel@git.drupal.org:sandbox/kmadel/1084984.git
   3baa11c..99fc324  master -> master
Branch master set up to track remote branch master from origin.
```

3. Next, we will open up the Drupal.org page for the sandboxed Colorbox File module.

kmadel's sandbox: **Colorbox File**

View   Version control   Edit   Maintainers

Posted by kmadel on *March 8, 2011 at 12:26pm*

Experimental Project
This is a sandbox project, which contains experimental code for developer use only.

Visit the Version control tab for full directions.
Integrates Colorbox with the Media module via a custom colorbox file formatter.

Promote to full project

4. To start the process for promoting a sandbox module to a full project, you just need to click on the **Promote to full project** link.

5. On the **Promote** page, I will check both checkboxes, enter `media_colorbox` as the short name, and click next the **Promote to full project** button.

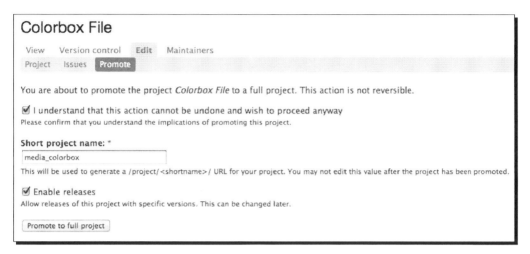

6. The next page asks if I am sure that I want to promote the module, and I am sure, so I will click next the **Promote** button:

7. Now, it is no longer a sandbox project and Drupal provides some important instructions regarding the remote repository for the project. The `git` command in the following screenshot needs to be executed before any new changes can be pushed to the remote repository, because Drupal moved it to a new location for full projects and to match the new short project name.

8. You may notice that although the short project name was changed to `media_colorbox`, the title of the module is still Colorbox File. We can click on the **Edit** link to modify the project title and description for the **Media Colorbox project** page.

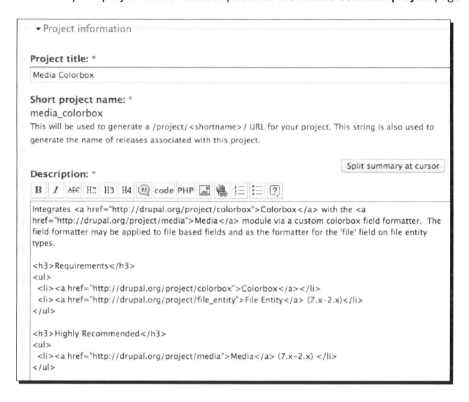

After updating the project name and description, the project will reflect the new name and the updated description.

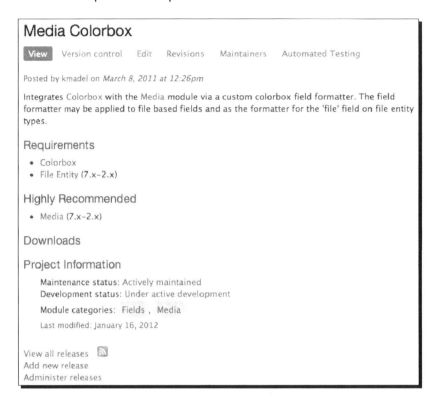

Now, we need to create a dev release for the Media Colorbox module, so that it is easier to download and install. Drupal provides instructions on the Version control page of a full project page for creating a branch for a dev release with git (These instructions are only displayed for module maintainers).

9. Executing the following `git` commands on our local Media Colorbox repository will create a new dev branch.

```
git checkout -b 7.x-1.x
git push -u origin 7.x-1.x
```

10. Now that we have a new dev branch in the Media Colorbox repository, we will be able to add a dev release to the project. On the **View** page of the Media Colorbox module, there is a **Add new release** link below the **Project information**. Clicking on that link will bring us to **Create Project release** page.

11. The **Create Project release** page lists only one Git release tag or branch to select from, the dev branch we just created, so we just need to click on the **Next** button.

12. On the **Create Project release details** page, we will enter some **Release notes**, and click on the **Save** button; the other fields will already be filled because this is the first dev release.

We have successfully promoted the Media Colorbox module to full project status, and have created an initial dev release.

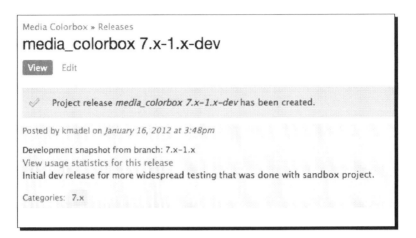

Drupal.org will automatically generate `tar.gz` and `zip` files, and attach them to the project, but it may take as long as 12 hours for a dev release (official non-dev releases are published within five minutes). Until then, only an unpublished release node will appear on the **Releases for Media Colorbox** page.

Summary

In this chapter, we learned more about the Views module, and have seen how a good Views plugin, along with some custom CSS, enabled us to create a very appealing rotating banner component for our d7dev site.

We learned that Drush has some hooks of its own, and saw how easy it is to add a simple Drush integration enhancement to the Views Slideshow module that will save others a bit of time when they install the module.

We also learned a bit about the Drupal `.install` file and how to use it to clean up after ourselves when our module is uninstalled. Finally, we learned how a module is promoted from a sandbox project to a full project.

In the next chapter, we are going to be introduced to `SimpleTest`. `SimpleTest` is a custom functional testing framework that was a contributed module for Drupal 6, and has been added to core for Drupal 7. After an overview of `SimpleTest` in core, we will write some of our own `SimpleTest` tests to test some of the code we have written in previous chapters.

10

Test Your Code with SimpleTest

There never seems to be enough time in the day to write additional code for testing your code. I have to admit that I am not a test first developer by nature. However, I do understand the importance and value that tests provide. Tests can be written and run whenever we add new functionality to our code. This will quickly let us know if our changes break any of the previously existing functionality. Drupal 7 includes a testing framework called **SimpleTest** *that makes writing tests for Drupal easier.*

The following topics will be covered in this chapter:

◆ An introduction to the SimpleTest testing framework for Drupal 7

◆ An overview of how SimpleTest is used with Drupal core

◆ Code Examples: Writing our own SimpleTest test cases

What is SimpleTest?

SimpleTest (`http://www.simpletest.org/`) is a PHP test framework similar to the **JUnit** test framework for Java. The purpose of the SimpleTest PHP framework is to make it easier to write unit tests and functional tests for PHP code.

> A **unit test** is intended to test the smallest testable part of an application from the programmer's perspective.
>
> A **functional test** (also known as **black-box testing**) is intended to test a component against a design or specification from a user's perspective. Functional tests are sometimes referred to as **web tests** in PHP and more specifically Drupal.

SimpleTest (`http://drupal.org/project/simpletest`) for Drupal is a Drupal-specific testing API that is modeled after the SimpleTest PHP framework. It is integrated with Drupal in order to make writing functional or web tests much easier than using the SimpleTest PHP framework by itself. Drupal SimpleTest was first introduced as a contributed module for Drupal 5, and was initially dependent on the SimpleTest PHP framework. However, as of the 6.2-x release of the SimpleTest module it is no longer dependent on any external libraries. Beginning with Drupal 7, the SimpleTest module was added to core.

Although the Drupal SimpleTest framework supports unit testing, it is primarily focused on functional or web testing.

SimpleTest in Drupal Core

As mentioned previously, SimpleTest was added as a core module to Drupal 7. It was also used extensively to develop Drupal core for the Drupal 7 release. Take a look into any of the core modules, and you will see one or more `.test` files. It has been noted by many core developers that Drupal 7 development was much quicker because of the use of SimpleTest. Anytime any major changes were made to the core code base, all of the core tests could be run to see if the new code broke any existing functionality. Without the SimpleTest test cases, it would have taken a person or persons hours, days, or even weeks to identify the same issues that are quickly identified by the SimpleTest test cases. You can see how continuously running these tests against any changes in your code, especially a code base as large as Drupal core, can speed up development. But, we first have to actually write the tests for our code!

SimpleTest web interface

The SimpleTest web interface for Drupal 7, located at `admin/config/development/testing`, enables you to run the test cases included with any installed module.

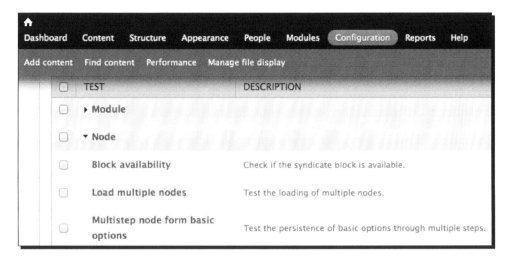

The tests are organized by groups specified in the test case definition (similar to the way that modules are organized by the package property in a modules .info file), and the **Testing configuration** screen enables you to run all available tests, run all of the tests for the selected test group or run individual test cases. The output for running the **NODE SAVE** test should look similar to the following screenshot (unless you wrote some code that broke the core Node module):

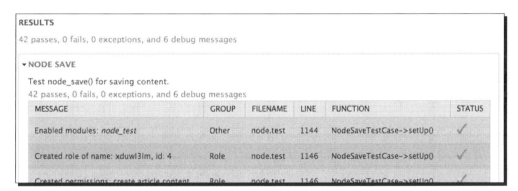

Test files structure for modules

There is some inconsistency regarding where the test files should be located within the module folder. Documentation on drupal.org (http://drupal.org/node/394888) states:

> All tests for a module are to be placed in a central test file in root of a
> module directory.

However, if you take a look at the directory structure of the core file and node modules, you will see the inconsistency. The core test file, `node.test`, for the node module is in the base `node` folder (even though there is also a `test` sub-folder). But, for the file module, the core test file, `file.test`, is placed in the `test` sub-folder:

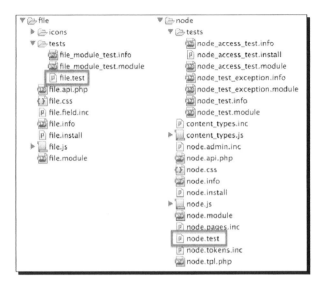

Although the documentation specifies placing the `.test` file at the root of the `module` directory, it makes a lot of sense to create a folder to keep a clean and organized module structure. The most important (and required) thing is that the module `.info` file specifies the location correctly. If the `.test` file isn't listed in the `.info` file, then it won't be useable regardless of where it is located. If you look at contributed modules that have tests, you will see a mixture of the `.test` file location much as we see here with core modules.

The SimpleTest class

SimpleTest is an OOP (recall the introduction to Object Oriented Programming for Drupal in *Chapter 8, Recipe Lists and More with Views*) framework with a base abstract class `DrupalTestCase`. The SimpleTest framework includes two base concrete classes that are to be extended by module-specific test cases:

1. `DrupalUnitTestCase`: This class cannot interact with the Drupal database nor call any functions that require a database. The `DrupalUnitTestCase` class does not enable any modules by default; all modules must be manually enabled.

2. `DrupalWebTestCase`: This class installs a temporary Drupal test environment that includes a database, and is stood up and torn down every time tests are run. It also enables the core modules.

All SimpleTest-based test classes will typically include the following two functions: `getInfo` **and** `setUp`.

The getInfo function

The `getInfo` function provides Drupal with the required information about the test. It consists of an array with the following properties:

- ◆ `name`: The name of the test as it will show up in the Drupal Testing configuration page.

- ◆ `description`: The description of the test, is displayed along with the name on the Drupal Testing configuration page.

- ◆ `group`: The group of tests this test case should fall under. This is usually the name of the module, but sometimes there are groups that contain tests for multiple modules.

The setUp function

The `setUp` function creates an initial starting state for a test. The `DrupalUnitTestCase` and `DrupalWebTestCase`, each have their own distinct version of the `setUp` function. In the case of web test cases, it will actually install a standalone Drupal test environment, and a custom test case will extend the function to include custom code to create any Drupal objects needed to run the test case. The `setUp` function for the `DrupalUnitTestCase` class does not install a temporary Drupal environment.

The `setUp` function is also used to enable any non-core modules needed to run the test case. By default, the only modules that are enabled for `DrupalWebTestCase` are the core modules. If you are testing a custom module, then you will need to, at the very least, enable that module.

Test functions

Test functions are the heart of a SimpleTest test case and where the actual test logic will be added. An extended SimpleTest class may have any number of test functions. The test functions, in turn, may do additional function-specific setup, and will make assertions about what is being tested.

Test assertions

Test assertions are the actual tests of SimpleTest. `DrupalUnitTestCase` and `DrupalWebTestCase` share a common set of assertion functions defined in the `DrupalTestCase` class. In addition to those shared assertions, `DrupalWebTestCase` includes a number of additional assertions that are specific to testing the web functionality of Drupal.

Unit Testing with the Drupal SimpleTest module

Although typically used for functional testing, the SimpleTest framework does support writing unit tests. Unit tests are created by extending the `DrupalUnitTestCase` class provided by the SimpleTest module. As the primary focus of the SimpleTest module is for functional or web test cases, it should be noted that there is not one unit test included with Druapl core. But, the **examples** module (`http://drupal.org/project/examples`) does include a unit test example.

> The examples module (`http://drupal.org/project/examples`) for developers is a great resource for code examples. It offers the example code for most of the major APIs and unique code constructs that are part of Drupal 7, to include writing a unit test with the SimpleTest framework. If you haven't already, I highly recommend that you download the examples module from the URL provided.

Take a look at the following SimpleTest code example from the examples module:

```
class SimpletestUnitTestExampleTestCase extends DrupalUnitTestCase {

  public static function getInfo() {
    return array(
      'name' => 'Simpletest Example unit tests',
      'description' => 'Test that simpletest_example_empty_mysql_date
        works properly.',
      'group' => 'Examples',
    );
  }

  function setUp() {
    drupal_load('module', 'simpletest_example');
    parent::setUp();
  }

  /**
    * Call simpletest_example_empty_mysql_date and check that it
      returns correct
   * result.
    *
    * Note that no environment is provided; we're just testing the
      correct
   * behavior of a function when passed specific arguments.
    */
  public function testSimpletestUnitTestExampleFunction() {
```

```
    $result = simpletest_example_empty_mysql_date(NULL);
    $message = t('A NULL value should return TRUE.');
    $this->assertTrue($result, $message);

    $result = simpletest_example_empty_mysql_date('');
    $message = t('An empty string should return TRUE.');
    $this->assertTrue($result, $message);

    $result = simpletest_example_empty_mysql_date('0000-00-00');
    $message = t('An "empty" MySQL DATE should return TRUE.');
    $this->assertTrue($result, $message);

    $result = simpletest_example_empty_mysql_date(date('Y-m-d'));
    $message = t('A valid date should return FALSE.');
    $this->assertFalse($result, $message);
  }
}
```

Notice how this `SimpletestUnitTestExampleTestCase` class extends
`DrupalUnitTestCase`. Once again, SimpleTest test cases for Drupal are typically extensions
of one of the two concrete classes (sometimes a complex module may have its own `base`
test class that extends one of the core concrete test classes). Then, within that class, there
will always be a `getInfo` function and usually a `setUp` function (especially in the case of
a web test case). The `getInfo` function provides the SimpleTest framework with required
information about the test, and the `setUp` function provides the initial state of a test. The
`setUp` function for a web test will typically be much more involved than it is for a SimpleTest
unit test, as you can see in the code that the `setUp` function is only loading a module and
executing the parent `setUp` function.

Functional or web testing with Drupal SimpleTest

The examples module also has an example of a functional test.

```
class SimpletestExampleTestCase extends DrupalWebTestCase {
  protected $privileged_user;

  public static function getInfo() {
    return array(
      'name' => 'Simpletest Example',
      'description' => 'Ensure that the simpletest_example content
        type provided functions properly.',
      'group' => 'Examples',
    );
  }
```

```
public function setUp() {
    parent::setUp('simpletest_example');  // Enable any modules
        required for the test
    // Create and log in our user. The user has the arbitrary
        //privilege
    // 'extra special edit any simpletest_example' which the code
        //uses
    // to grant access.
    $this->privileged_user = $this->drupalCreateUser(array('create
        simpletest_example content', 'extra special edit any "
        simpletest_example'));
    $this->drupalLogin($this->privileged_user);
}

// Create a simpletest_example node using the node form
public function testSimpleTestExampleCreate() {
    // Create node to edit.
    $edit = array();
    $edit['title'] = $this->randomName(8);
    $edit["body[und][0][value]"] = $this->randomName(16);
    $this->drupalPost('node/add/simpletest-example',
        $edit, t('Save'));
    $this->assertText(t('Simpletest Example Node Type @title has
        been created.', array('@title' => $edit['title'])));
}

...

}
```

Notice that this functional test extends the `DrupalWebTestCase` class rather than the `DrupalUnitTestCase` class. This test also includes the `getInfo` and `setUp` functions as did the previous unit test case example. Although there is not much more `setUp` code versus the unit test example, you will notice that the `setUp` function for this functional test case calls a function that will interact with the database: `drupalCreateUser`. The `DrupalUnitTestCase` class does not support any interaction with the database.

Time for another recipe

We will switch things up a bit, and have some desert. This rich and creamy Chocolate Joe-Joe ice cream should satisfy chocolate lovers and cookie lovers alike.

- ◆ `name`: Chocolate Joe-Joe Ice Cream

- ◆ `cuisineType`: American

- ◆ `description`: This rich and creamy chocolate ice cream includes delicious Joe-Joe cookies.

- ◆ `recipeYield`: Eight servings

- ◆ `prepTime`: 20 minutes

- ◆ `cookTime`: 150 minutes

- ◆ `ingredients`:

  - ❑ Two cups heavy cream

  - ❑ One cup whole milk

  - ❑ One cup cocoa powder

  - ❑ Three-fourth cup brown sugar

  - ❑ Three-fourth cup granulated sugar

  - ❑ One tablespoon vanilla extract

- ❑ One pinch salt
- ❑ One cup coarsely chopped Joe-Joe cookies (may substitute Oreos)
- ❑ One tablespoon crushed red pepper

◆ `instructions:`

1. Combine brown sugar, granulated sugar, and salt in a large mixing bowl.
2. Pour milk into sugar mixture, and use electric mixer to beat until sugar is dissolved.
3. Slowly add heavy cream, using a whisk to thoroughly combine with the sugar mixture.
4. Add vanilla and whisk to combine.
5. Add cocoa powder, and stir with whisk until completely combined.
6. Pour the mixture into an air-tight container, and place it in the freezer for one hour.
7. Take the mixture out of the freezer, and pour it into ice cream machine.
8. Mix for 30 minutes or a bit longer if it doesn't start to thicken.
9. Pour the mixture into an air-tight container, and place it in the freezer for two hours.
10. Before serving, remove it from freezer and let sit for ten minutes at room temperature.

Writing our own SimpleTests

We are going to write a SimpleTest test for the duration integer field formatter that we developed back in *Chapter 2, Custom Content Types and an Introduction to Module Development*. We will start by creating a unit test case, and create a web test case.

Time for action – creating a unit test case for the D7Dev duration formatter

If you recall, the duration formatter (`d7dev_integer_duration`) is defined in the d7dev module. The GCD function used in the `d7dev_field_formatter_view` function is a perfect candidate for a unit test, as it is completely self-contained, and does not depend on any external modules nor database interaction.

1. Expand the `sites/all/modules/custom/d7dev` folder in Aptana Studio, then right-click on that folder, and create a new folder named `tests`.

2. Next, right-click on the newly created tests folder, and create a new file named `d7dev.test`.

3. Now, open up the `d7dev.info` file, and add the following file setting:

```
files[] = tests/d7dev.test
```

Remember, it doesn't matter where you place your test files within a module as long as the location is correctly specified in the `.info` file.

4. Switch back to the `d7dev.test` file, and add the following code:

```php
<?php

/**
 * @file
 * Tests for d7dev.module.
 */

/**
 * Unit test for d7dev_integer_duration formatter
 */
class DurationFormatterUnitTestCase extends DrupalUnitTestCase{

}
```

Along with some documentation, you can see that we are extending the `DrupalUnitTestCase` class.

5. Next, we will add the necessary `getInfo` function:

```php
public static function getInfo() {
  return array(
    'name'  => 'Duration formatter unit test',
    'description'  => 'Unit test the gcd function for the
      duration formatter.',
    'group' => 'D7Dev'
  );
}
```

As discussed previously, the `getInfo` function returns an array that will register our test case with Drupal, and control what is displayed on the **Testing configuration** page.

6. Now we will add the `setUp` function:

```
function setUp() {
  parent::setUp('d7dev');
}
```

Not much to it, we are just telling the SimpleTest framework to load the `d7dev` module, so that we will be able to call its GCD function in our `test` function. Now that we have the test defined and set up it, is time to create a test function.

7. Add the following test function after the `setUp` function:

```
/**
 * Test greatest common denominator function.
 */
function testNumberDurationField() {
  $gcdResult = gcd(40, 60);//expect this to be 20
  //use assertEqual to check if we get the expected value
  $this->assertEqual(20, $gcdResult, t('Greatest common
    denominator for 60 and 40 is @result.', array('@result' =>
    $gcdResult)));
}
```

First, we are calling the GCD function from `d7dev.module`. Then, we use the `assertEqual` function from the base `DrupalTestCase` class to test or assert that the outcome of the GCD function is equal to the expected result of 20. Now, we are ready to run the tests in the browser.

8. Load the d7dev site in your browser, click on the **Configuration** link in the **Admin** toolbar, then click on the **Performance** link under the `Development` section.

9. On the **Performance administrative** screen, click on the **Clear all caches** button.

Our Drupal environment will not pick up our new tests until we clear the caches.

10. Next, click on the **Configuration** link in the **Admin** toolbar, then click on the **Testing** link under the **Development** section.

11. On the **Testing administrative** screen, scroll down to and expand the `D7Dev` group that we specified in the `getInfo` function of our test case, and you will see the new unit test case we added.

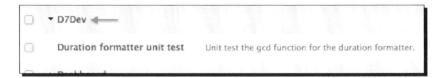

12. Now, select the checkbox for our **Duration formatter unit test**, then scroll down and click on the **Run tests** button. You will see the following output on the **Test result** screen:

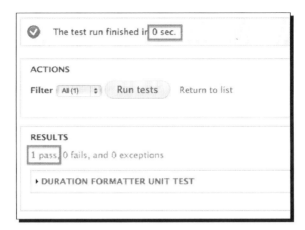

Note that the test ran in only **0** seconds and under **RESULTS**, there was **1pass**. We only made one assertion in our unit test, so we will only have one result.

13. Next, expand the **DURATION FORMATTER UNIT TEST** section, and you will see a detailed summary of the test we just ran.

What just happened?

We created our first SimpleTest test, a simple unit test for our custom duration field formatter.

Now that we have created a simple unit test for our custom field formatter, we will now create a web test case.

Time for action – creating a web test case for the D7Dev duration formatter

The `d7dev_integer_duration` formatter is a perfect candidate for a web test case.

1. In Aptana Studio, open the `d7dev.test file`, and add the following code after the unit test case we just added:

```
/**
 * Web test for d7dev_integer_duration formatter.
 */
class DurationFormatterWebTestCase extends DrupalWebTestCase {

}
```

Rather than extending `DrupalUnitTestCase`, we are extending the `DrupalWebTestCase` class.

2. Now, we will add some global variables and the required `getInfo` function:

```
protected $field;
protected $instance;
protected $test_user;

public static function getInfo() {
  return array(
    'name'  => 'Duration formatter web test',
    'description'  => 'Test the creation and display of number
    field with duration formatter.',
    'group' => 'D7Dev'
  );
}
```

Again, the `getInfo` settings will be displayed on the **Testing configuration** page. The global variables defined above the `getInfo` function will be used throughout the test case.

3. Next, the necessary `setUp` code to execute our web test case, is as follows:

```
function setUp() {
  parent::setUp('d7dev');
  $this->test_user = $this->drupalCreateUser(array('access
content','create article content'));
  $this->drupalLogin($this->test_user);
}
```

In addition to loading the d7dev module, we are creating a test user, and then logging into the Drupal test environment installed by the parent `setUp` function code with that test user. The `drupalCreateUser` and `drupalLogin` functions are provided by the `DrupalWebTestCase` class that we are extending, and are not available in a `DrupalUnitTestCase`. The `drupalCreateUser` takes an array of permissions to be applied to our test user for interaction with our test case, and we log that user in with the `drupalLogin` function.

4. Now that we have a logged in user, we can start doing stuff with that user. Add the following test function below our `setUp` function:

```
/**
 * Test the d7dev_integer_duration formatter output.
 */
function testNumberDurationField() {

}
```

5. The first thing we will have our test user do is create a new `number_integer` field on the article content type to include applying our custom duration formatter.

```
// Create a field with the d7dev_integer_duration formatter.
$this->field = array(
  'field_name' => drupal_strtolower($this->randomName()),
  'type' => 'number_integer',
);
field_create_field($this->field);
$this->instance = array(
  'field_name' => $this->field['field_name'],
  'entity_type' => 'node',
  'bundle' => 'article',
  'widget' => array(
    'type' => 'number',
  ),
  'display' => array(
    'default' => array(
      'type' => 'd7dev_integer_duration',
    ),
  ),
);
field_create_instance($this->instance);
```

Note the use of the `randomName` function (wrapped with the `drupal_strtolower` function) that is used as the value for the `field_name`. The `randomName` function belongs to the `DrupalTestCase` class, so it is available for both unit test cases and web test cases. Then, we set the default display to `d7dev_integer_duration`, so that this field will use our custom formatter. Finally, we use the `field_create_instance` function to create the field we defined. The `field_create_instance` function is a function in the core field module, and even though we didn't explicitly enable the field module in our test case `setUp` function, it is available because the `DrupalWebTestCase` class `setUp` function enables all core modules.

6. Next, we need to have the test user create a new article content item, set the value of the `number_integer` field we just added, and then save the new article.

```
// Display creation form.
$this->drupalGet('node/add/article');
$langcode = LANGUAGE_NONE;

// Submit a integer value; formatted it should become '1 and
  3/4'.
$value = '105';
$edit = array(
  'title' => $this->randomName(),
  "{$this->field['field_name']}[$langcode][0][value]" =>
    $value,
);
$this->verbose('$edit: ' . var_export($edit, TRUE));
$this->drupalPost(NULL, $edit, t('Save'));
```

First, we used the `drupalGet` function (a `DrupalWebTestCase` function) to load the add article form. We then created a `$edit` array that will set the value for our `number_integer` to 105, and we also set the `title` field as it is a required field for a node form. Then, before we call the `drupalPost` function to save the new article node, we make use of the verbose function. The verbose function will create a link to a page that will output the resulting `$edit` array, and will allow us to see that the `number_integer` field we added has the correct value of 105.

7. Now, it is just a matter of asserting that our custom formatter is formatting the `number_integer` field with a value of 105 correctly:

```
//the d7dev_integer_duration should convert the integer to
  //hours and fraction of an hour
$this->assertRaw('1 and <sup>3</sup>&frasl;<sub>4</sub>',
  t('Value formatted correctly.'));
```

The assertion that we will use is the `assertRaw` function (again, a `DrupalWebTestCase` class specific function). The `assertRaw` function returns `true` if the raw (or HTML fragment) text being passed into the function is found in the HTML source of the page being loaded. Now, we are ready to run our web test case.

8. Load the d7dev site in your browser, click on the **Configuration** link in the **Admin** toolbar, then click on the **Performance** link under the **Development** section.

9. On the **Performance administrative** screen, click on the **Clear all caches** button. Anytime that you add another test case to your `.test` file, you will have to clear the caches, so that it is picked up by Drupal.

10. Next, click on the **Configuration** link in the **Admin** toolbar, and click on the **Testing** link under the **Development** section.

11. On the **Testing administrative** screen, scroll down to and expand the **D7Dev** group that we specified in the `getInfo` function of our test case, and you will see the new web test case we added.

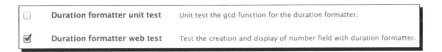

12. Now, select the checkbox for our **Duration formatter unit test**, then scroll down and click on the **Run tests** button. First, you will notice that it took a good deal longer for this test case to run than it took for our unit test case. Then, you will see the following output on the **Test result** screen:

13. This web test case took much longer than the unit test that we wrote. That is mainly due to the fact that the `setUp` function for the `DrupalWebTestCase` basically does a Drupal install every time you run a test case that extends that class (the installed test Drupal environment is temporary as it is "torn" down by the `DrupalWebTestCase` tearDown function). Also notice that there were 14 passes even though we only made one literal assertion in our test case:

```
$this->assertRaw('1 and <sup>3</sup>&frasl;<sub>4</sub>',
  t('Value formatted correctly.'));;
```

Many of the DrupalWebTestCase functions will make their own assertions.

14. Expand the **DURATION FORMATTER WEB TEST** link to view the detailed results of our web test case.

MESSAGE	GROUP	FILENAME	LINE	FUNCTION	STATUS
GET http://d7dev.local:8888/user/2 returned 200 (7.36 KB).	Browser	d7dev.test	55	DurationFormatterWebTestCase->setUp()	✓
Valid HTML found on "http://d7dev.local:8888/user/2"	Browser	d7dev.test	55	DurationFormatterWebTestCase->setUp()	✓
Verbose message	Debug	d7dev.test	55	DurationFormatterWebTestCase->setUp()	⚠
User yUTpLMn4 successfully logged in.	User login	d7dev.test	55	DurationFormatterWebTestCase->setUp()	✓
GET http://d7dev.local:8888/node/add/article returned 200 (15.08 KB).	Browser	d7dev.test	84	DurationFormatterWebTestCase->testNumberDurationField()	✓
Valid HTML found on "http://d7dev.local:8888/node/add/article"	Browser	d7dev.test	84	DurationFormatterWebTestCase->testNumberDurationField()	✓
Verbose message	Debug	d7dev.test	84	DurationFormatterWebTestCase->testNumberDurationField()	⚠
Verbose message	Debug	d7dev.test	93	DurationFormatterWebTestCase->testNumberDurationField()	⚠
GET http://d7dev.local:8888/node/1 returned 200 (11.78 KB).	Browser	d7dev.test	94	DurationFormatterWebTestCase->testNumberDurationField()	✓
Valid HTML found on "http://d7dev.local:8888/node/1"	Browser	d7dev.test	94	DurationFormatterWebTestCase->testNumberDurationField()	✓
Verbose message	Debug	d7dev.test	94	DurationFormatterWebTestCase->testNumberDurationField()	⚠
Value formatted correctly. ⟵	Other	d7dev.test	97	DurationFormatterWebTestCase->testNumberDurationField()	✓

Basically, enabling of modules with the `setUp` function, successful creation of certain objects (in this case, the creation of a role, permissions, and a user with the `drupalCreateUser` function), gets, and posts of actual pages with `drupalGet` and `drupalPost`, and of course any explicit assertion, such as `assertRaw`, will result in a SimpleTest pass or a fail. Also, besides our explicit call to the verbose function, many of the parent test case functions (the test case we are extending) will generate a Verbose message—basically, anytime there is any type of HTML markup generated, there will be a verbose message.

15. Right-click on the first **Verbose message** link to open it in a new tab, and you will see the actual physical output that these test functions are generating in the temporary test Drupal install created by the `setUp` function of `DrupalWebTestCase`.

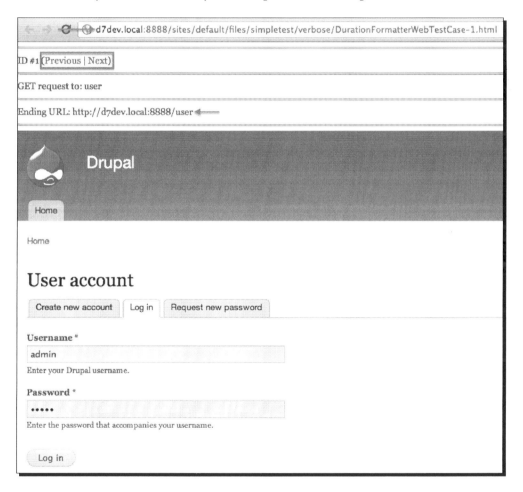

First, notice the actual URL of the page ends with `sites/default/files/
simpletest/verbose/DurationFormatterWebTestCase-1.html`. But,
also notice that the verbose output includes an ending URL, and in this case,
it is `http://d7dev.local:8888/user`. Remember, the `setUp` function of
`DrupalWebTestCase` actually installs a temporary Drupal test environment and
tears it down after the test case has completed. So, any time there is verbose output
to be generated, it is actually a static representation of the page written as an HTML
fragment to the files directory. Next, notice the **Previous** and **Next** links at the top of
the page. These links will allow us to navigate through all of the verbose output for
the current test case.

16. Click on the **Next** link, and continue to click on it until you get to `sites/default/
files/simpletest/verbose/DurationFormatterWebTestCase-5.html`.

In addition to displaying the actual output within the default theme, the verbose output also includes the PHP array that was posted to create the new article node by the call to `drupalPost`. You can see for yourself that our duration field formatter formatted the test integer field correctly.

What just happened?

We created a functional (or web) test case for our d7dev module that will test that the `duration` field formatter will properly format an integer field, and learned how web test cases are processed by the Drupal SimpleTest framework.

Summary

In this chapter, we have learned about unit testing, web or functional testing with the SimpleTest framework, and how to write tests for own custom Drupal code. To learn even more about what you can and can't do with SimpleTest test cases in Drupal, I recommend reading through the SimpleTest source code, specifically the classes defined in the `drupal_web_test_case.php` file. The code is very well documented, and available in any Drupal 7 install.

In the next chapter, we are going to take a look at another useful tool for developing and managing configuration between sites—the **Features** module.

11

Introduction to the Features Module and Configuration Management

*In this chapter, we are going to introduce you to the **Features module**, and show how it can be used to not only share Drupal components with other Drupal users' sites, but also to manage certain aspects of Drupal configuration between different environments of the same site (a development site versus a live site, for example).*

The following topics will be covered in this chapter:

◆ An introduction to the Features module

◆ An introduction to the concept of Drupal configuration management

◆ Using the Features module to create a reusable Recipe content type module

◆ Using Features to manage the updated configuration between two environments of the same site

Introduction to the Features module

The Features module (`http://drupal.org/project/features`) allows you to export certain Drupal site components (such as Content Types, Image styles, or Views, among many others) as code that is dynamically generated by the Features module, and added to a generated module or Feature. These Features-generated modules can then be installed and enabled on other sites to make those custom components instantly available without repetitive, and sometimes extensive, manual configuration, or the need to write any custom code.

For example, we may want to share our Recipe content type and recipe-related Views for use with other sites. The Features module would allow us to do this quite easily. Although the Features module was originally developed with the intent of sharing Drupal components with other Drupal users' sites, many Drupal developers quickly began using the Features module to manage the configuration of Drupal components between different environments of the same Drupal site.

Using Features to manage configuration

Again, the Features module was not initially developed with the intent of using it to manage configuration between environments. But, it has become one of the best options available for Drupal 7 configuration management between site environments. It should be noted that the vast majority of the configuration for a Drupal site is maintained as data in the Drupal database. At some point, you are going to want to deploy your Drupal 7 site from your local development environment to a publicly accessible host. Even if you intend on hosting your publicly-available Drupal 7 site yourself, it is a best practice to keep all active development separate from the live or publicly available version of your site. You never know when some code you are writing or some new module you want to try out may break your entire site. So, it is always best to test any and all changes in a local development environment. However, one of the biggest hurdles in maintaining two or more environments (in many cases there will be three or four different environments for one Drupal site—development, integration, QA, and production) for the same Drupal site is managing configuration between those sites. Since any configuration that is done using the Drupal web-based administrative UI is persisted to the Drupal database; managing that configuration involves figuring out how to get the necessary configuration data from the database of one site/environment to another site/environment.

Some options for managing configuration between different Drupal site environments include:

◆ **Migrating or synchronizing databases between environments**:

Migrating/synchronizing databases between environments may work fine if there is just one person developing and adding content to the site, and it is an excellent way to initially set up a new environment (for example, when setting up a live/production site for the first time). However, this approach becomes especially difficult to manage if there are multiple developers, or when administrators are directly configuring the live site and/or content authors are directly adding content to the live site. The development and production databases will quickly become out of sync, and it will become very difficult to merge changes between the development database and the live database.

◆ **Manually updating configuration between environments**:

Not only is this a tedious process for managing configuration between environments, but also it is prone to errors, and may result in a lot of headaches when you try to figure out why something doesn't look right or isn't working as expected between environments. Just go back and take a look at *Chapter 2, Custom Content Types and an Introduction to Module Development*, and see how many steps were involved to create the Recipe content type. In addition to a single custom content type, suppose you had three or four additional custom content types, several Views, and a few custom image styles. That would be a lot of custom configuration to manage manually.

◆ **Writing custom code for all configuration changes**:

We could have written custom code to create our D7Dev Recipe content type in a custom module rather than using the Drupal administrative UI. Enabling the module would enable the custom content type, and we would be able to use that content type across environments or sites by installing and enabling the custom module. If we wanted to add an additional field to that content type, then we would update the code of the Recipe content type module, and update that module in the other environments or sites. However, the Features module will generate all of the code needed to programmatically generate a content type that was created with the Drupal administrative UI. It only takes a few clicked checkboxes and button clicks. If you want to add a field, then you would use the Drupal administrative UI to add it, and then use the Features to update that feature. So, rather than writing a bunch of custom code to create a complex content type, why not let the Features module generate the code for us.

Managing configuration between different environments for a Drupal site has been recognized as an important capability to improve the Drupal platform. For Drupal 8, a core configuration management initiative has been announced, making the addition of configuration management to Drupal core a primary goal of the next major Drupal release. If you are interested in learning more about the Configuration Management Initiative for Drupal 8, then check out `http://groups.drupal.org/build-systems-change-management/cmi`.

Drupal components that can be managed with Features

There are two distinct categories of Drupal components that can be managed with the Features module: Drupal components supported by Features directly and Drupal components that are supported by additional Features-related modules.

Features supported components

The Features module includes custom code to support some of these components, and many more are supported by the excellent **CTools** integration that the Features module includes.

- **Content types**: Selecting a content type as a component of a feature will automatically include all the fields associated with that content type and Taxonomy vocabularies referenced by any Term reference field (although in the case of a Term reference field, Features will not include the vocabulary terms).

- **Fields**: Although individual fields may be selected as a component of a feature, fields are automatically added as dependencies when creating features with content type components, and are not typically added manually.

- **Image styles**: Custom image styles are available as components to be exported as features. You may recall from *Chapter 6, Adding Media to our Site*, that we created an image style with custom code. You may find that it is easier to use Features to create custom image styles. If you use the Image styles administrative UI to create a new image style and add it as a component to a feature, then you will find that the Features generated code is very similar to the custom code that we wrote in *Chapter 6*.

- **Text formats**: There is typically not as much configuration involved with text input filters as there is for content types or Views, but it is definitely easier to add any custom text format filter configuration to an easily-managed Features generated module, than it is to remember what text format filter changes you made in your development site that need to be manually configured when you are ready to launch the live version of your site.

- **Menus**: On large sites, menu entries can become quite extensive and tedious to manage manually. This is an especially useful Features component when developing custom code for displaying menus that more than one developer may be working on.

- **Taxonomies**: Although useful for exporting custom vocabularies that are associated to Term reference fields of an exported content type, the taxonomy Features component does not include the terms associated with the exported vocabularies.

- **Views**: Custom Views are an excellent candidate for a Features module. Just take a look back at *Chapter 8, Recipe Lists and More with Views*, to see how many steps might be needed to configure some more complex Views. Attempting to manually duplicate that configuration in any number of additional environments would be tedious to say the least. It should be noted that Views actually includes the ability to export the configuration for a custom view. However, this is exported as text, and must be managed manually between sites. Having a Views-based Features module that only needs to be installed and enabled as a module is a much more straightforward process.

- **Roles and permissions**: The ability to manage the configuration of roles and permissions on a simple site may not be all that useful. However, once you start modifying a number of permissions and adding more than a couple custom roles to your site, you will quickly come to appreciate the ability to manage this type of configuration with a Features-generated module.

- Again, every Drupal component that you are able to add to a Features module is that much less manual configuration that is necessary to manage between sites or environments.

 When managing configuration between environments with the Features module, it is important to be cognizant of any possible interdependencies between your custom Features modules. If at all possible, all of your Features modules should be self-contained and should not share common components between different Features modules. You should also try to minimize the number of components in any one given Features module. It is much easier to manage and maintain several custom Features module with no interdependencies and a limited number of components, than it is to manage just a few monolithic Features with a spider web of interdependencies.

Drupal components supported with additional modules

There are a number of contributed modules that were developed to add Features capabilities for unsupported components, or enhance support for some components already supported. The following list is not complete, but rather covers some of the components supported by Features add-on modules that I have found useful.

- **Core Blocks**: The Features module by itself does not support core blocks. The Features **Extra module** (`http://drupal.org/project/features_extra`) enables the ability to export custom block configuration as a feature. Another solution to managing blocks' configuration with Features is to use the **Context module** (`http://drupal.org/project/context`) for managing blocks layout to replace the core Blocks module with the **Boxes module** (`http://drupal.org/project/boxes`). Both the Context and Boxes modules have excellent Features support.

- **Content**: Typically, you wouldn't want to manage content between environments or different sites with Features. However, there are some cases where there is core content for a site that will be exactly the same between environments. Another interesting way that you may want to take advantage of a content type-based Features module is to populate a development environment with content from your live site to enable better testing of new features in development. The **UUID Features Integration module** (`http://drupal.org/project/uuid_features`) adds the ability to add specific content nodes as components of a feature.

Drupal 7 core modules and Drupal 7 contributed modules have introduced a concept of a machine name (the concept of a machine name was part of some Drupal 6 contributed modules, but was only introduced to core with Drupal 7). A machine name will be guaranteed to be unique for a single Drupal instance and a particular type of component. For example, you can't have two taxonomy vocabularies with the same machine name or two Views with the same machine name on the same site. This uniqueness is not guaranteed across different sites.

UUIDs are meant to provide a unique identifier across any and all Drupal instances of a given component across sites. A UUID makes it possible to copy unique components or entities between sites, and ensure that they do not collide with the system identifier of an already existing entity of the same type. That is why something like a node ID would not work. As an example, suppose you have two sites, and you would like to share content from one site with the other. You have created 10 nodes on the site where you want to add content from the other site, but the site from which you want to add content only has five nodes. The node ID of the nodes on your content origination site are 1 to 5, and the node ID of the nodes on the target site are 1-10. So, you could import those nodes and force a new node ID of 11 to 15 on them, but then there would be no way of updating those nodes with any changes that may occur on the origination site. A UUID would not only enable the initial export and import of nodes forms one site to another (that is the easy part), but it would also allow for on-going updates of the imported node of a target site based on any changes that may have been applied to the shared node on the originating site.

- **Vocabulary terms**: Many times, you will have a vocabulary with terms that are not meant to be manipulated by anyone, but administrative users. Or, you may have a custom view that uses a particular vocabulary term as the value for a term-based filter. These types of vocabularies are excellent candidates for managing as Features-generated modules. This extended Features functionality is provided by the UUID Features Integration module.

- **Variables**: Any variables that are in the Drupal variables table can be added as a component to a Features-generated module by installing the **Strongarm module** (http://drupal.org/project/strongarm).

In addition to these components, there are a number of contributed modules that include custom Features support to enable easy management of configuration, and the creation of shareable Features utilizing the functionality of those contributed modules. A list of some of these modules is available at http://drupal.org/taxonomy/term/11478.

Time for action – installing the Features module

Now, we will install the Features modules so that we can learn how to utilize it to help with Drupal configuration management.

1. Open the Terminal (Mac OS X) or Command Prompt (Windows) application, and change to the root directory of our d7dev site.

2. Use Drush to download and enable the Features module,

   ```
   $ drush dl features

   Project features (7.x-1.0-beta6) downloaded to /Applications/MAMP/
   htdocs/d7dev/sites/all/modules/features.  [success]

   $ drush en features

   The following extensions will be enabled: features

   Do you really want to continue? (y/n): y

   features was enabled successfully.                    [ok]
   ```

3. Now, open our d7dev site in your browser, and click on the **Structure** link in the **Admin** toolbar, then click on the **Features** link, and you will see the following **Features** administrative screen for managing Features.

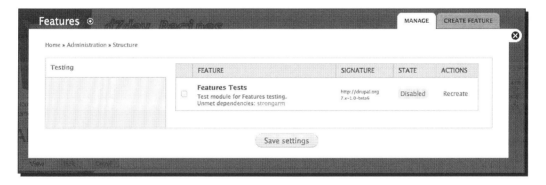

Typically, to enable a feature, you just select the checkbox of the feature on the **Features MANAGE** administrative screen, and click on the **Save settings** button. However, you will notice that you are not able to select the **Features Tests feature** checkbox in this screenshot. This is because that feature depends on the strongarm module that we mentioned, and we have not installed or enabled that module for our D7Dev site. The Features module is not only able to determine the external dependencies of a given feature, but it is also able to enforce the validation of those dependencies.

What just happened?

We enabled the Features module, and explored the administrative page for managing Features.

Adding a new Feature

Now, we are going to create our first D7Dev-specific feature, and enable that feature in a new live environment for our D7Dev site. We are going to create a Features module that will allow us to manage the configuration of our custom Recipe content type between a development and live environment.

Time for action – creating a Recipe content type feature

Now that we have installed the Features module, we are ready to create our first feature.

1. Open our d7dev site in your browser, and click on the **Structure** link in the **Admin** toolbar, then click on the **Features** link.

2. Once the **Features MANAGE** page loads, click on the **CREATE FEATURE** tab.

3. On the **CREATE FEATURE** page, enter `D7Dev Recipe content` type as the **Name**, `Content type for entering recipes.` as the **Description**, and `7.x-1.0-beta1` as the **Version**.

4. Next, select **Content types: node** from the **Edit** components select list, check the checkbox for our custom Recipe content type, and click on the **Download feature** button.

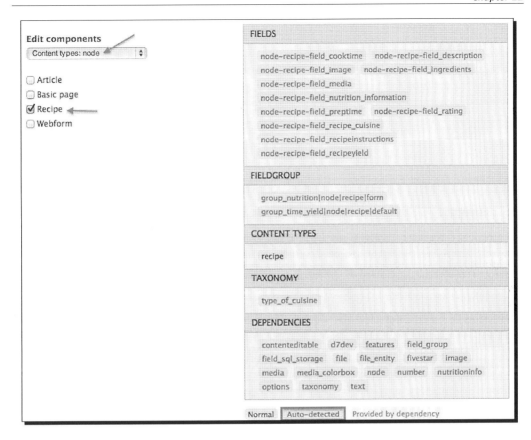

Notice the **Auto-detected** dependencies automatically included by the Features module. The Features module automatically included all of the fields that we created for the Recipe content type: the custom field groups, the vocabulary we associated with the recipe cuisine field, and all of the modules that the Recipe content type depends on (mainly for field formatters we specified on the **MANAGE DISPLAY** screen for our Recipe content type).

5. Next, we will use the following command to un-tar and copy the `d7dev_recipe_content_type` feature from your browser's `download` folder to a newly created `sites/all/modules/d7dev_features` folder in our d7dev site (the path to your downloaded feature may vary, so please check).

6. Open the Terminal (Mac OS X) or Command Prompt (Windows) application, and change to the root directory of our d7dev site.

```
$ cd /Applications/MAMP/htdocs/d7dev/

$ mkdir sites/all/modules/d7dev_features

$ tar -C /Applications/MAMP/htdocs/d7dev/sites/all/modules/d7dev_
features/ -xvf ~/Downloads/d7dev_recipe_content_type-7.x-1.0-
beta1.tar

x d7dev_recipe_content_type/d7dev_recipe_content_type.features.
field.inc

x d7dev_recipe_content_type/d7dev_recipe_content_type.field_group.
inc

x d7dev_recipe_content_type/d7dev_recipe_content_type.features.inc

x d7dev_recipe_content_type/d7dev_recipe_content_type.features.
taxonomy.inc

x d7dev_recipe_content_type/d7dev_recipe_content_type.info

x d7dev_recipe_content_type/d7dev_recipe_content_type.module

$
```

7. Now, we are going to use Drush to enable the `recipe` feature for our D7Dev site.

```
$ cd /Applications/MAMP/htdocs/d7dev/

$ drush en d7dev_recipe_content_type

The following extensions will be enabled: d7dev_recipe_content_
type

Do you really want to continue? (y/n): y

d7dev_recipe_content_type was enabled successfully.          [ok]

$
```

> Even though enabling our `d7dev_recipe_content_type` feature will not change or add anything to our Recipe content type, we still enable it so that any future changes to our custom Recipe content type will result in the feature state being overridden, signifying the need to update the feature.

8. Before we create a new Drupal site for a live environment, we are going to add and commit the feature we just copied to our d7dev Git repository:

```
$ cd /Applications/MAMP/htdocs/d7dev/

$ git add -A

$ git commit -m 'add recipe content type feature'

[master 8903cd1] add recipe content type feature

 13 files changed, 1039 insertions(+), 166 deletions(-)

 create mode 100644 sites/all/modules/d7dev_features/d7dev_recipe_
content_type/d7dev_recipe_content_type.features.field.inc

 create mode 100644 sites/all/modules/d7dev_features/d7dev_recipe_
content_type/d7dev_recipe_content_type.features.inc

 create mode 100644 sites/all/modules/d7dev_features/d7dev_recipe_
content_type/d7dev_recipe_content_type.features.taxonomy.inc

 create mode 100644 sites/all/modules/d7dev_features/d7dev_recipe_
content_type/d7dev_recipe_content_type.field_group.inc

 create mode 100644 sites/all/modules/d7dev_features/d7dev_recipe_
content_type/d7dev_recipe_content_type.info

 create mode 100644 sites/all/modules/d7dev_features/d7dev_recipe_
content_type/d7dev_recipe_content_type.module

$

Now we will create a live environment for our D7Dev site by using
Git to clone a copy of our D7Dev site.

$ cd /Applications/MAMP/htdocs/

$ git clone /Applications/MAMP/htdocs/d7dev/ d7live

Cloning into d7live...

done.

$
```

By adding and committing the `d7dev_recipe_content_type` feature to our D7Dev site Git repository before we used Git to clone it to our new D7Live site, we now have that feature available to be enabled in the D7Live site, once it is up and running.

9. Once the Git clone process is complete, follow the instructions from *Chapter 1*, *Getting Set up*, for creating a database, substituting the name d7live for d7dev, then visit the new site at http://localhost/d7live/. You should see the default Drupal 7 setup screen:

10. Complete the setup process just as we did in *Chapter 1*, once again, ensuring that you substitute the d7live database for the d7dev database, and name the site D7Live.

11. Next, open the Terminal (Mac OS X) or Command Prompt (Windows) application, change to the root directory of our new d7live site, and use Drush to download and enable the Features module for our d7live site.

```
$ drush dl features

Project features (7.x-1.0-beta6) downloaded to /Applications/MAMP/
htdocs/d7dev/sites/all/modules/features.  [success]

$ drush en features

The following extensions will be enabled: features

Do you really want to continue? (y/n): y

features was enabled successfully.                    [ok]
```

12. Next, enter the drush command within the d7live folder; you will see that there are a set of Features-specific Drush commands available.

```
$drush

All commands in features: (features)
 features-add (fa)      Add a component to a feature module.

 features-diff (fd)     Show the difference between the default and
overridden state of a feature.

 features-export (fe)   Export a feature from your site into a
module.

 features-list (fl,     List all the available features for your si
te.

 features)

 features-revert (fr)   Revert a feature module on your site.

 features-revert-all    Revert all enabled feature module on your
site.

 (fr-all, fra)

 features-update (fu)   Update a feature module on your site.

 features-update-all    Update all feature modules on your site.

 (fu-all, fua)
```

13. Next, in your browser, click on the **Structure** link of the **Admin** toolbar of the new D7Live site, and click on the **Features** link. You will see the D7Dev Recipe content type feature in a **Disabled STATE**.

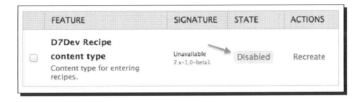

14. Click on the **Disabled** link in the **STATE** column, and you will see an overview screen for the feature that includes a table of dependency with a status of **Enabled** or **Disabled**.

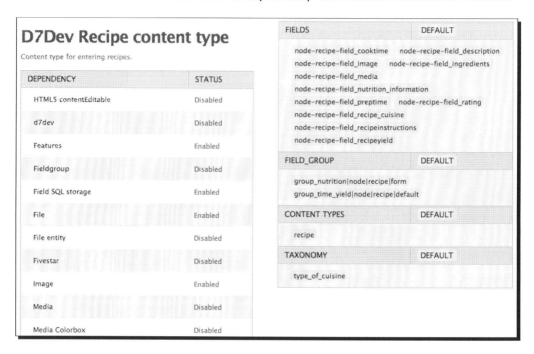

15. Now, with the Mac OS X Terminal application or the Windows Command Prompt, we will use Drush to enable d7dev_recipe_content_type, and all of the required but disabled dependencies.

Theoretically, it should be as easy as enabling d7dev_recipe_content_type and relying on Drush to enable the necessary dependencies. However, there is an issue with the order in which Drush enables the dependent modules. Specifically, as shown in the following code snippet, the media module is enabled before the views module, resulting in the following error:

```
$ drush en d7dev_recipe_content_type
```

The following extensions will be enabled: nutritioninfo, colorbox, media_colorbox, media, votingapi, fivestar, file_entity, field_ group, features, ctools, views, d7dev, entity, contenteditable, d7dev_recipe_content_type

Do you really want to continue? (y/n): y

Drush command terminated abnormally due to an unrecoverable error. [error]

```
Error: Call to undefined function views_get_enabled_views() in /
Applications/MAMP/htdocs/d7live/sites/all/modules/media/media.
module, line 1054
$
```

16. Therefore, we will use Drush to enable the media module along with its dependencies, and enable our recipe feature.

```
$ drush en media

The following extensions will be enabled: views, ctools, file_
entity, media

Do you really want to continue? (y/n): y

ctools was enabled successfully.         [ok]

file_entity was enabled successfully.    [ok]

media was enabled successfully.    [ok]

views was enabled successfully.    [ok]

$ drush en d7dev_recipe_content_type

The following extensions will be enabled: nutritioninfo, colorbox,
media_colorbox, votingapi, fivestar, field_group, features, d7dev,
entity, contenteditable, d7dev_recipe_content_type

Do you really want to continue? (y/n): y

colorbox was enabled successfully.                  [ok]

contenteditable was enabled successfully.           [ok]

d7dev was enabled successfully.                     [ok]

d7dev_recipe_content_type was enabled successfully.    [ok]

entity was enabled successfully.               [ok]

fivestar was enabled successfully.             [ok]

media_colorbox was enabled successfully.       [ok]

nutritioninfo was enabled successfully.        [ok]

votingapi was enabled successfully.            [ok]

field_group was enabled successfully.          [ok]

features was enabled successfully.             [ok]

$
```

17. Now that the recipe feature is enabled, return to our D7Live site in your browser, click on the **Structure** link in the **D7Live Admin** toolbar, then click on the **Features** link. On the **Features MANAGE** page, you will see that our D7Dev Recipe content type feature is enabled.

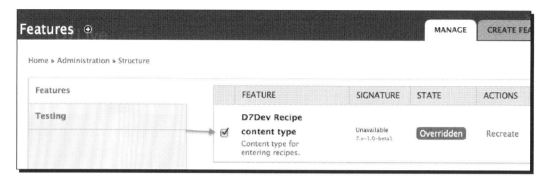

The **D7Dev Recipe content type** feature is enabled, but notice that the **STATE** is specified as **Overridden**.

This is one of the few, but nagging issues with some exported Features components. In this case, not only does the exported `type_of_cuisine` vocabulary not include the terms that we added for our D7Dev site, the Features module has marked it as **OVERRIDDEN**. In many cases, as in this one, there is not a clear reason why this is the case.

18. Next, in the **Admin** toolbar, click on the **Structure** link, click on the Content **types** link, and you will see our Recipe content type listed.

19. Now, on the **Content types** administrative page, click on the **manage fields** link for our Recipe content type, and you will see that all of the fields that we added to our D7Dev Recipe content type are there.

LABEL	NAME	FIELD	WIDGET	OPERATIONS	
+ name	title	Node module element			
+ description	field_description	Long text	Text area (multiple rows)	edit	delete
+ image	field_image	Image	Image	edit	delete
+ recipeYield	field_recipeyield	Text	Text field	edit	delete
+ prepTime	field_preptime	Integer	Text field	edit	delete
+ cookTime	field_cooktime	Integer	Text field	edit	delete
+ ingredients	field_ingredients	Text	Text field	edit	delete
+ recipeInstructions	field_recipeinstructions	Long text	Text area (multiple rows)	edit	delete
+ nutrition	field_nutrition_information	Nutrition Information	Nutrition Information form	edit	delete
+ Media	field_media	File	Media file selector	edit	delete
+ rating	field_rating	Fivestar Rating	Stars (rated while viewing)	edit	delete
+ recipeCuisine	field_recipe_cuisine	Term reference	Select list	edit	delete

What just happened?

The Features module enabled us to add the Recipe content type that we manually configured for our D7Dev site to our new D7Live site, without writing any code or doing any manual configuration. In addition to that, the feature can be version-controlled for deployment between the two environments of our D7Dev site, and can even be shared with other Drupal users' sites as long as they have all of the dependent modules (but remember, some of those dependent modules are custom modules that we have created in this book, so we would have to share those modules in addition to sharing the Recipe content type feature).

Managing updates to Feature components

The true power of using Features to manage configuration between site environments is highlighted by the Features update process. We are going to add a new vocabulary to categorize our D7Dev recipes by Dietary Consideration (Vegetarian, Vegan, Gluten-free, and so on), and add a new taxonomy field to our Recipe content type. We will then see how the Features module enables the migration of this configuration from our development site to our live site through the generated code.

Time for action – updating our Recipe content type feature

Now, we will be updating our Recipe content type feature.

1. Open our d7dev site in your browser, and click on the **Structure** link in the **Admin** toolbar, then click on the **Taxonomy** link.

2. Next, on the **Taxonomy** administrative page, click on the **Add vocabulary** link.

3. Enter Dietary Consideration as the **Name**, 'Allows categorization of recipes based on dietary considerations such as gluten-free or vegan.' as the **Description**, uncheck the **Handle as an item in microdata** checkbox, and click on the **Save** button.

4. At this point, we won't worry about adding any terms to our new vocabulary. So, click on the **Structure** link in the **Admin** toolbar, then click on the **Content types** link, then the **manage fields** link for our Recipe content type.

5. Scroll down the **MANAGE FIELDS** page to the **Add new field** row. Enter recipeDiet as the **Label**, recipe_diet as the **Field name**, select **Term reference** as the field type, select Autocomplete term widget (tagging) as the field widget, and click on the **Save** button.

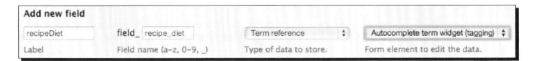

6. On the **FIELD SETTINGS** page, select **Dietary Consideration** as the **Vocabulary**, and click on the **Save field settings** button.

7. Next, on the recipeDiet field EDIT page, scroll down to the Number of values select list in the RECIPEDIET FIELD SETTINGS section and select Unlimited, and then click the Save settings button.

8. Now, open the Terminal (Mac OS X) or Command Prompt (Windows) application, change to the root directory of our d7dev site, and use the Features Drush `fu` command to update our `d7dev_recipe_content_type` feature.

```
$ cd /Applications/MAMP/htdocs/d7dev/

$ drush fu d7dev_recipe_content_type

Module appears to already exist in sites/all/modules/d7dev_
features/d7dev_recipe_content_type

Do you really want to continue? (y/n): y

Created module: d7dev_recipe_content_type in sites/all/modules/
d7dev_features/d7dev_recipe_content_type      [ok]

$
```

Now, the new `dietary_consideration` vocabulary and the new `field_recipe_diet` field are part of our recipe feature on our d7dev development environment.

9. Next, we need to add and commit it to the d7dev Git repository, so that we can use Git to pull those changes into the d7live environment.

```
$ cd /Applications/MAMP/htdocs/d7dev/

$ git add -A

$ git commit -m 'added recipeDiet term reference field'

[master 1c16903] added recipeDiet term reference field

 4 files changed, 120 insertions(+), 0 deletions(-)

$ cd ../d7live

$ git pull

remote: Counting objects: 21, done.

remote: Compressing objects: 100% (11/11), done.

remote: Total 11 (delta 8), reused 0 (delta 0)

Unpacking objects: 100% (11/11), done.

From /Applications/MAMP/htdocs/d7dev
```

```
   8903cd1..1c16903  master      -> origin/master
Updating 8903cd1..1c16903
Fast-forward
 .../d7dev_recipe_content_type.features.field.inc  |   74
++++++++++++++++++++
 .../d7dev_recipe_content_type.features.inc         |   10 +++
 ...d7dev_recipe_content_type.features.taxonomy.inc |   32
+++++++++
 .../d7dev_recipe_content_type.info                 |    4 +
 4 files changed, 120 insertions(+), 0 deletions(-)
$
```

10. Now that the updated recipe feature code has been pulled into our d7live environment, we can use the Features Drush `fr` or `features-revert` command to revert the database configuration to what is represented by the updated recipe features code.

```
$ cd /Applications/MAMP/htdocs/d7dev/
$ drush fr d7dev_recipe_content_type
```

Note: The `features-revert` command will overwrite any database configuration related to the `d7dev_recipe_content_type` feature. We could also revert the feature on our d7dev site to ensure that the feature is the same between the d7dev and d7dev live sites.

11. Next, open our d7dev site in your browser, click on the **Structure** link in the **Admin** toolbar, click on the **Features** link, then click on the **Overridden STATE** link for our D7Dev Recipe content type feature. You will see that the feature now includes the new field and the new vocabulary that we had added in our D7Dev development environment.

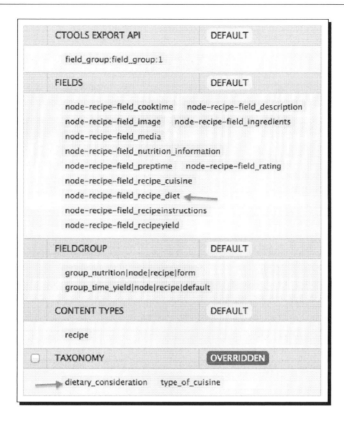

What just happened?

We used the Features module to manage configuration changes to our Recipe content type between our development and live environments. All of the changes are actually maintained as versioned code in the Git repositories associated with each of our site environments, and if we need to, we could easily revert to a different version of our Recipe content type without any manual configuration.

We also discovered some very useful Features Drush commands that make it very easy to manage Features-based configuration from the command line.

Features for sharing Drupal components

The idea of using the Features module to create self-contained packages of reusable Drupal components is popular enough that there is a category dedicated to it on the **Modules search** page (`http://drupal.org/project/modules`) on Drupal.org.

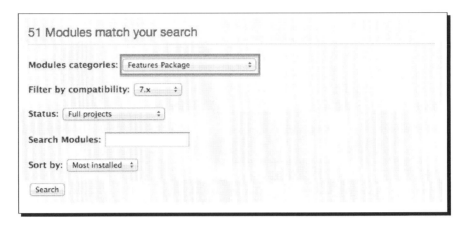

Note, however, that not all of the 51 modules categorized as belonging to the Features Package category are actually features. A number of modules that extend the capabilities of the Features module are also included, such as the UUID Features Integration module that we mentioned earlier in the chapter.

Summary

In this chapter, we have learned about some of the advantages of using the Features module to manage configuration between different environments of a Drupal site. The Features module generates modules and makes it easy to manage Drupal components, like our Recipe content type, between environments as version controlled code. This alleviates the necessity of duplicating the steps of manually configuring a number of Drupal components between sites, and as your development environment becomes more complicated and the number of Drupal components becomes more numerous, this will be a huge time saver.

Pop quiz Answers

Chapter 1, Getting Set up

Pop quiz – PHP and MySQL configuration for Drupal

1	b

Index

About Packt Publishing

Packt, pronounced 'packed', published its first book "*Mastering phpMyAdmin for Effective MySQL Management*" in April 2004 and subsequently continued to specialize in publishing highly focused books on specific technologies and solutions.

Our books and publications share the experiences of your fellow IT professionals in adapting and customizing today's systems, applications, and frameworks. Our solution based books give you the knowledge and power to customize the software and technologies you're using to get the job done. Packt books are more specific and less general than the IT books you have seen in the past. Our unique business model allows us to bring you more focused information, giving you more of what you need to know, and less of what you don't.

Packt is a modern, yet unique publishing company, which focuses on producing quality, cutting-edge books for communities of developers, administrators, and newbies alike. For more information, please visit our website: www.packtpub.com.

About Packt Open Source

In 2010, Packt launched two new brands, Packt Open Source and Packt Enterprise, in order to continue its focus on specialization. This book is part of the Packt Open Source brand, home to books published on software built around Open Source licences, and offering information to anybody from advanced developers to budding web designers. The Open Source brand also runs Packt's Open Source Royalty Scheme, by which Packt gives a royalty to each Open Source project about whose software a book is sold.

Writing for Packt

We welcome all inquiries from people who are interested in authoring. Book proposals should be sent to author@packtpub.com. If your book idea is still at an early stage and you would like to discuss it first before writing a formal book proposal, contact us; one of our commissioning editors will get in touch with you.

We're not just looking for published authors; if you have strong technical skills but no writing experience, our experienced editors can help you develop a writing career, or simply get some additional reward for your expertise.

Made in the USA
Lexington, KY
15 September 2012